HLT
PUBLICATIONS

TORT

Suggested Solutions

**UNIVERSITY OF LONDON
JUNE EXAMINATION 1990**

HLT PUBLICATIONS
200 Greyhound Road, London W14 9RY

Examination Questions © The University of London 1990
Solutions © The HLT Group Ltd 1990

ISBN 1 85352 629 0

British Library Cataloguing-in-Publication.

A CIP Catalogue record for this book is available from the British Library.

Printed and bound in Great Britain.

FOREWORD

HLT Publications are written specifically with the student in mind. Whether they are studying for A Levels, a degree or professional qualification they will find our publications clear, concise and up-to-date.

All our publications are written by specialists, the majority of whom have direct practical teaching experience. Each year all our materials are carefully reviewed and updated as appropriate.

HLT Publications is the publishing arm of Holborn College, which has experience of over twenty years as an independent college with a current student population of over 2,000. We are ideally placed to understand and respond to the needs of students. Most importantly, we are able to test our publications directly in our own lecture theatres.

Proof of the high quality of our texts is that they are widely used by students at universities, polytechnics and colleges throughout the United Kingdom and overseas, as well as by practitioners seeking an update or overview on recent changes. Given the comprehensive range of topics covered, whatever syllabus you are studying, our texts will be invaluable to you.

Textbooks provide an invaluable foundation and comprehensive introduction to the subject and aim to equip the student with a sound grasp of the basic principles involved. They include discussions of the current state of the law as well as considering practical issues.

Casebooks have been produced as companion volumes to the relevant textbooks, and aim to supplement and enhance students' understanding and interpretation of a particular area of the law, and to provide essential background reading. They contain the appropriate statutes as well as all the important cases, and include extracts from judgments together with detailed commentaries as appropriate.

Revision WorkBooks are a new series of questions and answers for students preparing for law examinations. They are arranged in the order of the topics to which they apply. This valuable revision aid is supported by key points and question analysis for each subject, recent cases and statutes, and concise notes on how to study and plan effective revision strategies.

Suggested Solutions to past examination papers are available for LLB, Bar and Solicitors' Finals examinations. They are available either as single papers covering the last examinations or in packs covering a number of preceding years' examinations. These are not intended as model answers but may be used as both a revision aid and a guide to examination techniques.

Law Update published annually in March/April gives law students at degree and professional levels, and other students with law elements in their courses, a review of the most recent developments in specific subject areas - an essential revision aid for the next examinations. Practitioners seeking a quick update will also find this a useful guide on recent changes.

Publications are available from most academic bookshops or by mail order from the publisher. An order form appears at the back of this book.

HOLBORN COLLEGE COURSES

SPECIALIST DIPLOMAS IN LAW & BUSINESS

Validated by the University of Oxford Delegacy of Local Examinations at degree level.

9 month course.

Diplomas in: Contract Law • Commercial Law • Company Law • Revenue Law • European Community Law • Criminal Law • Evidence • Constitutional Law • English Legal System • Land Law • Organisational Theory • Economics • Accounting and Business Finance • Computer Systems & Information Technology • Maths for Economists • Statistics

Entry: Evidence of sufficient academic or work experience to study at degree level.

FUNDAMENTALS OF BRITISH BUSINESS

Examined internally by Holborn College

To familiarise European and other overseas business studies students with UK business practice. Courses are tailor-made for groups of students on a College to College basis. Courses run for ten to seventeen weeks and permit part-time relevant work experience.

Past courses have included: Aspects of Organisational Behaviour • Marketing • Statistics • Business English & Communication Skills • Economics • International Trade • Company Law

LAW

Examined externally by the University of London.

Three year course.

LLB Law.

Entry: 2 'A' levels grade E and 3 'O' levels.

ACCOUNTING & MANAGEMENT DEGREES

Examined externally by the University of London.

Three year course.

BSc (Econ) Accounting • BSc (Econ) Management Studies • BSc (Econ) Economics & Management Studies

Entry: 2 'A' levels grade E and 3 'O' levels to include Maths and English.

DIPLOMA IN ECONOMICS.

Examined externally by the University of London.

One year full time, two year part time courses.

Completion of the Diploma gives exemption from the first year of the BSc (Econ) Degree programmes reducing them to two years.

Entry: Mathematics and English 'O' level equivalent. Minimum age 18.

THE COMMON PROFESSIONAL EXAMINATION

Examined externally by Wolverhampton Polytechnic.

9 month, 6 month and short revision courses.

Entry: Acceptance by the Professional Body.

THE BAR EXAMINATION

Examined by the Council of Legal Education for non-UK practitioners.

9 month course.

Entry: Acceptance by the Professional Body.

THE SOLICITORS' FINAL

Examined by the Law Society.

6 month re-sit and short revision courses.

Entry: Acceptance by the Professional Body.

THE INSTITUTE OF LEGAL EXECUTIVES FINAL PART 2

Examined by the Institute of Legal Executives.

9 month course and short revision courses.

Entry: Acceptance by the Professional Body.

A & AS LEVEL COURSES

Examined by various UK Boards.

9 month course and short revision courses

Subjects offered: Law • Constitutional Law • Economics • Accounting • Business Studies • Mathematics Pure and Applied • Mathematics and Statistics • Sociology • Government and Politics

Entry: 3 'O' levels.

FULL-TIME, PART-TIME, REVISION & DISTANCE LEARNING

ACKNOWLEDGEMENT

The questions used are taken from past University of London LLB (External) Degree examination papers and our thanks are extended to the University of London for the kind permission which has been given to us to use and publish the questions.

Caveat:

The answers given are not approved or sanctioned by the University of London and are entirely our responsibility.

They are not intended as 'Model Answers', but rather as Suggested Solutions.

The answers have two fundamental purposes, namely:

a)   To provide a detailed example of a suggested solution to examination questions, and

b)   To assist students with their research into the subject and to further their understanding and appreciation of the subject of Laws.

Note:

Please note that the solutions in this book were written in the year of the examination for each paper. They were appropriate solutions at the time of preparation, but students must note that certain caselaw and statutes may subsequently have changed.

INTRODUCTION

Why choose HLT publications

Holborn College has earned an International reputation over the past ten years for the outstanding quality of its teaching, Textbooks, Casebooks and Suggested Solutions to past examination papers set by the various examining bodies.

Our expertise is reflected in the outstanding results achieved by our students in the examinations conducted by the University of London, the Law Society, the Council of Legal Education and the Associated Examining Board.

The object of Suggested Solutions

The Suggested Solutions have been prepared by College lecturers experienced in teaching to this specific syllabus and are intended to be an example of a full answer to the problems posed by the examiner.

They are not 'model answers', for at this level there almost certainly is not just one answer to a problem, nor are the answers written to strict examination time limits.

The opportunity has been taken, where appropriate, to develop themes, suggest alternatives and set out additional material to an extent not possible by the examinee in the examination room.

We feel that in writing full opinion answers to the questions that we can assist you with your research into the subject and can further your understanding and appreciation of the law.

Notes on examination technique

Although the SUBSTANCE and SLANT of the answer changes according to the subject-matter of the question, the examining body and syllabus concerned, the TECHNIQUE of answering examination questions does *not* change.

You will not pass an examination if you do not know the substance of a course. You *may* pass if you do not know how to go about answering a question although this is doubtful. To do *well* and to guarantee success, however, it is necessary to learn the technique of answering problems properly. The following is a guide to acquiring that technique.

1   *Time*

        All examinations permit only a limited time for papers to be completed. All papers require you to answer a certain number of questions in that time, and the questions, with some exceptions carry equal marks.

        It follows from this that you should never spend a disproportionate amount of time on any question. When you have used up the amount of time allowed for any one question STOP and go on to the next question after an abrupt conclusion, if necessary. If you feel that you are running out of time, then complete your answer in *note form*. A useful way of ensuring that you do not over-run is to write down on a piece of scrap paper the time at which you should be starting each part of the paper. This can be done in the few minutes before the examination begins and it will help you to calm any nerves you may have.

2   *Reading the question*

        It will not be often that you will be able to answer every question on an examination paper. Inevitably, there will be some areas in which you feel better prepared than others. You will prefer to answer the questions which deal with those areas, but you will never know how good the questions are *unless you read the whole examination paper.*

You should spend *at least* 10 MINUTES at the beginning of the examination reading the questions. Preferably, you should read them more than once. As you go through each question, make a brief note on the examination paper of any relevant cases and/or statutes that occur to you even if you think you may not answer that question: you may well be grateful for this note towards the end of the examination when you are tired and your memory begins to fail.

3   *Re-reading the answers*

Ideally, you should allow time to re-read your answers. This is rarely a pleasant process, but will ensure that you do not make any silly mistakes such as leaving out a 'not' when the negative is vital.

4   *The structure of the answer*

Almost all examination problems raise more than one legal issue that you are required to deal with. Your answer should:

i)   *identify the issues raised by the question*

      This is of crucial importance and gives shape to the whole answer. It indicates to the examiner that you appreciate what he is asking you about.

      This is at least as important as actually answering the questions of law raised by that issue.

      The issues should be identified in the first paragraph of the answer.

ii)   *deal with those issues one by one as they arise in the course of the problem*

      This, of course, is the substance of the answer and where study and revision pays off.

iii) *if the answer to an issue turns on a provision of a statute, CITE that provision briefly, but do not quote it from any statute you may be permitted to bring into the examination hall*

      Having cited the provision, show how it is relevant to the question.

iv)   *if there is no statute, or the meaning of the statute has been interpreted by the courts, CITE the relevant cases*

      'Citing cases' does not mean writing down the nature of every case that happens to deal with the general topic with which you are concerned and then detailing all the facts you can think of.

      You should cite *only* the most relevant cases - there may perhaps only be one. No more facts should be stated than are absolutely essential to establish the relevance of the case. If there is a relevant case, but you cannot remember its name, it is sufficient to refer to it as 'one decided case'.

v)   *whenever a statute or case is cited, the title of statute or the name of the case should be underlined*

      This makes the examiner's job much easier because he can see at a glance whether the relevant material has been dealt with, and it will make him more disposed in your favour.

vi)   *having dealt with the relevant issues, summarise your conclusions in such a way that you answer the question*

      A question will often say at the end simply 'Advise A', or B, or C, etc. The advice will usually turn on the individual answers to a number of issues. The point made here is that the final paragraph should pull those individual answers together *and actually give the advice required*. For example, it may begin something like: 'The effect of the answer to the issues raised by this question is that one's advice to A is that ...'

vii)   *related to (vi), make sure at the end that you have answered the question*

For example, if the question says 'Advise A', make sure that is what your answer does. If you are required to advise more than one party, make sure that you have dealt with all the parties that you are required to and no more.

5   *Some general points*

You should always try to get the examiner on your side. One method has already been mentioned - the underlining of case names, etc. There are also other ways as well.

Always write as *neatly* as you can. This is more easily done with ink than with a ball-point.

Avoid the use of violently coloured ink eg turquoise; this makes a paper difficult to read.

Space out your answers sensibly: leave a line between paragraphs. You can always get more paper. At the same time, try not to use so much paper that your answer book looks too formidable to mark. This is a question of personal judgment.

NEVER put in irrelevant material simply to show that you are clever. Irrelevance is not a virtue and time spent on it is time lost for other, relevant, answers.

UNIVERSITY OF LONDON

LLB EXAMINATION

PART I

for External Students

LAW OF TORT

Wednesday, 6 June 1990: 10.00 to 1.00

Answer **FOUR** of the following EIGHT questions

1   "Can a mere failure to speak ever give rise to liability in negligence under *Hedley Byrne* principles? In our
        view it can, but subject to the all-important proviso that there has been on the facts a voluntary assumption
        of responsibility in the relevant sense, a reliance on that assumption." (*Banque Financiere de la Cite CA* v
        Westgate Insurance Co Ltd (1989)).

        Discuss.

2   "The general rule is that, if conduct is presumptively unlawful, a good motive will not exonerate the
        defendant, and that, if conduct is lawful apart from motive, a bad motive will not make him liable."
        (Winfield and Jolowicz).

        Discuss this statement. Should the law of tort attach more importance to the defendant's motives?

3   Keith is a lecturer in law at the University of Slumsville. One of his duties is to organise moots and mock
        trials. He arranged with Lucy, a mathematics student, and Mark, a law student, that they would stage an
        incident which would be the basis of a mock trial. In accordance with the arrangement, as Lucy walked into
        a mathematics lecture, Mark seized her from behind, tore her shoulder bag from her and rushed from the
        room. Lucy collapsed and another student, Noel, sprang from his seat and tackled Mark. In the ensuing
        scuffle, Mark suffered a dislocated shoulder and Noel lost several teeth.

        Lucy suffered from a rare medical condition and the incident caused a spasm which constricted her throat and
        she died of asphyxiation. Neither Lucy nor anyone else had known that she suffered from this condition,
        but the evidence now is that she could have died at any time if she suffered severe shock. Mark's shoulder
        injury did not respond to treatment and he is likely to have a permanent disability. He was so distressed by
        learning of Lucy's death that he suffered a complete nervous breakdown and is unlikely to be able to resume
        his studies.

        Advise Mark, Noel and Lucy's father as to any possible claims in tort.

4   Lord Steeple opened his mansion house and gardens to the public one day. All proceeds were to be donated
        to the local church restoration fund. A notice at the entrance read: "All visitors enter these premises at
        their own risk." Lord Steeple's private quarters were not open to the public and notices were clearly placed
        on doors, saying, "Private. Closed to Visitors." In the grounds are the ruins of an earlier house. A notice
        at the outside read: "This building is dangerous. Visitors are asked to keep their children under control."

        Vestry visited the house, accompanied by his small son Pew. While visiting the ruins, Pew struggled free
        of Vestry's grasp and squeezed under a railing. He fell six feet to a lower level and suffered severe cuts and
        bruises and a broken arm. When Vestry saw that he was injured, he ran into the main house and through a
        door marked "Private. Closed to Visitors." He was set upon by an alsatian dog which Lord Steeple's
        butler, Aisle, had, without Lord Steeple's knowledge, been training as a guard dog. The dog caused Vestry
        severe injuries.

        Advise Vestry and Pew.

5 Anna, Betty, Clara and Daphne occupied adjoining houses in a terrace. Clara had a temporary posting overseas for two years starting in October 1989. She let her house for two years to Edward, whose hobby is carpentry. Edward has spent a great deal of time building furniture and other large wooden objects in the garden at the back of the house. This has annoyed Daphne, a nurse, who is frequently on duty at nights and is unable to sleep during the day when Edward is working. Edward has refused to desist from noisy work when Daphne is trying to sleep. Sawdust has blown over the fence into Betty's garden. Some of this was eaten by a dog belonging to Betty's sister, Emily, who came to stay permanently with Betty in January. The dog was severely ill as a result and eventually died. The sawdust was extremely difficult to pick up and after a heavy rainstorm in April sawdust was carried into the drain in Betty's garden. The drain was blocked and, in the ensuing flood, water flowed into Betty's and Anna's houses. During the storm a piece of coping blew off the roof and damaged Anna's car which was parked in the road. Neighbours had told Edward earlier that they could see that the coping had worked loose.

Advise Daphne, Emily, Betty and Anna.

6 Harriet established a fund to award a substantial prize each year for the best work of art submitted for consideration by an artist under thirty. Two of the six trustees of the fund are Jeremy and Kenneth. One of the candidates for the prize in 1990 was Lionel. In his report to the other trustees, Jeremy stated that "Lionel's work is devoid of all artistic originality". Lionel has recently been divorced by Jeremy's daughter. Kenneth's report stated, "I hear from various sources that Lionel was concerned in a recent scandal involving the production of artistic fakes. It would be better not to consider him until the position is clear." Kenneth had his report typed by his wife, Molly, who is the secretary to the director of an art gallery. She used the word-processor in her office and did not immediately delete the document in case it required corrections. Before she could do so, her employer, in searching for another document, came upon Kenneth's report. He abandoned plans to hold an exhibition of Lionel's work.

Advise Lionel.

7 Tyrant Industries plc decided to install a light railway to transport raw materials and finished goods between its factory premises and a railway station three miles away. They reached an agreement with Farmer Fred that for part of the distance they would utilise disused tracks which ran on an embankment across Fred's land. The local authority gave planning permission on condition *inter alia* that the embankment would be suitably landscaped and that the landscaping scheme would be approved by the Foliage Consultancy Council, a body established by the government to advise on certain environmental protection policies. Tyrant Industries contracted with Sleepers plc to carry out the main construction work. The contract permitted Tyrant Industries to nominate sub-contractors to carry out parts of the work and provided that Sleepers would not be liable for the neglect or wilful default of subcontractors. Tyrant Industries nominated Greenmadness Ltd as sub-contractors for the landscaping work. Greenmadness Ltd submitted a scheme which was approved by the Foliage Consultancy Council. The work was carried out in 1988. Tyrant Industries also contracted with Cleaners Ltd that Cleaners would maintain the tracks for a period of five years for a fixed annual sum.

As a result of the dry summer of 1989 and the ensuing mild winter the trees chosen by Greenmadness grew very rapidly and proved to be unsuitable for the embankment, which has become weakened. It poses no danger in itself but is at present insufficiently strong to carry trains. Tyrant Industries have had to purchase a fleet of heavy lorries to transport goods and have to meet the much higher transport costs involved. Because the tracks are not in use, the maintenance work is much more complex and Cleaners Ltd find that their contract has become more onerous.

Advise Tyrant Industries and Cleaners whether they have any claims in tort.

8   Sam is a trainee fireman with the Waterside Fire Brigade. While undergoing instruction in driving a fire engine, he was ordered by his instructor Tom to drive at high speed along a country road with his blue lights flashing and bell sounding. Sam could see that the driver of the car ahead, Ursula, had become agitated, but he kept going. Ursula panicked in trying to make room for the fire engine and collided with a lamp post. Ursula received serious eye injuries but was released immediately. Her passenger Violet was trapped in the car. Ursula needed urgent medical treatment and was taken to a nearby hospital. However, there had been a major railway accident a short time earlier and the hospital was unable to admit other casualties. Ursula was therefore removed to another hospital six miles away; the hospital was unable to save her sight, but this would have been possible if she had been able to receive prompt treatment. Violet was released after two hours. She was not seriously hurt but was taken by ambulance to hospital for examination. On the way the ambulance was involved in a further accident (without negligence on anyone's part) and Violet sustained two broken legs.

Advise Ursula and Violet.

QUESTION 1

General comment

It is vital to note that this essay question is not a general essay on negligent misrepresentation since *Hedley Byrne*, but is aimed at only a small part of this topic. The question also demonstrates the need to keep up to date in this area, as it can only be answered by candidates with a good knowledge of recent cases.

Suggested solution

It has long been established that as regards careless acts the law will impose liability, but it will not impose liability in respect of omissions, ie liability in negligence is confined to misfeasance and not non-feasance - see, for example, the speech of Lord Goff in *Smith* v *Littlewoods Organisation* (1), where Lord Goff stated this general rule and identified four exceptions. By analogy, in negligent misstatement, one might assume that while liability may arise in respect of a negligent misstatement, no liability will arise from a failure to speak. Essentially, the statement from *Banque Financiere* says that no liability will attach to a failure to speak subject to just one exception, namely where there has been a voluntary assumption of responsibility in the relevant sense and reliance on that assumption.

One might begin by asking what the Court of Appeal meant by the phrase 'voluntary assumption of responsibility' as in *Smith* v *Eric Bush* (2) the House of Lords rejected the view stated in *Hedley Byrne* v *Heller* (3) that a duty of care as regards negligent misstatement arose from a voluntary assumption of responsibility and this view was repeated by the House in *Caparo Industries* v *Dickman* (4). In *Smith* it was said that the phrase 'assumption of responsibility' can only have any meaning if it is understood as referring to the circumstances in which the law will deem the maker of the statement to have assumed responsibility to the person who acts on the advice, which essentially has turned the test from a subjective to an objective test.

It is this interpretation of the phrase 'voluntary assumption of responsibility' which should be borne in mind when discussing the quote given. Thus what was said in *Banque Financiere* can be rephrased by saying that a failure to speak can give rise to liability only where the law will deem the non-speaking party has assumed responsibility to the other, ie a failure to speak will give rise to liability only where a duty to speak arises.

Reduced to these simple terms, the statement in *Banque Financiere* seems obvious.

However, the Court of Appeal has decided in several recent cases that a duty can be owed in the absence of a voluntary assumption of responsibility. In *Banque Financiere* itself the court held that in an appropriate case the court could hold that having regard to the special circumstances and the relationship between the parties, a defendant could be treated in law (even though not in fact) as having assumed a responsibility to the plaintiff.

In *Reid* v *Rush & Tompkins* (5) Ralph Gibson LJ stated that a duty not to cause economic loss may be owed without an assumption of responsibility by the person giving advice or reliance by the person receiving it, although both May LJ and Neil LJ reserved their positions on this point.

Finally, in *Van Oppen* v *Clerk to the Bedford Charity Trustees* (6), Balcombe LJ stated that exceptionally in some cases of pure economic loss the court may be prepared to find the existence of a duty of care and to treat the defendant in law as having assumed a responsibility to the plaintiff.

It would seem, therefore that the quotation in the question, although accurate in so far as it goes, is incomplete in that it makes no reference to those situations where the defendant is deemed to have assumed a duty or responsibility unless one reads 'voluntary assumption of responsibility' to include this situation, following *Smith* v *Eric Bush* and *Caparo Industries* v *Dickman*, in which case it is both accurate and complete as the law currently stands.

References

1   [1987] AC 241
2   [1989] 2 All ER 514
3   [1964] AC 465
4   [1990] 1 All ER 568
5   [1989] 3 All ER 228
6   [1989] 3 All ER 389

QUESTION 2

General comment

This is a lengthy question which covers a wide range of the law of tort, including malicious prosecution and falsehood, nuisance and the economic torts.

Suggested solution

Perhaps the best known case on lawful conduct not being made unlawful by a bad motive is *Bradford Corporation* v *Pickles* (1), where the defendant was held not liable for intentionally intercepting water flowing through his land via undefined channels. The defendant's motive in doing this was to coerce the plaintiff into buying the defendant's land at the defendant's price, and it was held that as his act was lawful his motive could not make it unlawful. This was re-emphasised by the House of Lords a few years later in *Allen* v *Flood* (2). *Chapman* v *Honig* (3), where a landlord maliciously served a notice to quit on a tenant, and *Wyld* v *Silver* (4), where persons exercised a long-defunct right to hold a fair solely to prevent the erection of buildings for which planning permission had been granted, are more modern examples.

Clearly, however, there are some areas of the law of tort where motive is relevant. Thus malice will have to be shown in malicious prosecution or malicious falsehood, and in defamation the presence of malice will destroy the defence of fair comment or qualified privilege.

Another area in which motive is relevant is nuisance. While malice is by no means an essential ingredient of this tort, the presence of malice may mean that an interference is deemed unreasonable, as in *Hollywood Silver Fox Farm* v *Emmett* (5) where the defendant was held to have committed a nuisance when he acted maliciously, and it seems clear that in the absence of malice no nuisance would have been found. *Christie* v *Davey* (6) is a similar example of malice being taken into account.

Finally, it is in the area of economic torts that motive may be relevant. Thus in *Mogul Steamship* v *McGregor, Gow & Co* (7), it was held that the motive of the defendant was irrelevant and a cause of action would only arise where the defendant's action was unlawful. A few years later in *Allen* v *Flood* (2) the House of Lords reached a similar conclusion. However, in *Quinn* v *Leatham* (8) the House of Lords held that a tort had been committed where the defendants acted lawfully but with a malicious motive. The anomalous finding in *Quinn* has been confined to cases of conspiracy to injure. Motive is relevant to this tort which can be carried out (inter alia) by the doing of a lawful act by unlawful means by two or more persons: *Mulcahy* v *R* (9). This leads to the strange conclusion that if an individual carried out the acts they would be lawful, ie the motive would be irrelevant, but if carried out by more than one person the acts would become actionable because of the motive, as in *Huntley* v *Thornton* (10) where the reason for denying the plaintiff employment was to uphold the dignity of certain union officials. By contrast in *Crofter Hand Woven Harris Tweed* v *Veitch* (11), where the defendants' motive was to protect their members' interests, it was held no action would lie.

In addition conspiracy may be to injure by unlawful means, but it was held in *Lonrho* v *Shell Petroleum* (12) and *Metall Und Rohfstoff* v *Donaldson Lufkin & Jenrette* (13) that an essential ingredient of this form of the tort was a sole or predominant purpose of injuring the plaintiffs' interests, so again motive is relevant.

In the tort of inducing a breach of contract, the relevant defences were summarised in *Edwin Hill* v *First National Finance Corporation* (14). It was stated that absence of malice was irrelevant: *South Wales Miners' Federation* v *Glamorgan Coal* (15), but that a moral duty to induce a breach of contract, as in *Brimelow* v *Casson* (16) was a defence, so again motive may be relevant.

Lastly, in the tort of interference with trade by unlawful means, it was held in *Lonrho* v *Al-Fayed* (17) that an essential ingredient of this tort was an intent to harm the plaintiff or to direct the unlawful act against the plaintiff, so again motive is relevant here.

Thus it can be seen that while traditionally the law has disregarded motive, there are some important exceptions to this rule in both nuisance and defamation and in the relatively new and still developing area of economic torts the courts seem more ready to pay attention to the defendant's motives.

The difficulty of attaching more importance to the defendant's motives is that often the criterion used in fixing liability is objective, rather than subjective, as well as the difficulty of ascertaining the defendant's motive, especially as unreasonable behaviour does not necessarily prove the existence of malice. As public law (eg planning law) controls a person's freedom to act in detriment to the interests of the community, and the law of tort regulates behaviour between individuals, it might seem as an unwarranted infringement on personal liberty to delve into a person's motives and make lawful acts unlawful. Even greater problems could arise if unlawful acts were to be made lawful because of a good motive; eg an employer removes a guard from dangerous machinery to enable the employee to work faster and obtain higher wages - the employee is injured and would not have been if the guard had been kept in place. Should the employer's good motive exonerate him? On the other hand why should a malicious defendant be able to rely on a defence of justification in defamation? The reliance on motive would also tend to create uncertainty as regards the liability of a particular defendant.

Overall, therefore, it is submitted that a case has not been made out for attaching more importance in tort to the defendant's motives.

References

1	[1895] AC 587	10	[1957] 1 WLR 321
2	[1898] AC 1	11	[1942] AC 435
3	[1963] 2 QB 502	12	[1982] AC 173
4	[1963] 1 QB 169	13	[1989] 3 All ER 14
5	[1936] 2 QB 392	14	[1989] 3 All ER 801
6	[1893] 1 Ch 316	15	[1905] AC 239
7	[1892] AC 25	16	[1924] 1 Ch 302
8	[1901] AC 495	17	[1989] 2 All ER 65
9	(1868) LR 3 HL 306, 317		

QUESTION 3

General comment

This problem concerns trespass to the person and the relevant defences. The possibility of vicarious liability should also be briefly considered.

Suggested solution

As regards the incident between Lucy and Mark and its consequences, as Mark's act is intentional we must consider trespass to the person and in particular the tort of battery which consists of the intentional and direct application of force to another person. In *Letang* v *Cooper* (1) it was held that where the act which caused the damage was intentional the cause of action lies in trespass to the person, and this was accepted by the Court of Appeal in *Wilson* v *Pringle* (2). Thus it would appear that there is no overlap between the torts of trespass to the person and negligence.

Clearly Mark's actions constitute an intentional and direct application of force to Lucy. However, Lucy has a problem in establishing liability in that in *Wilson* v *Pringle* it was held that the act of touching the plaintiff had to be a 'hostile touching'. In view of Lucy's agreement with Mark to stage the incident the touching would appear to be non-hostile. A further problem for Lucy is that she has consented to the physical contact by Mark and volenti would provide a complete defence to Mark. Even if Lucy was unaware of the exact incident, providing she was aware in general terms of what was to happen this would be enough to support the defence of volenti: *Chatterton* v *Gerson* (3).

Noel has committed a battery on Mark as Noel's actions were direct and intentional. Noel would seek to raise the defence of acting in support of the law as he thought that Mark had stolen Lucy's property. By s24(4) Police and Criminal Evidence Act 1984 a person may arrest without warrant any person who is, or who he suspects with reasonable cause to be, in the act of committing an arrestable offence. Section 24(5) also allows any person who has reasonable cause to believe that a person is guilty of an arrestable offence to arrest that person without warrant if that arrestable offence has in fact been committed. Thus Noel has fallen foul of the trap in *Walters* v *W H Smith* (4) in that he must prove that an offence has actually been committed, and it is no defence to show there were reasonable grounds for believing the person arrested to be guilty. Hence Noel cannot rely on the defence that he was acting in support of the law and is liable to Mark in battery. Noel will be prima facie liable for the damage to Mark's shoulder and as regards Noel's lost teeth, he will be regarded as the author of his own misfortune.

Noel could also attempt to justify his attack on Mark on the grounds that Mark was a trespasser in so far as Mark is a law student and the lecture was a mathematics lecture. However, as Noel is not the occupier of the lecture theatre he will have to show that he has the authority of the occupier to eject a trespasser, which seems unlikely. Noel would also have to show that Mark was requested to leave the premises, had a reasonable opportunity to do so, and failed to leave. As no request was made for Mark to leave Noel cannot raise this defence.

As regards the injury to Mark's shoulder, as Noel intended to inflict harm on Mark no question of remoteness of damage will arise: *Quinn* v *Leatham* (5); *Doyle* v *Olby (Ironmongers) Ltd* (6) and Noel will be liable for the damage to Mark's shoulder. As regards Mark's nervous breakdown the question of causation arises, ie what event caused the breakdown. We are told that it was caused by Mark's distress at Lucy's death. Turning to Lucy's death we are told Lucy collapsed after Mark removed her shoulder bag and that Noel attacked Mark after this occurrence. I assume that the 'incident' referred to in the problem which caused the spasm was therefore the removal of the bag by Mark. As Mark intended to harm Lucy then again no question of remoteness of damage would arise and Mark would be liable to Lucy's death, but as we have seen Lucy's consent will provide a total defence to Mark's actions.

Thus we should advise Mark that he can sue Noel in respect of his dislocated shoulder, but that he has no remedy for the nervous breakdown he has suffered. We should advise Noel that he is liable to Mark for Mark's shoulder injury, but has no remedy as regards his lost teeth. We should advise Lucy's father that he has no claim.

We could also consider whether Keith is vicariously liable for the actions of Lucy or Mark. Keith is not the employer of Lucy or Mark but we should consider whether an ad hoc agency has arisen as in *Ormrod* v *Crossville Motor Services* (7) where Keith is the principal and Lucy and Mark are his agents acting on his behalf. If so, the University of Slumsville would be liable for Keith's acts as they are his employer, Keith is their employee and Keith was organising the incident in connection with a mock trial and so was acting in the course of his employment. However, this would not affect the liabilities of the parties as described above.

References

1   [1965] 1 QB 232
2   [1987] QB 237
3   [1980] 3 WLR 1003; [1981] QB 432
4   [1914] 1 KB 595
5   [1901] AC 495
6   [1969] 2 QB 158
7   [1953] 1 WLR 1120

QUESTION 4

General comment

This question concerns the Occupiers Liability Act 1957, the Occupiers Liability Act 1984 and the Animals Act 1971.

Suggested solution

Lord Steeple is the occupier of the mansion house and its grounds under the Occupiers Liability Act 1957, *Wheat* v *Lacon* (1), and Vestry and Pew are his visitors and as such are owed the common duty of care by the occupier, Lord Steeple; s2(1) 1957 Act.

As regards Pew, by s2(3) 1957 Act an occupier must be prepared for children to be less careful than adults. In the case of very young children both the guardian of the child and the occupier must act reasonably and each is entitled to assume that the other will act reasonably: *Phipps* v *Rochester Corporation* (2). In view of the warning notice by the ruins, and the fact that we are told Pew 'squeezed' under a railing, it could be argued that Lord Steeple is not in breach of the common duty of care that he owes to Pew. This would be especially true if the danger was obvious, even to a child: *Liddle* v *Yorks (North Riding) CC* (3).

Turning to the warning by the ruins, s2(4)(a) 1957 Act provides that a warning is not by itself sufficient to discharge the occupier from liability unless in all the circumstances it was enough to enable the visitor to be reasonably safe. In Lord Steeple's case there is not only a warning but also a railing which would seem to discharge the duty under the 1957 Act. It was held in *Hogg* v *Historic Buildings Commission* (4) that the antiquity of a building is a factor to be taken into account in determining whether or not the occupier has taken reasonable care, and in *Rae* v *Mars UK* (5) it was held that where an unusual danger exists, the visitor should not only be warned but a barrier or notice should be placed to show the immediacy of the danger. Taking these factors and those in the previous paragraph into account Lord Steeple appears to have complied with the duty imposed as regards Pew.

Lord Steeple may also seek to rely on the defence that by the notice at the entrance he has excluded any duty he owes under the 1957 Act. By s2(1) of the 1957 Act the occupier can exclude his duty by agreement or otherwise (ie via a non-contractual notice) in so far as he is free to. Such an exclusion clause will be subject to the provisions of the Unfair Contract Terms Act 1977 by s1(1)(c) of that Act. However the Unfair Contract Terms Act 1977 only applies to business liability (s1(3) 1977 Act) and as Lord Steeple only opens his house on one day per year and donates all proceeds to the church restoration fund it would seem that Lord Steeple is not granting access for his business purposes and thus the Unfair Contract Terms Act 1977 will not apply to the notice and it will be a valid exclusion of duty to Pew.

Considering now Vestry, when Vestry ran through the door marked 'Private. Closed to Visitors', Vestry was no longer Lord Steeple's visitor. An occupier may give a visitor permission to enter some parts of his premises but not others: *The Calgarth* (6). An occupier who wishes to do this must take steps to bring the limitation to his visitor's attention: *Gould* v *McAuliffe* (7) and Lord Steeple has done this by means of the notice on the door. Hence as regards this part of the premises Vestry is a trespasser and any duty owed to Vestry is governed by the Occupiers' Liability Act 1984. By s1(3) of the 1984 Act the occupier of premises owes a duty of care to a non-visitor if:

a)   he is aware of the danger or has reasonable grounds to believe it exists

b)   he knows or has reasonable grounds to believe that the visitor is in the vicinity of the danger concerned or may come into the vicinity of the danger, and

c)   the risk is one against which, in all the circumstances, he may reasonably be expected to offer the non-visitor some protection.

In Vestry's case, Lord Steeple does not satisfy conditions (a) or (b) as he is unaware that the dog is being trained as a guard dog and is unaware of Vestry's presence in the private quarters. Thus a duty under the 1984 Act will not arise.

We must now consider whether any liability to Vestry arises under the Animals Act 1971 or the Guard Dogs Act 1975.

Lord Steeple is the keeper of the dog (assuming that Lord Steeple owns the dog) by s6(3) of the Animals Act 1971, and the dog is a non-dangerous species as defined by s6(2) of the 1971 Act. By s2(2) 1971 Act the keeper will be liable if:

a)   the damage is of a kind which the animal, unless restrained, was likely to cause or which, if caused by the animal, was likely to be severe; and

b)   the likelihood of the damage or of its being severe was due to characteristics of the animal which are not normally found except at particular times or in particular circumstances; and

c)   those characteristics were known to that keeper or were at any time known to a person who had charge of the animal or that keeper's servant.

Requirements (a) and (b) are met in this case, the damage from a bite by an alsatian dog being likely to be severe and alsatians are not normally vicious except in the particular circumstances of their being kept as guard dogs: *Cummings* v *Grainger* (8). In addition, the servant of the keeper must have charge of the animal to make his knowledge relevant, which seems to be the case here. Thus Lord Steeples is prima facie liable to Vestry under s2(2) 1971 Act and note that s2(2) does not require negligence on the part of the keeper: *Curtis* v *Betts* (9).

However, Lord Steeple has several defences available to him under s5 of the 1971 Act. By s5(1) he will not be liable if the damage is wholly due to Vestry's fault, and while this is unlikely to succeed, by s10 Lord Steeple may rely on contributory negligence on Vestry's part to reduce any damages payable. If Vestry voluntarily accepted the risk there will be no liability, but again this seems unlikely in the given circumstances. Section 5(3) of the 1971 Act provides a defence against a trespasser if the animal was not kept for the protection of persons or property, but we are told it was being trained as a guard dog, or if it was kept for this purpose that it was reasonable to do so. In *Cummings* v *Grainger* it was held reasonable to have a guard dog in a scrap metal yard 'in the East End of London where persons of the roughest type come and go' (per Lord Denning). Whether it would be reasonable to have a guard dog in a stately home would be a matter for the court to decide, but in view of the burglaries that occur in such premises a court might well find that the keeping of a guard dog was not unreasonable. Although criminal liability may arise under s1 Guard Dogs Act 1975, s5(1) of that Act expressly provides that it confers no civil right of action.

Hence the advice to Pew is that he cannot sue Lord Steeple, and the advice to Vestry is that if he sues Lord Steeple he at best only has a slight chance of success.

References

1	[1966] AC 552	6	[1927] P93
2	[1955] 1 QB 450	7	[1941] 2 All ER 527
3	[1934] 2 KB 101	8	[1977] QB 397
4	Current Law, March 1989, Para 285	9	[1990] 1 All ER 769
5	Times Law Report 15 February 1989		

QUESTION 5

General comment

This question involves primarily a consideration of the law of private nuisance, with an element of *Rylands* v *Fletcher* and negligence.

Suggested solution

Edward's activities may constitute a private nuisance. Nuisance may be defined as an unreasonable interference with a person's use or enjoyment of his land. It thus follows that only a person who has an interest in land may bring an action for private nuisance: *Malone* v *Laskey* (1), and that the interference must be unreasonable.

As regards *Daphne*, it is well established that noise can constitute a nuisance: *Halsey* v *Esso Petroleum* (2); *Tetley* v *Chitty* (3), and while there must be give and take between neighbours, so not all interferences give rise to liability: *Walter* v *Selfe* (4), an amount of noise which prevents sleep is unreasonable. We are told that Edward spends a great deal of time on his hobby, which is relevant, as a short or temporary disturbance is not likely to be a nuisance: *Harrison* v *Southwark & Vauxhall Water Co* (5). The character of the neighbourhood will also be a relevant factor in determining whether an interference with health and comfort amounts to a nuisance: *Bamford* v *Turnley* (6), but even if the terrace lies in a town centre the interference would seem to be unreasonable. Daphne has one problem, however, which is that Edward could claim that she is an abnormally sensitive plaintiff as she is trying to sleep in the day. In *Robinson* v *Kilvert* (7) and *Heath* v *Mayor of Brighton* (8) it was held that a person cannot increase his neighbour's liability by putting his land to a special use, and Daphne by sleeping in the day may not be able to bring an action in nuisance.

Turning to Betty, the sawdust blowing into her garden may constitute a nuisance: *Leakey* v *National Trust* (9). The fact that the sawdust was difficult to pick up affords Edward no defence as it is no defence in nuisance to show that the defendant took all reasonable, or even all possible, care. Provided the defendant caused the nuisance he is liable. Thus Edward is liable for the intrusion of the sawdust into Betty's garden. As regards the blocked drain the question arises as to whether or not this damage is too remote to impose liability on Edward. It was held in *The Wagon Mound (No 2)* (10) that in nuisance the test for remoteness of damage was reasonable foreseeability. It would seem reasonably foreseeable that if large quantities of sawdust are left to blow into a neighbour's garden that a drain may become blocked and flooding ensue, and if so Edward would be liable for the flooding of Betty's and Anna's houses.

Emily can only sue in nuisance if she has some interest in land eg as a tenant: *Malone* v *Lasky* (above). We are not told of Emily's status, which may be that of a tenant or that of a guest. If the former, Emily can sue in nuisance for any damage that has actually occurred eg vet's bills and cost of a replacement dog. If the latter, she is without a remedy.

Anna can sue Edward for the flooding to her house as discussed above. Edward may claim that Betty's failure to sweep up the sawdust broke the chain of causation, but as we are told that the sawdust was extremely difficult to pick up this seems unlikely to succeed as Betty's failure to sweep up the sawdust was foreseeable and is just the sort of event Edward should have foreseen and guarded against: *Stansbie* v *Troman* (12). Turning to the damage to Anna's car, Edward as occupier of premises close to the highway is under a duty to keep his premises in repair: *Tarry* v *Ashton* (13), and in *Wringe* v *Cohen* (14) it was said that this duty arose whether the occupier knew of the danger or not. As Edward was aware of the coping being loose he cannot claim the benefit of the exception to the rule in *Wringe* v *Cohen*, namely that the damage arose from a 'secret and unobservable operation of nature' and hence Edward is liable for the damage to Anna's car.

Clearly all the plaintiffs should be advised to sue Edward as he is the creator of the nuisance. Clara would only be liable if she let the premises for purposes which constitute a nuisance: *Tetley* v *Chitty*, which she has not done.

Edward may also be liable for the escape of the sawdust under the rule in *Rylands* v *Fletcher* (15), as all the criteria for the operation of the rule appear to be satisfied. Betty and Anna may wish to plead this as an alternative cause of action in respect of the flooding. It would not apply to the escape of the coping as the coping was not brought onto the land by Edward nor was its presence a non-natural use of the land.

Edward may also be liable in negligence. Edward is under a duty to ensure that his activities do not cause harm to others - see *Caparo Industries* v *Dickman* (16) for the most recent formulation of the criteria for imposing a duty of care. He is in breach of this duty by failure to sweep up the sawdust and this breach caused the damage which followed and thus damage was reasonably foreseeable as regards the flooding and a similar liability in negligence will arise in respect of the damage to Anna's car. Whether it is reasonably foreseeable that Emily's dog would eat the sawdust and die is debateable.

As regards Daphne, as Edward's actions are deliberate rather than careless any alternative action would lie in trespass to the person rather than negligence, and as there has been no direct interference with her person Daphne has only the questionable action in nuisance against Edward.

Thus the advice to Daphne would be that she has only a slim chance of success in nuisance; Betty has a good case in both nuisance and negligence, and also *Rylands* v *Fletcher*. Emily has some chance of success in nuisance depending on her status, but a limited chance of success in negligence; Anna can claim for the flooding and the damage to her car in both nuisance and negligence and claim under *Rylands* v *Fletcher* for the flooding.

References

1	[1907] 2 KB 141	9	[1980] QB 485
2	[1961] 1 WLR 683	10	[1967] AC 617
3	[1986] 1 All ER 663	11	[1933] 1 KB 551
4	(1851) 20 LJ Ch 433	12	[1948] 2 KB 48
5	[1891] 2 Ch 409	13	(1876) 1 QBD 314
6	(1860) 3 B & S 62	14	[1940] 1 KB 229
7	(1889) 41 Ch D 88	15	(1868) LR 3 HL 330
8	(1908) 98 LT 718	16	[1990] 2 WLR 358

QUESTION 6

General comment

This question calls for a discussion of the elements of defamation and defences such as justification, qualified privilege and fair comment.

Suggested solution

We must consider whether Lionel has been defamed by Jeremy, Kenneth or Molly.

The reports by Jeremy and Kenneth are in permanent form and so any defamation that has occurred will take the form of libel. As regards Molly's use of the wordprocessor, this would also appear to be a communication in permanent form (as indeed it lasted long enough for her employer to see it), so this would also be libel if it were defamatory. In fact, as the allegation in the word processor imputes a crime punishable by imprisonment, and also would tend to disparage the plaintiff in any business or calling, if it were to be slander it would be actionable per se and require no proof of special damage (see s2 Defamation Act 1952) which from Lionel's point of view is the most important difference between the statement being held to be slander rather than libel.

To succeed in an action for defamation Lionel must prove that the statement complained of was defamatory; that it could reasonably be understood to refer to Lionel; and that it was published to a third party.

The usual test of a statement being defamatory is that it tends to lower the plaintiff in the estimation of right thinking members of society generally: *Sim* v *Stretch* (1) or which expose him to hatred, contempt and ridicule: *Parmiter* v *Coupland* (2).

Jeremy's statement is prima facie defamatory as it would tend to lower Lionel in the estimation of right thinking members of society, and the fact that Jeremy did not intend to defame Lionel is irrelevant: *Cassidy* v *Daily Mirror Newspapers* (3).

As regards Kenneth's statement the situation is a little more complex. In *Lewis* v *Daily Telegraph* (4) it was held that to say a person was being investigated for fraud was not the same as saying that he was guilty of fraud. However, Kenneth has stated that he has heard that Lionel was concerned with fakes rather than being investigated for fakes; Kenneth might argue that his recommendation to delay a decision rather than to refuse Lionel the prize is implying that he is not claiming that the allegation is true, but is rather awaiting clarification of the situation. In *Hartt* v *Newspaper Publishing* (5) the Court of Appeal held that the approach to adopt was that of the ordinary hypothetical reader who was neither naive nor unduly suspicious but who might read between the lines and be capable of loose thinking. Ultimately it would be a question for the jury to decide, but we shall continue the discussion on the assumption that the statement is prima facie defamatory.

Lionel must also prove that the statements refer to him and have been published to a third party. As regards both Jeremy and Kenneth there is no problem here as Lionel is mentioned by name and Jeremy has sent his report to the other trustees. I assume that Kenneth has also sent his report to the other trustees, but if he has not the fact that Molly's employer has seen it is sufficient publication.

We must now consider Molly. Assuming that Kenneth's statement is defamatory, and it clearly refers to Lionel, there has been a publication by Molly to her employer as every repetition of the statement constitutes a fresh publication and gives rise to a fresh cause of action: *Cutler* v *McPhail* (6). The publication need not be intentional, negligent publication is sufficient: *Theaker* v *Richardson* (7). Hence prima facie Molly has defamed Lionel.

Let us now turn to any defences which are available to the defendants.

One defence that is available to all defendants is justification ie truth of the statement concerned, but the facts of the problem do not tell us whether this is so and we shall assume that a plea of justification will fail.

Jeremy may seek to rely on the defence of qualified privilege on the grounds that he has a legal, social or moral duty to make the statement to the other trustees and that they have a corresponding interest to receive it: *Watt* v *Longsdon* (8). It seems clear from the facts of the problem that such a duty exists on both sides and would provide a defence to Jeremy. However, the defence of qualified privilege can be destroyed by showing that the defendant was actuated by malice, and as Lionel has recently been divorced by Jeremy's daughter, Jeremy may have made the statement with a malicious motive. By malicious is meant that Jeremy has no honest belief in the truth of his statement: *Horrocks* v *Lowe* (9). If Jeremy honestly believes his statement, malice cannot be inferred merely because Jeremy's belief is unreasonable or unfair: *Horrocks* v *Lowe*; lack of honest belief is essential.

Jeremy may also claim that his statement is fair comment based on true facts made in good faith on a matter of public interest. The courts tend to define public interest widely: *London Artists* v *Littler* (10), and the award in question would be a matter of public interest. The comment must be fair in the sense that the defendant honestly believed the opinion stated: *Slim* v *Daily Telegraph* (11). However, the question arises, has there been a comment based on facts or has Jeremy merely made a statement of fact? It seems that Jeremy has merely made a statement of fact and not opinion, there being no sub-stratum of fact as in *Kemsley* v *Foot* (12). Again the presence of malice will destroy this defence: *Thomas* v *Bradbury, Agnew* (13).

Kenneth may seek to rely on the defence of qualified privilege as regards publication to the other trustees, and as with Jeremy the duty to make and to receive the statement exists and there is no reason to impute malice to Kenneth.

As regards the publication by Kenneth to Molly, as this is a husband and wife communication it attracts absolute privilege and no action will lie in respect of it. The publication would also be covered by qualified privilege: *Bryanston Finance* v *De Vries* (14).

Considering the publication by Molly to her employer, Molly cannot use the defence of qualified privilege as although her employer may have an interest in receiving the statement, Molly appears to have no interest in making the statement to her employer: *Watt* v *Longsdon*. Molly may seek to rely on the defence that she is an innocent republisher and as such she will not be liable if she did not know the statement contained a libel and could not reasonably be expected to know this: *Sun Life Of Canada* v *W H Smith* (15).

Thus Lionel should be advised to sue Jeremy, Kenneth and Molly although of these Kenneth would appear to have the best defence.

References

1	[1936] 2 All ER 1237	9	[1975] AC 135
2	(1840) 6 M & W 105	10	[1969] 2 QB 375
3	[1929] 2 KB 331	11	[1968] 2 QB 157
4	[1964] AC 234	12	[1952] AC 345
5	Times Law Report 10 November 1989	13	[1906] 2 KB 627
6	[1962] 2 QB 292	14	[1975] QB 703
7	[1962] 1 WLR 151	15	[1934] 150 LT 211
8	[1930] 1 KB 130		

QUESTION 7

General comments

This problem concerns pure economic loss and requires a discussion of *Junior Books* and its subsequent interpretation by the courts. It is a good example of the need to keep up to date in the rapidly changing area of duty of care and those situations in which the duty is restricted.

Suggested solution

It is clear from the facts of the problem that the loss suffered by Tyrant Industries and Cleaners is pure economic loss. We must therefore consider the situations in which the law will allow recovery for such loss.

The traditional approach of the courts was to deny recovery of economic loss that was not consequent upon damage to the person or property of the plaintiff: *Spartan Steels & Alloys v Martin* (1).

However, in 1983 in *Junior Books v Veitchi* (2) the House of Lords allowed recovery for economic loss suffered by the plaintiff when a firm of sub-contractors, with whom the plaintiff had no contractual relationship, laid a floor defectively. It was held that there was such a relationship of proximity between the plaintiff and the defendant that the defendant owed the plaintiff a duty of care to avoid economic loss. *Junior Books* was decided when the two-tier test of Lord Wilberforce in *Anns v Merton London Borough Council* (3) was still used to determine the existence of a duty of care and the House of Lords relied heavily on the fact that the plaintiff had nominated the defendant to lay the floor and had relied on the defendant to carry out this work properly, that this reliance was known to the defendants and that the damage was a direct and foreseeable result of the defendants' negligence. Interestingly, Lord Brandon dissented on the grounds that the decision effectively created contractual obligations while circumventing contractual concepts such as privity and consideration.

Recent subsequent cases have not followed *Junior Books*; in parallel with the retreat from *Anns*, which formed the basis for *Junior Books*, the latter case has been the subject of much judicial analysis and criticism. In *Muirhead v Industrial Tank Specialities* (4) *Junior Books* was not followed and in *Aswan Engineering Establishment v Lupdine* (5) it was said that where the defect renders the product less valuable the plaintiff's remedy lies in contract, and where the defect creates a danger to others the remedy lies in tort, and that *Junior Books* was the first case to cross this line.

In *Simaan General Contracting v Pilkington* (6) there was a nominated sub-contractor situation but *Junior Books* was not applied, and in *Greater Nottingham Co-operative Society v Cementation Piling & Foundations* (7) there was a contract between the plaintiff and the defendants who were nominated sub-contractors. The defendants carried out their work carelessly but the contract related only to the materials and not the way in which the work was to be carried out. The Court of Appeal held that no duty of care arose in tort because the contractual relationship between the parties precluded this and exhaustively defined the obligations between the plaintiff and the defendant.

In *D & F Estates v Church Commissioners* (8) the House of Lords held that a builder was not liable in tort for the cost of remedying defects in a building constructed by him if the defects did not pose an imminent threat of physical injury to the building or occupants or damage other property of the plaintiff, and where the only purpose of the remedial works was to render the buildings fit for their intended use, which seems to be the situation in the question set. In *D & F Estates* Lord Bridge stated that the consensus of judicial opinion seemed to be that *Junior Books* cannot be regarded as laying down any principle of general application in the law of tort and Lord Oliver stated it was really of no use as an authority on the general duty of care. In *Simaan Contracting* Dillon LJ went even further and said that the case had been the subject of so much analysis and discussion with differing explanations of the case that the case cannot now be regarded as a useful pointer to any development of law and that he found it difficult to see that future citation from *Junior Books* could ever serve any useful purpose.

Given this extensive and detailed criticism of *Junior Books* Tyrant and Cleaners must be advised that there is no chance of successfully suing Greenmadness in tort for the economic loss they have suffered. The fact that Tyrant nominated Greenmadness as nominated sub-contractors is not enough to allow Tyrant to sue: *Simaan General Contracting*, nor do Cleaners have the required proximity.

The next aspect we must consider is whether Tyrant and Cleaners can sue the Foliage Consultancy Council in negligence for the economic loss they have suffered. To see whether or not Foliage owe a duty of care to these parties one would use the test for duty of care laid down in *Caparo Industries* v *Dickman* (9) by the House of Lords, viz, foreseeability of damage, proximity of relationship and the reasonableness or otherwise of imposing a duty. The problem for Tyrant and Cleaners is that in *Curran* v *Northern Ireland Co-ownership Housing Association* (10) the House of Lords held that although the defendants had to be satisfied under regulations that certain building work was to be carried out properly, the purpose of the regulations was to ensure that public money was spent properly and not to protect the interests of the plaintiff; see also *Mariola Marine* v *Lloyd's Register* (11). In the present problem the purpose of approval by Foliage is to protect the environment and not the interests of Tyrant or Cleaners. Hence Tyrant and Cleaners cannot sue Foliage.

There is no point in Tyrant suing Sleepers in tort because following *Greater Nottingham Co-operative* the contract between Tyrant and Sleepers would define any liability for economic loss, and it is stated in the contract that there will be no liability on Sleepers' part for the neglect or wilful default of Greenmadness.

If Cleaners were to sue Sleepers, they would be met by the earlier agreement regarding the difficulties of imposing a duty of care in respect of economic loss.

Thus our advice to Tyrant and Cleaners is that they have no claims in tort.

References

1	[1973] 1 QB 27	7	[1988] 2 All ER 971
2	[1983] 1 AC 520	8	[1988] 3 WLR 368
3	[1978] AC 728	9	[1990] 1 All ER 568
4	[1986] QB 507	10	[1987] AC 178
5	[1987] 1 All ER 135	11	Times Law Report 21 February 1990
6	[1988] 2 WLR 761		

QUESTION 8

General comment

This question involves a consideration of breach of duty and causation in negligence, with particular reference to the possibility of a novus actus interveniens breaking the chain of causation. Finally the question of vicarious liability should also be considered.

Suggested solution

It is well established law that Sam as a driver owes a duty of care to all other road users and would clearly be able to meet the latest formulation of the criteria laid down for the imposition of a duty of care in *Caparo Industries* v *Dickman* (1). In carrying out this duty of care Sam must act as a reasonable man: *Blyth* v *Birmingham Waterworks* (2); this is an objective test which means that the standard of care required of a trainee driver is the same standard as required of an experienced and competent driver: *Nettleship* v *Weston* (3), and it is by this standard that Sam must be judged. When Sam drives at high speed along a country road he is prima facie in breach of his duty as a reasonable man would not act in this way. If Sam were en route to an emergency then his actions would be those of a reasonable man: *Watt* v *Hertfordshire County Council* (4), but this is not the situation here. Ursula's collision is caused by Sam's breach of duty so prima facie Sam is liable for any injuries caused. Sam may seek to argue that Ursula did not make room for the fire engine to pass, but acted instead in a careless manner and that she caused her own injuries, ie that her panic and collision was a novus actus interveniens. As Ursula has been placed in an emergency or difficult situation by Sam's negligence however, the court is unlikely to make this finding if Ursula acted reasonably in the agony of the moment, even if with hindsight she could have avoided the accident: *Jones* v *Boyce* (5). But it is open to the court to find contributory negligence on Ursula's part and to reduce any damages awarded by s1 Law Reform (Miscellaneous Provisions) Act 1945 having regard to Ursula's fault in causing the accident. All that Sam will have to show is that Ursula failed to look after herself properly: *Davies* v *Swan Motor* (6).

Hence Sam is liable for the eye injury initially suffered by Ursula (subject to any reduction in damages); the question arises, however, is Sam liable for Ursula's subsequent loss of sight or is the earlier railway accident a novus actus interveniens? The new act (ie the railway accident) is an act of a third party and we must decide whether this act is the true cause of Ursula's loss of sight. From the facts of the problem it seems that the loss of Ursula's sight was caused only by the delay, and so Sam would not be liable for this additional damage: *Knightley* v *Johns* (7). It is not a situation where the delay was a natural and probable consequence of the first accident and was foreseeable as in *Rouse* v *Squires* (8); instead there has been a break in the chain of causation. [Note that the question that must be decided here is one of causation and not foreseeability as Sam is liable for any personal injury that ensues in the accident as he need only foresee the kind of damage and not the extent: *Smith* v *Leech, Brain* (9)].

Similarly Sam will be liable for Violet's slight injuries suffered in the collision but not for her two broken legs, as the cause of the broken legs was a novus actus interveniens which was not a natural and probable consequence of the first collision (see above).

As we are told that Sam was undergoing instruction and is a trainee fireman, it is clear that Sam is an employee, the Waterside Fire Brigade (or the appropriate local authority) is his employer, and Sam was acting in the course of his employment. The fact that Sam was doing so in a negligent manner is irrelevant: *Century Insurance* v *Northern Ireland Road Transport Board* (10).

Thus the Waterside Fire Brigade (or the appropriate local authority) will be responsible for Sam's actions and Ursula and Violet are advised to sue the Fire Brigade in respect of the injuries first suffered in the collision; as regards the later more serious injuries they are without a remedy. Ursula and Violet should also be advised that if they failed to wear seat belts and the wearing of a seat belt would have reduced their injuries that a reduction will be made for contributory negligence on their part: *Froom* v *Butcher* (11).

References

1	[1990] 1 All ER 568	7	[1982] 1 WLR 349
2	(1856) 11 Ex 781	8	[1973] QB 889
3	[1971] 2 QB 691	9	[1962] 2 QB 405
4	[1954] 1 WLR 835	10	[1942] AC 509
5	(1816) 1 Stark 493	11	[1975] 3 WLR 379
6	[1949] 2 KB 291		

ORDER FORM

SOLICITORS' FINAL

	TEXTBOOKS Cost £	REVISION WORKBOOKS Cost £	SUGGESTED SOLUTIONS PACKS (a) Winter Cost £	PACKS (a) Summer Cost £	SINGLE PAPERS (b) Winter Cost £	SINGLE PAPERS (b) Summer Cost £
Accounts	14.95	9.95	14.95	14.95	2.25	2.25
Business Organisations & Insolvency			11.95	§ 11.95	2.25	2.25
Consumer Protection & Employment Law	14.95		11.95	§ 11.95	2.25	2.25
Conveyancing I & II	14.95		14.95	14.95	2.25	2.25
Family Law	14.95		14.95	14.95	2.25	2.25
Litigation	14.95		14.95	14.95	2.25	2.25
Wills, Probate & Administration	14.95	9.95	14.95	14.95	2.25	2.25
Final Exam Papers (Set) 1989				9.95		
Final Exam Papers (Set) 1990			9.95	9.95		

INSTITUTE OF LEGAL EXECUTIVES

	Cost £
Company & Partnership Law	18.95
Constitutional Law	13.95
Contract Law	13.95
Criminal Law	13.95
Equity and Trusts	13.95
European Law & Practice	17.95
Evidence	17.95
Land Law	13.95
Revenue Law	16.95
Tort	13.95

§ Limited to new syllabus from Summer 1986.

(a) Packs consist of either collected Winter or Summer papers. They change in April to include the previous Summer & Winter papers respectively.

(b) Single papers are published in April & October and are the previous Winter & Summer papers respectively, together with final examination papers.

LLB PUBLICATIONS

	TEXTBOOKS Cost £	CASEBOOKS Cost £	REVISION WORKBOOKS Cost £	SUG. SOL. 1985/89 Cost £	SUG. SOL. 1990 Cost £
Administrative Law	17.95	18.95		14.95	3.00
Commercial Law Vol I	17.95	18.95	9.95	14.95	3.00
Vol II	16.95	18.95			
Company Law	18.95	18.95	9.95	14.95	3.00
Conflict of Laws	17.95	16.95		14.95	3.00
Constitutional Law	13.95	16.95	9.95	14.95	3.00
Contract Law	13.95	16.95	9.95	14.95	3.00
Conveyancing	16.95	16.95		14.95	3.00
Criminal Law	13.95	16.95	9.95	14.95	3.00
Criminology	16.95				3.00
European Community Law	17.95	16.95		*7.95	3.00
English Legal System	13.95	14.95		14.95	3.00
Equity and Trusts	13.95	18.95	9.95	14.95	3.00
Evidence	17.95	17.95	9.95	14.95	3.00
Family Law	16.95	18.95	9.95	14.95	3.00
Jurisprudence	14.95		9.95	14.95	3.00
Labour Law	15.95				
Land Law	13.95	18.95	9.95	14.95	3.00
Public International Law	18.95	16.95	9.95	14.95	3.00
Revenue Law	16.95	18.95	9.95	14.95	3.00
Roman Law	19.95				
Succession	16.95	17.95	9.95	14.95	3.00
Tort	13.95	18.95	9.95	14.95	3.00

CPE PUBLICATIONS

	Cost £
Criminal Law	13.95
Constitutional & Administrative Law	13.95
Contract Law	13.95
Equity and Trusts	13.95
Land Law	13.95
Tort	13.95

BAR PUBLICATIONS

	TEXTBOOKS Cost £	CASEBOOKS Cost £	SUG. SOL. 1985/89 Cost £	SUG. SOL. 1990 Cost £
Conflict of Laws	16.95	17.95	† 3.95	3.95
European Community Law & Human Rights	17.95	16.95	† 3.95	3.95
Evidence	17.95	17.95	14.95	3.95
Family Law	16.95	18.95	14.95	3.95
General Paper I	19.95	16.95	14.95	3.95
General Paper II	19.95	16.95	14.95	3.95
Law of International Trade	16.95	16.95	14.95	3.95
Practical Conveyancing	16.95	16.95	14.95	3.95
Procedure	19.95	16.95	14.95	3.95
Revenue Law	16.95	16.95	14.95	3.95
Sale of Goods and Credit	17.95	17.95	14.95	3.95

* 1987-1989 papers only † 1988 and 1989 papers only

HLT PUBLICATIONS

All HLT Publications have two important qualities. First, they are written by specialists, all of whom have direct practical experience of teaching the syllabus. Second, all Textbooks are reviewed and updated each year to reflect new developments and changing trends.

They are used widely by students at polytechnics and colleges throughout the United Kingdom and overseas.

A comprehensive range of titles is covered by the following classifications.

- **TEXTBOOKS**
- **CASEBOOKS**
- **SUGGESTED SOLUTIONS**
- **REVISION WORKBOOKS**

The books listed overleaf can be ordered through your local bookshops or obtained direct from the publisher using this order form. Telephone, Fax, or Telex orders will also be accepted. Quote your Access or Visa card numbers for priority orders. To order direct from publisher please enter cost of titles you require, fill in despatch details and send it with your remittance to The HLT Group Ltd.

Please complete Order Form overleaf

DETAILS FOR DESPATCH OF PUBLICATIONS

Please insert your full name below

Please insert below the style in which you would like the correspondence from the Publisher addressed to you

TITLE Mr, Miss etc. INITIALS SURNAME/FAMILY NAME

Address to which study material is to be sent (please ensure someone will be present to accept delivery of your Publications).

POSTAGE & PACKING

You are welcome to purchase study material from the Publisher at 200 Greyhound Road, London W14 9RY, during normal working hours.

If you wish to order by post this may be done direct from the Publisher. Postal charges are as follows:

UK - Orders over £30: no charge. Orders below £30: £2.00. Single paper (last exam only): 40p

OVERSEAS - See table below

The Publisher cannot accept responsibility in respect of postal delays or losses in the postal systems.

DESPATCH All cheques must be cleared before material is despatched.

SUMMARY OF ORDER Date of order:

Cost of publications ordered: £

Add postage and packing: UNITED KINGDOM:

OVERSEAS:	TEXTS		Suggested Solutions (last Exam only)
	One	Each Extra	
Eire	£3.00	£0.50	£1.00
European Community	£7.50	£0.50	£1.00
East Europe & North America	£8.50	£1.00	£1.50
South East Asia	£10.00	£1.50	£1.50
Australia / New Zealand	£12.00	£3.50	£1.50
Other Countries (Africa, India etc)	£11.00	£3.00	£1.50

Total cost of order: £

Please ensure that you enclose a cheque or draft payable to The HLT Group Ltd for the above amount, or charge to ☐ ☐ VISA

Card Number

Expiry Date______ Signature______

HAYNES GREAT CARS

PORSCHE
911

HAYNES GREAT CARS

PORSCHE
911

A celebration of the world's most revered sports car

MICHAEL SCARLETT

A catalogue record for this book is available from the British Library

ISBN 1 84425 124 1

Library of Congress catalog card number 2005926084

Published by Haynes Publishing,
Sparkford, Yeovil, Somerset BA22 7JJ, England

Tel: 01963 442030 Fax: 01963 440001
Int. tel: +44 1963 442030 Int. fax: +44 1963 440001
E-mail: sales@haynes.co.uk
Website: www.haynes.co.uk

Haynes North America Inc.
861 Lawrence Drive, Newbury Park, California 91320, USA

Edited by Warren Allport
Designed by Richard Parsons

Printed and bound in Great Britain by J. H. Haynes & Co. Ltd

PHOTOGRAPH CREDITS
All photographs are from the Porsche Photographic Archive except where credited otherwise.
National Motor Museum, Beaulieu 2-3, 6, 24-25, 118-119
John Colley 56-57

CONVERSION DATA

Metric to non-metric:

1mm	= 0.0394in
1km (kilometre)	= 0.621 miles
1cu dm (cubic decimetre)	= 0.035cu ft
1 litre (1,000cc)	= 1.760 Imperial pints
	= 2.10 US pints
	= 0.220 Imperial gallons
	= 0.264 US gallons
	= 61.023cu in
1kg (kilogramme)	= 2.205lb
1 tonne (metric ton)	= 0.984 ton
1bar	= 14.504psi
1PS (metric horsepower)	= 0.986bhp (James Watt)
	= 0.724kW
1kW (kilowatt)	= 1.341bhp
	= 1.360PS
1Nm (Newton metre)	= 0.738lb ft
1mkg (metre kilogram)	= 0.102Nm
1kph (km per hour)	= 0.621mph
100kph	= 62.137mph
litres/100km to mpg	= 282.473 divided by litres/100km

Non-metric to metric:

1in	= 25.4mm
1ft	= 304.8mm
$\frac{1}{4}$ mile	= 402.32 metres
1 mile	= 1.609km
1cu in (cubic inch)	= 0.0164cu dm
1cu ft (cubic foot)	= 28.317cu dm
1 pint	= 0.568 litre
1 Imperial gallon	= 4.546 litres
1 US gallon	= 3.785 litres
1lb (pound)	= 0.454kg
1 ton	= 1.016 tonne
1psi (pound per sq in)	= 0.069bar
1bhp (James Watt)	= 1.014PS
	= 0.746kW
1lb ft (pound foot)	= 1.357Nm
	= 0.138mkg
1mph (miles per hour)	= 1.609kph
60mph	= 96.56kph
100mph	= 160.93kph
mpg to litres/100km	= 282.473 divided by the mpg figure

Contents

Introduction   6

Acknowledgements   9

Design and development   10

First decade   24
1963–1973   The 911 goes into production

Second decade   56
1974–1983   The first 911 turbo

Third decade   84
1984–1993   Turbo and all-wheel-drive era

Fourth Decade   118
1994–2005   Proper location and proper cooling

Index   160

Introduction

I have to confess that when Haynes Publishing invited me to write this book on the Porsche 911 in their Great Cars series, I accepted with secretly very mixed feelings. After all, many of the book's potential buyers will be enthusiasts for the car and will expect something extolling its virtues but I am on record, if mostly anonymously as is the tradition for *Autocar* road tests, as a repeated critic of the 911's handling. This was born of experience between 1967 and 1984 of sampling its behaviour on the Motor Industry Research Association's superb test tracks, some of whose corners are perfect for safely exploring the on- and over-the-limit cornering performance of test cars.

Freelances, which I have been since 1984, do not all enjoy the same facilities as full-time magazine motoring journalists. So although I had driven most models of 911 on Porsche press driving launches since that time, such events (always on public roads) do not usually provide MIRA-type corners on which one may safely conduct handling experiments at any car's limit. I knew from such launches that the improvements in tyres and, after the 993-series, decent rear suspension had pushed the limit at which one might suffer the old 911 devil to such a high level that one rarely had the chance to play with the car safely to see what its limit

behaviour was like outside a test track.

So it was a wonderful thing to attend the British press launch of the 2005 997-series Porsche 911 Carrera and Carrera S at Oulton Park earlier this year, to be able to test that latest (at the time of writing) 911 properly and find that it really does drive very reasonably and safely at extremely high cornering rates. The result was a near St Paul-on-the-road-to-Damascus conversion, which made writing this book much more straightforward.

For there was always so very much that one could admire in these Porsches, even in the less well-endowed earlier days: the standard of finish and functionality, so

Few cars illustrate as well as the Porsche 911, the old adage in car styling that a good, simple shape won't date.

The 911's functional beauty and cleanliness of line have seen it survive lustily – and still lusted after – for more than 40 years.

pure and unadulterated with the effeminacies and phoney excesses and vulgarities of so much, if not all, styling; the superb engineering always evident in any Porsche; the fit and finish of its parts; the ingenuity and thought of so much of its design, in the original mechanical sense of the word before it got hijacked by stylists.

This book is radically different from previous *Haynes Great Cars* titles, not just because it is the first non-British one but because the 911 has existed, mostly with huge commercial and competition success, for over 40 years – something that was not even approached by any of the sports cars in the series so far. It is also a car whose history cannot be told without relating its mechanical history – the mostly constant development of the car is the story, which is why there is so much to say about it from a technical viewpoint, leaving no room for quotations from sales brochures.

To reflect typical views of the motoring press on the 911 throughout its life to date, there are however occasional quotations, mostly from road tests conducted by *Autocar* magazine. I was a full time employee of the Iliffe, then IPC-owned *Autocar* in the 18 years after the change from my engineering career in the aircraft, then embryonic British motor racing industry in 1966. I started at the magazine

as a road test rookie, becoming its technical editor and therefore running the road test team in 1976, so what must be said about *Autocar* road tests may look unpardonably immodest.

However, I must defend myself by pointing out that traditionally, and still to this day, *Autocar* road tests are unsigned

because they are, and always have been, a team effort. Though written by one team member, its road tests are the fusion of the opinions and judgements of the whole team. It is this that, in not only my humble view, makes them the most authoritative sources of informed judgement on all cars so tested.

A 1995 Carrera RS 3.8 coupé.

The 3.8-litre Carrera S, with 355PS, was more powerful than its 3.6-litre Carrera sibling (right).

Acknowledgements

For readers whose appetite may be whetted by this brief effort, and who have not seen the book, I most warmly recommend *Porsche 911 Story – the entire development history* by Paul Frère, a great former racing driver, motoring journalist of the highest calibre and innate modesty, and a colleague whom I count myself very fortunate to know. Again published by Haynes, it is now in its seventh edition and an invaluable reference source, which was a great help in writing this book. Also to be recommended as a general Porsche reference is Karl Ludvigsen's superb three-volume book *Porsche – Excellence Was Expected* (Bentley Publishers, 1,574 pages). The parent company, Dr. Ing. h.c. F. Porsche AG, in the very friendly and helpful guise of Michael Schimpke, another old friend, and his equally co-operative colleague Michael Baumann, have been wonderfully helpful and patient with my insistent and constant pestering for information. So also has the British end of the company, Porsche Cars Great Britain Ltd, and Geoffrey Turral, its sales manager, and Nick Perry, media relations officer, to both of whom I am most grateful. Very few people begin to exceed all others in their helpfulness, patience, and understanding: Steve Rendle, commissioning editor of the Books Division of Haynes Publishing, is one and my wife Alison is the other. She has put up with my unsocial retreats to my study to get on with the job of writing and played so encouraging a role, during a particularly daunting and distracting period of our lives caused by the extended negotiations of the selling and purchase of a house.

Michael Scarlett, October 2005

Opposite: 1978 selection: 911SC 3.0 Targa, 911SC 3.0 coupé, and Turbo 3.3 coupé showing its tea-tray rear wing.

Overall victory at Le Mans in 1998 with the 911 GT1 – close to the day 50 years before when the first Porsche sports car appeared.

Design and development

Ferdinand Porsche, born on 3 September 1875, was a remarkable automotive engineer by any standards. His name in the old Austro-German world was first made by the design of the electric Lohner-Porsche of 1900, when he was but 25 years old. Employed for the next 29 years by a variety of famous makes (including Daimler in Austria, Daimler and Daimler-Benz in Germany, then Steyr, Auto Union and the infant Volkswagen), he had established his own design consultancy by the end of 1930 in southern Germany.

The Porsche company was officially founded in March 1931, by the end of which year it boasted 19 employees, and had moved to its future Zuffenhausen, Stuttgart, home by 1938 with 138 employees, necessary to meet the challenge of the Volkswagen project. Porsche had been helped by investor friends at the beginning but the success of the young company allowed him and his family to assume full ownership in that same year. The family members involved included his daughter Louise (born in 1904), his son Ferdinand Anton Ernst (1909), called 'Ferry', and Louise's husband, Anton Piëch. Ferry took up the reins of the company after his father, but all of them were to play important roles in the Porsche story.

Porsche beginnings – and that engine position

The tale of the first 17 years of the Porsche company, tortuous just before and after the Second World War, is too complex to detail here and has been well told by others. However, there are aspects relevant to the story of the Porsche 911 that are important to mention.

The most significant is the reason for the fundamental layout of all road-going production Porsche sports cars apart from the mid-engined 914 of 1967 (and, of course, the Boxster of 1993) – the choice of a rear engine placed behind the rear-drive axis rather than in the so-called 'mid-

engine' position between the driver and back 'axle'.

There is a temptation for some car enthusiasts to believe that the transformation of Grand Prix racing cars from front-engine to mid-engine was brought about by the remarkable Cooper-Climaxes of the late 1950s – it is true that they and their various later rivals, understanding wheel location better, were vastly more successful than earlier mid-engined racers. However, Ferdinand Porsche deservedly takes huge credit in the history of the post-Vintage period for the

design of the Auto Union grand prix cars that fought with the front-engined Mercedes in the GP races of 1937–39. These astonishing monsters were mid-engined, their reputation for difficult handling due to the less happy choice of swing-axle wheel location at the rear and not the position of their vast engines.

Ferdinand Porsche is said to have first considered adding car manufacture to design consultancy as far back as 1922. During that pre-war period and the work on the Volkswagen KdF-Wagen (*Kraft durch Freude*, Strength through Joy), the idea for a

Opposite: Ferry Porsche with his father Ferdinand in a 1934 portrait. The son, who was to lead the Porsche car manufacturing firm 14 years later, had worked in his father's office since the Dr. Ing. h.c. F. Porsche GmbH design consultancy was established in 1931.

Below: The 1963 Type 901 2-litre coupé. Note the narrow tyres and rear overhang.

Porsche sports car sprang up after the rejection by VW of a project for a Beetle-based sports car. In 1938, Porsche planned the F-type or Type 114. This remarkable suggestion proposed a V10 1.5-litre engine, mid-mounted with transmission behind the rear axle in an oval-tube ladder chassis clothed in an elegant streamlined coupé body, with trailing arm swing-axle rear suspension and parallel trailing arms in front, all torsion-bar sprung.

The war stalled any thoughts of production but at least one copy of the stored plans survived hostilities. In 1947–48 the Porsche firm (still based in its late-war refuge in a former sawmill in the village of Gmünd, between Klagenfurt and Salzburg in Austria) was commissioned to design the Grand Prix Cisitalia, a mid-engined flat-12-cylinder air-cooled supercharged 1.5-litre – all subsequent Porsche all-out competition designs were to be mid-engined.

In 1947 Porsche was not the wealthy concern of later years, so reviving the ideas of the Type 114 was put aside in favour of the far less costly option of basing a production sports coupé on Volkswagen Beetle parts. However, at first the mid-engined ideal was preserved. The design proposed turning the VW layout round, to put the directly-air-cooled engine ahead of the rear-axle line. The blade arms, which in the Volkswagen trailed to locate the hubs longways, were to be sprung from the transverse torsion bars at their pivots and thus transformed into leading arms.

In the VW, the trailing arrangement ensured toe-in of the rear wheels under roll – helpful for stability in one respect (even if it made no difference to the two fatal disadvantages of camber change and, in extremis, jacking effect inevitable with swing-axle geometry). Changing to leading arm meant toe-out in roll – and therefore unwanted oversteer – plus non-standard lengthened arms and, with the torsion bar mounting much further aft, a heavier chassis to cope with the larger beam loading of the chassis. This combination swung the designers, anxious to minimise cost as well as weight, back to the Beetle's rear-engine layout.

There are undeniably contentious aspects to a rear- as opposed to mid-engined car – undesirable effects when cornering are the obvious ones – but the rear-engine layout has advantages. It is doubtful if the designers of what became the prototype of the Porsche 356 were anticipating the Issigonis philosophy eventually known as space efficiency – maximum interior space within minimum outside size exemplified first in the original BMC Mini two decades later – but putting the power unit behind the back wheels does allow more interior room than a mid-engined layout. Road-going Porches

have long enjoyed the advantage of relatively good interior space compared to mid- and many front-engined sports cars.

More relevant to a sports car are the rear-engined design's advantages in traction and braking. Both involve the effect of dynamic weight transfer, maximising load on the rear tyres during acceleration from rest for optimum getaway and minimising the chances of wasteful wheel-spin. Under braking, weight transfer forward works towards changing the typically one-third/two-thirds front-to-rear static weight distribution nearer to 50/50, ideal for the best possible braking balance.

Ancestor of the 911

Forget for a moment the contentious
handling issues of the Porsche design and
consider the 911 shape. The profile of that
first 911 is still basically the same as now,
41 years later. Only Britain's Morgan can
claim a longer-lived basic style of body,
dating back nearly twice that time. The
fact that the 911 shape has survived so
healthily for so long is as much as
anything else a tribute to the artistic
engineering eye of Ferdinand Alexander
(Butzi) Porsche (eldest son of Ferry Porsche
and grandson of the founder Dr Ferdinand

*Ferdinand
Alexander (Butzi)
Porsche with an
early Type 901.*

*A 901, forerunner of
the 911, in Porsche
works No 1.*

13

Erwin Komenda, the engineer largely responsible for the style and shape of the 356.

Porsche) and the abilities of Erwin Komenda, who rendered Butzi's sketches into metal. In later parlance Komenda would have been called the infant company's stylist (or today the debased word designer, which he deserved as he was an engineer as well as a stylist).

To engineers like those members of the Porsche family and firm, it is bordering on an insult to call that still utterly distinctive coupé profile 'styling' because the word 'styling', and today 'design' too, often are attached to shapes which are anything but functional. The coupé that is the root of all the subsequently added variant body types – Targa, Cabriolet, Speedster – is the embodiment of what ought to be for all body designers (but is still only for a select few) their dominating credo, that form should follow function. It is true that from an aerodynamic standpoint, function was distorted in that the shape was imperfect, generating a lot of high-speed lift which complicated the car's stability problems. When, in the light of later knowledge, this

was realised and acknowledged, it acquired, to some eyes, somewhat bizarre aero appendages. This was also true of other cars of that time, for example the allegedly aerodynamicist-developed Jaguar D-type.

The 356, the first production Porsche, first ran as a prototype chassis in March 1948. Its 16-year production run, of a total of 76,303 cars, lasted until September 1965, overlapping the 911 by two years if one counts – as one must – the appearance of the 901 prototype at the 1963 Frankfurt Show as the public beginning of the 911; the car started rolling off its Zuffenhausen production line in February 1964.

The 901 remained the name used for this considerable improvement on the 365 until '911' took its place in October 1965, the result of Peugeot's objections to infringement of its French-based trademark, which centred round two numbers with a zero between. The obeisance to Gallic sensitivities applied to road-going production Porsches, not the competition cars.

The engine seemed to be the main point of interest on the Porsche 901's first public appearance at the 1963 Frankfurt Show.

A 1964 shot of the 911 2.0 coupé (right) and its immediate predecessor, a 365C coupé.

Body-cum-chassis

The 911 differences began with its larger size. The body, a 2+2 like the latter-day 356's, sat on a 2,211mm wheelbase, 112mm longer than the 356's. It was therefore longer overall, at 4,163mm, if at 1,610mm not quite as wide, thanks to less-loosely tyre-enclosing wheel arches. In the light of 356 experience, the car was conceived to be roomier, if not a full four seater, with a front boot 'big enough to take a set of golf clubs' as Ferry Porsche insisted. Performance had to match that of the faster Carrera version of the 356 but with better refinement, better ride and handling, and less demanding maintenance – this last boiling down to eliminating grease nipples in suspension pivots, achieved by using elastomeric bushing.

Undeniably thanks to the company's work with the evolution and development of the Volkswagen and the notion of a fixed-head coupé as the starting point, the adoption of an integral body/chassis rather than any traditional separate chassis was probably taken for granted. The 901/911

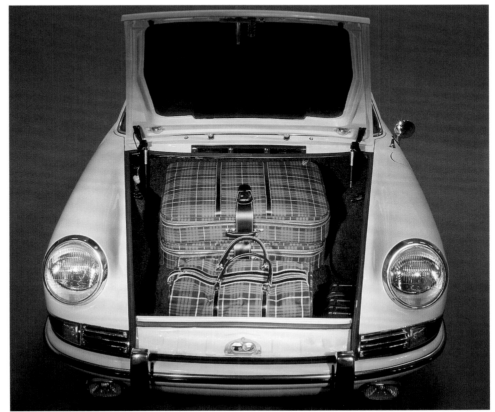

The 911 2.0 coupé's luggage space made to look its largest with tailored cases. A design requirement was space for a set of golf clubs.

bodyshell relied on relatively conventional integral design for its beam and torsional rigidity in the crucial occupant-containing centre box, with wide, quite deep side sills, a correspondingly deep centre box-section tunnel, and some longitudinal beam strength added by the roof and the slender A-pillars.

Transverse bracing was provided in the floor by wide, shallow box members each side of the centre tunnel at the front of the main seats, and smaller ribs formed in the floor. In front of the occupant cell, there was the considerable hoop supporting the facia and steering column with sill-wide feet each side; this was itself braced by its forward projection over the pedals. Ahead of the vertical wall ending the pedal area, extensions of the inward-swept sill sections were joined by a cross-member.

At the back of the cell, the floor was swept upwards from the cross-tube carrying the rear suspension torsion bars and diagonal link pivot brackets, forming a stiffening diagonal back diaphragm; this flattened to a multiple-ribbed deck ending in the small-section cross-member at the root of the roof sides. The rise of the side members formed by extending the sills ran the full length backwards to the tail, bridged transversely by the rear cross section, and further back by the considerable cross-member supporting the drivetrain.

Suspension and steering

Suspension was considerably different from the 365, particularly in front, where the previous transverse torsion bar-sprung parallel trailing link system – a Porsche favourite since at least Auto Union times – was replaced on each side by a strut formed by the telescopic damper (also acting as the steering pivot) and a bottom link pivoting on the longways-aligned torsion bar. An arrangement originally invented by Porsche engineering designer Wolfgang Eyb in 1952 (and very similar to the familiar MacPherson strut), this reduced the intrusion of suspension on luggage space thanks to its basic layout, further helped by using a torsion bar instead of the bulk of a coil spring coaxial

with the damper. A 13mm diameter anti-roll bar worked through rubber-bushed push/pull rods to the bottom of each suspension strut.

At the rear, the pure swing-axle design was supplanted by a semi-swing axle (semi-trailing arm), torsion bar-sprung. In detail design this was interesting and neat, with two torsion bars centre-located in the cross-tube in the back of the bodyshell. Each bar's outer end was splined to a deep but thin spring-steel blade arm trailing to the wheel hub carrier, which was part of the other suspension link, itself pivoting from a bracket on the torsion bar-containing cross-tube near to the centreline of the car.

A telescopic damper on each side ran upwards and slightly inwards, from the back of the hub carrier, to maximise damper stroke, and therefore effectiveness. This arrangement, of course, meant a new drive shaft, with the inboard universal joint accommodating plunge (longways movement) in itself, rather than depending on a splined telescoping shaft. Camber and toe-in could be adjusted via eccentrics. The trailing blade arm's easily twisted thinness meant it could accommodate twist imposed by the swing of the diagonal hub-carrying arm, while the effectively longer radius of the system produced less change of camber and toe-in of the wheel than the 356's plain swing-axle – better for handling and grip, if still not perfect.

For the first time on a Porsche, steering was by ZF rack and pinion, with the rack centrally mounted and a sharply angled double universal-jointed steering column, to make offering left- or right-hand drive easier. The fact that this layout also provided good passive safety in a head-on collision was, at that less passive safety conscious time, an incidental benefit. The pinion for the 16.5:1 overall ratio steering box ran in ball bearings, in a mounting spring-loaded against the rack, to

Steering wheel and control stalks give the date (1964) away but otherwise the instrument layout of this 911 2.0 coupé sets the pattern for most of the next four decades.

eliminate any play. The all-disc Ate brakes were partly carried over from the 356, using the same 284.5mm rear discs, but slightly larger 282mm discs in front, in place of 274mm. The 15in steel wheel sizes remained unchanged from the 365C, using 4½J rims – the widest recommended at the time for the tyre size, 165HR-15in front and rear. The relatively narrow dimensions were felt by the car's designers best to accommodate the camber change of the rear suspension.

Engine

The 911 had to be as quick as the previous Carrera version of the 365, but not as noisy. One route to refinement is a better choice of engine layout, which in the horizontally-opposed pattern set by 365 tradition and the rear-engine layout, was six instead of four cylinders. Work on such a larger capacity 2-litre engine with pushrod-operated overhead valves was started in 1961 but superseded the

following year by a same bore and stroke (80mm x 66mm), 1,991cc opposed six designed by a team led by Ferdinand Piëch.

The structure of the engine was an early example of the principle of partly exploiting the compressive strength of aluminium alloy and the tensile efficiency of steel, originally seen fully in the Rolls-Royce Merlin aero engine and, much later, Austin-Rover's neat little K-series engine. The two-part aluminium alloy crankcase, split longways along its vertical centreline, was bolted together. Cylinders, 'Biral' type, cast-iron centred with their aluminium alloy finned outsides, sat in machined recesses in the crankcase, sandwiched between it and the aluminium cylinder heads by long steel studs rooted each side of the main bearings. Cam boxes were separate castings bolted to the heads.

One 'overhead' camshaft to each trio of cylinders was mounted in the valve chest, not quite centrally, working 39mm diameter inlet valves and 35mm exhausts (set at 27° and 32° from the bore axis) through steel rocker arms, each rocker set on its own short shaft. Conventional methods to improve performance included sodium-filled exhaust valves to improve cooling, and double valve springs.

Camshaft drive was by one-to-one double-roller chain from a half-engine-speed intermediate shaft, gear-driven off the crank. Chain tensioning was done by a spring-loaded idler sprocket for each chain. The Bosch ignition distributor mounted at the flywheel end of the engine was skew-gear driven, again off the fully counterweighted crankshaft, with each individual con-rod bearing supported on each side, requiring a total of seven main bearings. An additional plain lead bearing was provided to carry the pinion drive for the half-speed shaft just beyond the nose of the crankshaft; it is this that causes some to label this crankshaft an eight-bearing one but structurally it is, of course, a seven-bearing crank.

The considerably short-stroke choice of bore and stroke meant that the comparative thinness of the crank webs was comfortably offset by the overlap of the 57mm diameter by 22mm wide main and connecting rod big end bearings, each

lined with steel-backed lead-indium bearing shells. Forged steel con rods had two-bolt-held big end bearings and fully floating gudgeon pins, with the flywheel held by six bolts after the original single-bolt arrangement had proved unreliable. Cast aluminium alloy pistons were fully skirted, with mildly domed crowns.

More severely than in an upright or even inclined design, reliable lubrication of any flat engine poses one challenge, all the more obvious in a sports car likely to be cornered hard – oil surge. To keep centre of gravity height down, Porsche clearly did not want to rely on one simple road-car way round this, using a deep-enough sump, and therefore went the

whole hog with a racing-style dry-sump system. Both the pressure and the larger scavenge gear-type pumps were placed on the front of the half-speed shaft, the pressure pump drawing oil from a reservoir at the back of the right-hand wing. The scavenge pump returned oil after its passage through bearings and the engine in general to the tank via an oil cooler and the full-flow oil filter.

Air-cooling, relative to the conventional way of ejecting engine heat via a liquid intermediary, is another challenge of this type of motor. Weight may be reduced but a much better job has to be done with a power-consuming and potentially noisy forced feed of air in a car, unlike a motor

The 2-litre flat-six engine with Solex carburettors installed in a 901.

An early 1963 prototype 911 2.0 litre (Type 901) poses against a background of 356 models awaiting delivery.

cycle. In the 356, Porsche had previously relied upon a VW-style radial-flow fan but for the 901/911 the designers went for the more efficient axial-flow type.

This 11-bladed aluminium alloy impeller was belt-driven off the back end of the crankshaft at 1.3 times crank speed, with the 490-watt alternator housed co-axially and tidily in its hub. Most of the fan's output was ducted by a shroud, largely moulded plastic or pressed metal close to hotter parts, over the entire engine and the oil cooler. Up to a tenth of its flow could be directed via heat exchangers round the exhaust pipes to warm the car's interior. Cockpit-controllable flap-valves either diverted this air to atmosphere or, via quietening spaces in the sills, to the cabin.

Fuelling the new engine began simply, with a Bendix electric pump. Then it grew a little complicated, with fuel fed to an 'overflow' tank on each cylinder bank, from which it went to each trio of Solex 30mm venturi 40 PI downdraught carburettors, each scavenged by a mechanical diaphragm pump driven off the back of the left-hand camshaft.

Transmission

Drive to the gearbox, which borrowed its type number 901 from the originally intended name of the car, was through a 215mm Fichtel & Sachs diaphragm spring clutch. The design of the transmission was impressively strong, setting a standard which was preserved hereafter in the 911's evolution – necessarily so, given one of the greatest advantages of the rear-engined layout, extraordinary traction by two-wheel-drive standards. This in turn demanded a higher degree of strength than usual to perform as the middle man in the battle between engine torque and the reaction of tyre grip during maximum acceleration. The one-piece sand-cast aluminium alloy casing of the main part of the gearbox housed both the five-speed gears and the two-planet-gear differential. As on a Volkswagen, the final drive was next to the clutch housing, the input drive shaft from the flywheel passing over the differential to form the upper shaft of the two-shaft change speed part in front, the lower gearbox shaft continuing rearwards as the final drive pinion shaft, and the selector shaft extending forward underneath.

Also as on a VW, the casing formed a tunnel. This was open at its front end to allow access to the gearbox, with a wall midway along its length between gearbox and the final drive end of the tunnel, closed again by the wall between the differential and gearbox, and open finally at the wide mouth of the clutch housing. Access to the differential was via a removable cover plate on the left side. The tunnel was closed at the front end by the end-cover casting, which carried the front bearings of the two gearbox shafts, the cantilevered first and reverse gear sets and, below, the gear-change selector shaft.

Gears themselves ran on needle-roller bearings on the input and output shafts, which were placed with their centres 68mm apart; the only exception was the input wheel of second gear, cut directly on the input shaft (first gear on Type 902 four-speed versions of the same gearbox). That integral gear apart, the design allowed the installation of different gear sets relatively easily to suit particular needs, such as those of customers interested in motor sport. Shafts were located endways by a double-row angular contact ball bearing in the end cover, and a roller bearing in the gearbox/differential wall. Gearbox and differential therefore shared the same lubricating oil. The selector shaft was supported by plain bearings in the differential wall at the back and in the tail of the end cover at the front. The shaft spacing and casing were good for a maximum design torque capacity of 186Nm, later (in 1969) raised to 201Nm with the change to a die-cast casing. This proved to be safely adequate for 911 models with engines up to 2.2 litres.

The two-star-wheel spiral bevel final drive used a seven-tooth pinion driving a 31-tooth crown wheel. Propulsion to the fixed-length drive shafts was initially through an unusual pair of universal joints, one to each differential housing side cover, designed and provided by the originally French-based, Nadella company, then normally known for the supply of needle-roller bearings, as their name would suggest. To allow for the axial 'plunge' movement dictated in the driveshafts by the semi-swing-axle suspension geometry, these relied on a hinged link in place of a plain Hooke joint's cross-centre link. Like a Hooke joint, these Nadella joints did not provide constant velocity transmission of drive when articulated, with the result that vibration occurred. It was not surprising therefore that three years later, on the introduction of what was then the fastest

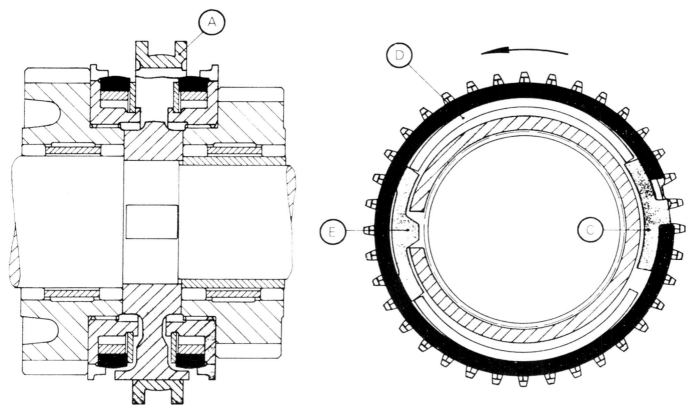

Porsche's famous split-ring synchromesh design, first seen on 1953 models of 356. As the driver's gearlever effort rises during gearchange, so does force on selector sleeve (A), and force on thrust block (C) to brake band (D) and anchor block (E), increasing synchronising force until gear-speeds match.

A 901, photographed in Porsche works No 1 with a model. Note the plain hubcaps with no badges.

model, the 911S, these were replaced by plunge-accommodating low-friction Rzeppa constant velocity balljoints. In varying sizes to suit increasing power and weight, these remain the Porsche 911 driveshaft UJs to this day.

That Porsche synchromesh

Porsche had earlier evolved its famous synchromesh system for the 1953 version of the 356, further improving it in 1959. A proper explanation and understanding of this legendarily effective design is only possible with the help of the engineering drawing on page 21 but basically it depended on a split ring synchroniser, which works on the same principle as the leading shoe brake drum idea, to provide very fast and effective gear-changing synchronisation.

Heating: a challenge

Inside the car, heating was a small challenge. With a water-cooled engine, it is relatively straightforward to bleed off some heat from the engine's cooling system by passing some of the liquid in the water-pump-engine-radiator circuit through a small 'radiator' – really a water-to-air heat exchanger – on the cabin side of the front bulkhead through which air from outside is passed into the car interior. First such heaters tried to provide temperature control by a cockpit-operated valve or tap, usually known as a water valve, which varied the volume and therefore flow of coolant through the heat exchanger.

This did not work ideally, temperature adjustment being slow and coarse. As road speed rose, so did the volume of air passing through the exchanger, requiring more heat for the same air temperature, so cabin air temperature dropped. In the late 1960s came the air-blending heater, which controlled temperature by mixing heated and unheated air regardless of flow variations due to road speed, which was perfect in response and in the variability and constancy of temperature.

When the engine is cooled directly and only by air with no intermediary of a liquid, the obvious thing to do is to place an exhaust-to-air heat exchanger in the exhaust system, fed by air forced through the

Power figures

Returning finally to the engine itself, in this first 2-litre manifestation, with a 9.0:1 compression ratio, it delivered 130PS (metric bhp) at 6,100rpm and 174Nm at 4,200rpm (then quoted as 17.8mkg). Maximum allowed engine speed was set by the rev-limiter in the distributor at 6,800rpm initially, later raised to 7,100rpm. Those output figures correspond to a specific power figure of 65.3PS/litre, respectable for the period, and a specific brake mean effective pressure of 11.03bar. Although its designers did not perhaps realise or require at the time, the basic design of this engine proved capable of a remarkable 88 per cent stretch, to an ultimate 3.75 litres, 30 years later.

exchanger by the engine's cooling fan. Porsche used two such exchangers, one to each side of the car. The heated air from each exchanger then passed through its own cockpit-controllable flap-valve, from whence it could be directed either to the windscreen demister vents (at first including the rear glass) and footwells or, if not wanted, diverted to the outside. Another cockpit flap-valve gave the occupants the ability to control the admission of unheated fresh air from an intake in front of the windscreen. To diminish the transmission of engine and fan noise, the ducts used were lined internally with sound-absorbing material.

In a way, like the water-valve control system, this system suffered from the variability of exhaust heat according to how hard or not the engine was working, how fast or slow. When driving in icy conditions, using little power, just when more cabin heat could be needed, the heater gave minimum heat, insufficient for both comfort and screen de-icing. Therefore early cars were equipped with an auxiliary petrol-fired heater, later (by the time of the A-series 911s introduced in 1967) becoming optional, before being dropped. Small improvements were gained by using extra electric blowers; separate controls for driver and passenger were provided.

FIRST DECADE
1963–1973

1963–1973
The 911 goes into production

The first 911's production birth was not untroubled. Besides the relatively minor matter of Peugeot's objection to 901, which meant that 911 became the car's name from the start of sales, more important problems surfaced. First, there was the car's handling, where the innate difficulties of a rear-engine layout were compounded by the need for extreme accuracy required in maintaining strict manufacturing tolerances in suspension geometry. Next came carburetion problems with the inadequately developed Solex system. Gearing of the transmission was also not ideal.

The combination of over-hung rear engine with narrow tyres of the same size front and rear, and a sideways centre of aerodynamic pressure relatively well forward of the centre of gravity was a problem in handling and, in particular, straight-line and side-wind stability. First efforts to tame the car's road behaviour centred on generating a degree of understeer in the front suspension to counter the natural oversteer of a rear weight bias (recalling the same philosophy behind the also rear-engined Hillman Imp's attempt to rival the Mini, launched the same year).

The 2-litre 911: basics of stability

Avoiding, or at any rate minimising, the handling challenge was not straightforward, however. With the drivetrain turning out to weigh more than it was intended to, reducing front tyre effectiveness relative to the rear's required too much degradation of the front's cornering ability in terms of excessive understeer. The simplest way round this initially was thought to be by adding weight at the front, putting supplementary 11kg iron weights at the tips of the front bumpers. This would change the weight distribution to something nearer to more front heavy, and increase polar moments of inertia both about the vertical and horizontal axes of the car.

This somewhat makeshift fix could not be tolerated for long. To remove the otherwise engineeringly objectionable addition of unnecessary weight, six years later in 1969, so-called B-series versions of the car replaced the single 60Ah 12-volt battery (originally mounted near the middle of the nose) with two 36Ah

Left: A 1967 2.0 coupé very sideways on an un-named circuit with the inside front wheel lifting – a situation very familiar to contemporary magazine road testers. It prompts the question of whether the driver was actually at the start of a spin when this photograph was taken.

Right: A 911 2.0 coupé pictured in 1964.

batteries wired in parallel and placed on each side in a well beneath each headlamp. This arrangement lasted until 1974, in G-series 911s, where reinforced bumpers required for export models took away space for the two batteries. At the same time, a larger 80-litre fuel tank and space-saver spare tyre became standard. The sideways weight split here was managed by reverting to a single 66Ah battery but mounting it far left, with the spare wheel on the right.

Then, returning to 1963, there was the poor carburetion of the Solex system on what had become known as the 901/01 first version of the engine. Strenuous efforts were made by both Solex and Porsche to overcome the serious 'flat spot' (momentary lack of power and throttle response) from low engine speeds. In the end, on the later 901/05 version, the engine was fitted with triple Weber 40 IDA carburettors, with which the engine's power, torque, and fuel consumption figures remained the same, but with no flat spots. Adjusting the gearing to better suit the engine's high-revving performance was not done by altering the 7/31 (4.429:1) final drive gears, but by lowering the ratios of each gear by an average of 7.2 per cent.

First attempt at a less-costly 911: the 912

The first evolution of the original 911 was the comparatively short-lived 912, introduced in the spring of 1965, coincident with the end of Porsche 356 production, and to some extent, intended to replace it. Short-lived maybe, but commercially successful, in that in its four-year life, over 30,000 912s were built and sold. An attempt to offer a less costly – though lower performing – version of the 911, the 912 appeared with the 90PS 1,582cc pushrod flat-four engine of the old 365C. However, this was replaced in 1967 with a detuned variant of the opposed six-cylinder Porsche-designed engine, its demise in 1969 bidding farewell to the last manifestation of any pure Volkswagen roots in a Porsche engine.

Styling and equipment economies included deleting the two outer dashboard instruments (the clock and combined oil pressure and level gauge), using a single horn button, and replacing the wood of

Above: Assembly of 1966 2-litre coupé in Porsche works No 2, Zuffenhausen. Here the drive unit is being lifted into place. The flat-six engine, with triple Weber carburettors, awaits installation.

Above: Departure from Porsche works No 1 for the 1965 Monte Carlo Rally. Left to right: Pauli Toivonen, Rolf Wütherich, Eugen Böhringer (in 904 on left), unidentified person, Peter Falk, Herbert Linge. The Linge/Falk 911 2.0 coupé is on the right.

Right: The royal palace in Monaco is the setting as Herbert Linge and Peter Falk receive their prize for fifth place in the overall classification on the 1965 Monte Carlo Rally.

the steering wheel rim with plastic. Outside, there were painted steel wheels instead of chromium-plated ones. Testers in the contemporary press commented favourably on one incidental benefit of downgrading to the wet-sump four-cylinder engine – its reduced weight, which improved the handling. *Autocar* magazine, which had been very critical of the 'often violent oversteer from the swing-axle rear suspension' of the 365, was positively enthusiastic about the 90PS 912's behaviour. Tested in the 24 September 1965 issue, soon after the first RHD 911 appeared in Britain, *Autocar*'s road testers extracted an average two-way maximum speed of 119mph and a 0–60mph time of 11.9sec – not bad for the time.

Not surprisingly in view of the substitution of semi-swing axle in place of pure swing axle of the 365 at the 911's introduction, they found its handling an improvement: 'It is in its handling that the new 912 shows the greatest advance on its predecessor [the Type 365 Super 90].... Driving fast to explore the adhesion on a very wet test track, we found the car hung on to the chosen line through bends beyond all reasonable limits almost regardless of speed until finally the tail swung out gently and progressively, and then came straight again immediately correction was applied.' Nevertheless, although for a while outselling the 911, the 912 still cost more than the 365 and so, not unpredictably, its production run ended in 1969.

A 1967 911S 2.0 coupé, displaying what were then its distinctive 'S'-identifying wheels.

First faster 911: the 911S

The more powerful 911S which came in the middle of the 912's time, in July 1966, owed some of its engine development and design to Porsche's racing type 901/20 described later. Changes to what was known as the 901/02 engine included an increased compression ratio of 9.8 instead of 9.0:1 gained by a higher piston crown; greater valve timing overlap from a new camshaft; larger bore ports with valve sizes up from 39/35mm inlet/exhaust for the 911, to 42/38mm for the 'S'; inlet valve lift increased very

slightly, and similarly different Weber 40 IDS carburettors that offered slightly larger diameter venturis, 32mm instead of 30; and a more efficient layout of the exhaust piping though the heat exchanger.

The result was a 30PS increase in engine power to 160PS at 6,600 instead of 6,100rpm and torque boosted by 2.2 per cent to 179Nm at 5,200rpm. To withstand the higher engine loading, pistons were upgraded from cast to forged aluminium alloy, gudgeon pin bosses were given

solid copper alloy bearing bushes instead of rolled bronze ones, and the con rods were soft-nitrided. The only gearing change was a slightly higher fifth.

Suspension now included a rear as well as front anti-roll bar to provide more sporting handling, while dampers were changed to adjustable Konis. Brakes themselves had larger calipers for ventilated discs. Outside, the 911S wore new forged aluminium alloy wheels, still 4½in rimmed. Style changes included a leather instead of wood steering wheel

Below left: Rear suspension of 1966 911S 2.0, showing the semi-trailing arm and ventilated disc brake.

Below: The 2.0's ventilated disc brake on hub and strut. This 1966 Porsche was the first 911 with ventilated disc brakes and claimed to be the first GT car in the world so fitted.

rim, and a choice of leather or vinyl with various cloth inserts for interior trim.

There were some appreciable performance gains for the 911S over the standard 911. *Autocar* in its 14 October 1966 911S road test measured the maximum speed as 137mph and its 0–60mph time as 8.0sec but commented: 'With something not far short of double the horsepower [of the 912] the 911S is not a car for the novice, and even the experienced driver must slow down when the road turns wet. Initially, there is stable understeer on corners, but power oversteer can be brought in with the right foot to any required degree. The driver needs to know the car well and what he is about.' The testers felt that in wet conditions, it was necessary to 'feed the throttles open carefully and progressively to prevent the tail twitching about, and to treat the polished surfaces in towns with considerable discretion'.

A 1966 publicity photograph of 2.0 with steel wheels and chrome hubcaps.

Specifications: 1966 911S

ENGINE

Capacity
1,991cc

Bore and stroke
80.0mm x 66.0mm

Compression ratio
9.8:1

Maximum power
160PS @ 6,600rpm

Maximum torque
179Nm @ 5,200rpm

Carburettors
Twin Weber 40 IDS

TRANSMISSION

Gearbox
Five-speed manual

BRAKES

Front
Dunlop-ATE4 disc, 269mm

Rear
Dunlop-ATE4 disc, 279mm

PERFORMANCE
Autocar road test, 14 October 1966

Top speed
137mph

Acceleration

0–60mph	8.0sec
0–100mph	20.5sec

KERB WEIGHT
1,047kg

Show launch of Targa body

Well before the 911's appearance, Porsche had enjoyed successful sales of an open version of the 365, so it was not a huge surprise when a Targa variant on the 911 body was revealed as a prototype at the 1965 Frankfurt Show. It took over a year, however, for the production version of this cross between a coupé and an open roadster to appear. At the time, its integral roll-over protection hoop was unique, indeed turning out to be an initiator of a new fashion. A broad section of sheet metal, faced with brushed stainless steel as distinct from the usual racing car steel tube, the hoop replaced a proportion of the stiffness contributed by the roof in the standard fixed-head coupé body, from which – to keep production costs down – the Targa was deliberately closely derived. Almost all the body below the waist was standard coupé 911.

The name 'Targa' was coined as a tribute cum reminder of Porsche victories in the world-renowned Targa Florio in Sicily; it has since entered the motoring lexicon as a word for an open car with a anti-roll-over hoop and usually, as on the Porsche original, a fixed glass rear window. On the Frankfurt Show prototype, there was intended to be a choice of designs for the roof panel between the windscreen frame and roll hoop – a hardtop in reinforced plastic or a roll of lightweight fabric for emergency use in a sudden shower. By the time the car was in production, the hardtop had been dropped in favour of a compromise piece of rubberised fabric with rigid side frames and folding scissor-fashion front and rear cross braces to tighten the fabric when extended.

This pre-production model of the 1965 2.0 Targa has an open rear compartment behind the T-bar.

A 2.0 Targa preproduction prototype in the grounds of Porsche's Zuffenhausen works with top and foldaway PVC rear window in place.

A second less expensive 911: the 911T

The end of the 912 did not solve one constant question in the company; how to provide a less expensive entry to the 911 world? A different attempt from the 912 at a lower-priced version of the 911 came in its replacement, the 911T of 1967. The 'T'

stood for Touring, and the six-cylinder 2 litre was made less costly to manufacture by reducing its power. This could be ensured with lower engine revs, and so a less sophisticated crankshaft, without balance weights, could be used at the cost of some increase in engine noise. Similarly, less elaborate cylinders than the Biral type could be replaced with plain cast-iron ones, while the steel rockers of the 911 were changed to less costly cast iron, a successful economy which in due course fed across to all 911 engines. However, the main de-tuning was achieved with a lower (8.6:1) compression ratio, gentler camshaft timing, and slightly reduced valve lift.

At first sight, the decision to use the larger-valved cylinder heads and Weber carburettors of the 911S engine looked contradictory in a car intended to be less expensive and powerful, but someone within Porsche had realised that a lower standard of equipment meant that the 911T would be the least heavy of the range,

so the better basis for later use as a competition car. Power did however come down, to 110PS at 5,800rpm and 157Nm of torque at the same 4,200rpm. A flatter torque curve providing a wider spread of useful power permitted a four- instead of five-speed gearbox, although customers could specify the five speed as an extra. The suspension had no anti-roll bars.

Autocar did not get its hands on a 911T until its 12 March 1970 issue, when the 2.2 carburettor engine had been uprated to 125PS at 5,800rpm and 176Nm at 4,200rpm. This was good enough for a 129mph maximum speed and a 0–60mph time of 8.1sec. The car's handling was described as: 'Cornering power on dry surfaces is very high and even the most exuberant driving seldom results in loss of adhesion. At the limit, it is generally the rear which slides first but front end bump-skidding was experienced on one or two occasions. In the wet, a great deal more discretion is necessary.'

Above: The 1967 911T 2.0 coupé regained the clock that had been omitted on the 912 and had a leather-rimmed steering wheel.

Right: The 1967 'T' 2.0 coupé. This 911 base model was favoured by users interested in motor sport because of its reduced equipment and therefore lighter overall weight.

The 911T of Vic Elford and David Stone displaying the initial understeer phase of 911 handling on the 1967 Monte Carlo Rally.

Below left: A 1967 2.0 Targa in one situation where its engine position was a great advantage traction-wise, if carefully driven.

Below: A 2.0 Targa visiting the Hockenheim Ring in 1967, with a racing Porsche in the background.

Right: A 1967 2.0 Targa with the roof off and rear window folded away, making it almost a full convertible.

Below: This side view of a 1967 911S 2.0 Targa displays its 'Alice band' roll-over protection hoop, which was to become a widely copied trademark of the Targa profile, and an early attempt at styled steel wheels.

Two-pedal 911

August of the same year, 1967, saw Porsche's first venture into two-pedal motoring with the introduction of an optional semi-automatic Type 905 Sportomatic gearbox, developed in collaboration with Fichtel & Sachs, designed to offer the 911 driver relatively normal gear changing on the open road, with the ease of two-pedal driving in town. The box consisted of a triple-element torque converter in series with an automatically operated diaphragm disc friction clutch worked via micro-switches in the gear lever and gear-change linkage connected to a solenoid-controlled vacuum diaphragm servo on the clutch release. The clutch was smaller than usual, because it was only needed and used for

gear changing, take-off from rest being the job of the torque converter. The four-speed gearbox itself was basically as the manual four-speed, but with a higher ratio final drive. As originally designed, the torque capacity was 172Nm, although when the casing was changed from sand-cast to die-cast, this was raised to 191Nm.

The reason for the longer-legged final drive ratio was not primarily an effort to compensate for the economy losses in a torque converter at cruise speeds as one might perhaps expect, certainly in a run-of-the-mill family car, if not an out-and-out high performance sports car. Contemporary manual box six-cylinder cars used a seven-tooth pinion to drive a 31-tooth crown wheel, whereas the Sportomatic version used the same pinion in conjunction with a 27-tooth crown wheel. Giving a 13 per cent lift in overall gearing, the reduction in the size of the crown wheel of the final drive was made to win some space to

accommodate the torque converter, an inherently space-consuming device. What American slang used delightfully aptly to call the 'slush pump' also forced the introduction of a differently formed one-piece casting for its housing, with lugs to provide mountings for the clutch-operating servo.

Autocar, testing the Sportomatic in a 140PS 911E in its 31 October 1968 issue, raved about 'the electric-cum-vacuum clutch control,' which its testers found 'so quick and precise that gear-changing really is as fast as one can move the lever; clutch release occurs as soon as there is any pressure against the lever, there is no jerk or delay as long as the throttle is released in the normal way. Heel-and-toe or "double declutching" are not necessary. Idling speed in gear is about 900rpm, with quite noticeable creep. It helps to avoid a nasty jolt if first gear is selected before the car has come to rest.'

Aerodynamic progress

Aerodynamically, the 911's predecessor had to some extent led its generation, with the original 356 body having a drag coefficient (Cd) of 0.36. The first 911 was similarly quite good, recording a Cd of 0.381. However, by the time of the first higher performance 911S model in its second manifestation, the B-series of 1968, it had dawned on the car's designers that a good degree of the 911's high speed instability and undue sensitivity to disturbance from side winds was perhaps an aerodynamic phenomenon.

Measurements in the wind tunnel at Stuttgart University showed that besides a worse Cd of 0.41 and increased frontal area due to wider tyres, there was some front lift and a lot more over the rear, as hindsight would suggest. With the car yawed to simulate the resultant angle off longways of forward road speed and a side wind, the lift worsened. Such an increase at the front was due to less flow – and therefore less

Above: Vic Elford and David Stone won the 1968 Monte Carlo Rally in this 911T on Porsche's first entry into this event. The 911T was chosen because it was lightest of the production cars. This one in rally trim weighed only 1,066kg and was fitted with the more powerful 911S engine, tuned here to 180PS, 10PS more than standard 'S' engine.

Left: The flat-six 2-litre engine of a 1967 coupé. Its cooling fan and carburettor throttle linkage are both conspicuous.

Above: In its element, a
2.0 coupé at speed at
Hockenheim in 1968.

Right: Spring blossom
frames a 911S 2.0.

Far right: This 1968 US
export model 911T 2.0
Targa is being tested on
a rolling road. Note the
rotating rear wheels
and chocked stationary
fronts. The red box
suspended in front of
the driver is the display
for the test-drive cycle.

downforce – over the downward slope of the bonnet because of the masking effect of the wings. This was corrected later, in 1971.

For the 1968 model year, Porsche introduced the 911L, basically a standard 2-litre 911 uprated with 911S equipment and the choice of a four- or five-speed or Sportomatic gearbox. This was supplanted by the 911E a year later, with Bosch plunger-pump sequential fuel injection and Boge hydropneumatic spring units. The latter did the job of suspension springs in place of the standard torsion bars; the spring rate rose progressively as the strut deflected and so eliminated the need for a front anti-roll bar, and also provided ride-height control in the front.

Top: Ferdinand Alexander (Butzi) Porsche in the styling studio with a scale model of the 911S Targa.

Above left: A 1968 'L' 2.0 coupé against a Dolomite-ish background.

Above: A 1968 'L' 2.0 coupé with unregistered production 911s in the background.

Left: Targa version of the 1968 model 2.0 'L'.

B-series brings longer wheelbase

This 1969 model year saw the introduction of the B-series cars, which brought the first piece of rear and valuable development in the 911, with the wheelbase lengthened by 57mm from 2,211mm to 2,268mm by means of longer trailing arms from the torsion bars, which, because of the increased leverage, went from 22mm to 23mm diameter. With the engine remaining in the same place, drive shaft joints therefore worked at an angle, requiring better, larger Rzeppa constant velocity joints.

More importantly from the handling viewpoint, extending the wheelbase relative to the back of the cockpit but not to the drive unit, by the simple expedient of lengthening the trailing blade arms of the rear suspension, meant that the rearwards overhang behind the back wheels of the engine was reduced slightly. Additionally, its lower weight (brought about by changing the crankcase alloy from aluminium to magnesium) contributed further, improving weight

distribution between front and back wheels a little, from 41.5/58.5 to 43/57 per cent front/rear. An improvement in grip on 911 'E' and 'S' models was made with the introduction of 6in rims with 70 per cent aspect ratio tyres.

Magnesium alloy was also used for the gearbox casing later in B-series production. Fuel injection, a mechanical system, was introduced on all but 911T. The Bosch six-plunger sequential system had been used first in competition Porsches. In the production engine, the pump was belt-driven off the left-hand camshaft. The amount of injected fuel was sensitive to throttle opening, engine speed, barometric pressure, and temperature. The system also provided overrun cut-off down to just above idle speed, an aid to economy. Fuelling was adjusted mechanically by a toothed rack moving a plunger up or down relative to ports in the pump.

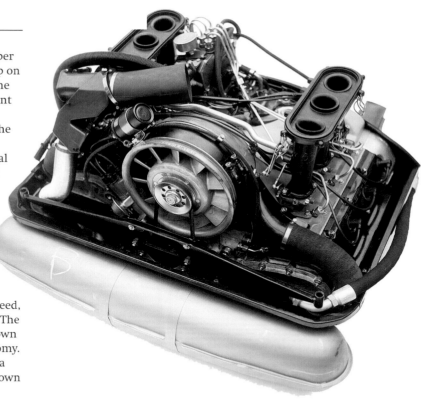

Above: The 1969 2-litre mechanically fuel-injected engine of the 911S.

Left: Ferry Porsche pictured in the yard of Porsche No 2 plant in Stuttgart-Zuffenhausen in 1968. Behind him (right to left) are his sons Ferdinand Alexander and Hans-Peter with his nephew Ferdinand Piëch. Ferdinand Porsche ran the design studios from 1961 and played a major part in styling the 904 and 901/911. Hans-Peter became production manager in 1965. Ferdinand Piëch joined Porsche KG as an experimental engineer in 1963, responsible for testing the new 901/911 six-cylinder engine and developing the sports-racing cars that were to prove so successful.

Left: A 1969 911S 2.0 Targa, now with glass rear window and longer wheelbase, in company with many 911 brethren.

These first fuel-injected engines also included substituting a constant flow rotary fuel pump for the previous Bendix diaphragm pump – its higher current demand (plus that of the newly introduced heated rear window) required a 16 per cent larger capacity 770W alternator. A finer fuel filter was fitted to minimise the chance of blocked or damaged pump or injectors. The ignition system was updated to a capacitor-discharge system, if still dependant for switching on a contact breaker. The higher spark discharge voltage eliminated any risk of misfires in cars running in slow traffic for too long, which in turn improved sparking plug life, and therefore reduced service costs. On the 911S engine an extra oil cooler was placed in the front wing and introduced into the scavenge circuit of this dry-sump-lubricated design, in addition to the standard engine-mounted cooler. Flow through the added cooler was controlled via a thermostatic valve, which only brought in the heat exchanger when the oil temperature rose above 70°C.

Valve timing on the 911E went back to that on the previous normal 2-litre engine, and the compression ratio was raised a tenth to 9.1:1. The main gains of adopting fuel injection for the 911 owner were improved drivability, most noticeable when forced to drive at slow traffic speeds, plus 10PS more for the 911E, now 140PS at 6,600rpm instead of 6,100, and 170PS at 6,800rpm instead 6,600 for the 911S. Torque on the 911E was unchanged, apart from occurring 300rpm higher at 4,500rpm, whereas on the 911S there was a small (3Nm) increase to 182Nm at 5,500rpm.

Above: Departure of 911S 2.0 rally team from Porsche works No 1 for the 1969 Monte Carlo Rally. Team cars (left to right) were: 25 (P. Toivonen/K. Lehto), 37 (B. Waldegaard/ L. Helmer), 31 (G. Larrousse/ J. C. Perramond), and 28 (V. Elford/D. Stone). Waldegaard won the event and was followed by Larrousse in second place.

Right: 1969 911E 2.0 Targa.

Steering improvements

Handling and grip were improved further with the 911E and 911S moving on to 6in rims and 185/70VR-15 tyres; aluminium alloy calipers for the 911S gave less unsprung weight, while aluminium alloy instead of steel for the engine cover and rear panel further reduced rear-end overhung weight. When it came to steering, the 911's predecessor, the Porsche 365, had used a worm and roller system from Gemmer. In company with others at that time, the simplicity and innately greater directness of rack-and-pinion steering, first used in mass production by Citroën before the Second World War, was regarded as a production economy. German manufacturers in particular traditionally preferred other

Top: 1969 911E 2.0 coupé with rubber-faced bumpers and overriders.

Above left: A 1969 911T 2.0 Targa pauses in the autumn sunshine.

Above: 1969 911T 2.0 with 110PS engine.

Left: The Kremer/Gall 911S 2.0 lifts a wheel during the 1969 Spa-Francorchamps 24-hour race. Erwin Kremer had won the race in 1968.

systems that steered the front wheels through a right-angle gearing mechanism. It was felt that there could be wear problems at the point either side of straight ahead, at which the most use occurs.

For this reason, the decision to move to rack and pinion was predicated on sturdiness and avoiding play between the pinion and rack teeth. In the elegantly engineered rack-and-pinion box in O- and A-series 911s, the pinion was supported on ball bearings on either side. The carrier block for the bearings sat on the rack, which passed under the pinion and was pressed against the pinion by a pad spring-loaded from the block's interior. The block was located on the rack longways by a grease-lubricated outer case within which the block could 'float' vertically, thus ensuring that the pinion's

mesh with the rack was always tight without introducing needless friction. It worked as its designer intended, very well, but it was not the least expensive way to do things.

A considerably less costly rack and pinion was introduced for the B-series. It did away with the floating block and separate pinion housing by casting the pinion housing in unit with the rack housing and designing the rack just flexible enough in beam strength to allow a simple pad to be spring-loaded against the underside of the rack from an access cap bolted to the housing, as used in most other manufacturers' rack-and-pinion systems. At the same time, the overall ratio of the steering around the mid, straight-ahead position was lowered in gearing terms, being numerically raised from 16.5 to 17.78:1.

Above: The 1970 911T coupé also had the 2.2-litre engine, with two Zenith carburettors and extra 15PS.

Right: The 1970 911E 2.2 coupé now had 155PS at 6,200rpm.

First steps up the engine size ladder

July 1969 saw the end of 2-litre engine production, being replaced in that August by the first step in larger capacity power for the 911, with the introduction of the 2.2-litre version. The least powerful 2.2 in the 911T used two three-choke carburettors, Zenith instead of Weber, and offered 125PS at 5,800rpm against the former 110PS; the previously 140PS 911E moved up to 155PS at 6,200rpm and the 160PS 911S to 180PS at 6,500rpm. Corresponding torque increases were from 157Nm to 177Nm at 4,200rpm for the 'T', from 176Nm to 192Nm at 6,200rpm for the 'E', and from 182Nm to 200Nm at 5,200rpm for the 'S'.

Details irrelevant to the increases in power were structural: the previous

Above: 1970 911T 2.2 Targa.

Left: A 1970 911S 2.2 Targa, dwarfed by a German air force Lockheed Starfighter F-104 (Widowmaker).

Helicoil (steel coil) reinforced sparking plug threads were replaced by threads now tapped directly in the aluminium alloy cylinder head, while fuelling was revised with the removal of the cold start solenoid from the fuel injection, its job being done well enough by the thermostatic control. Obviously, the power increases were mainly thanks to the 4mm increase in cylinder bore to 84mm – with the 66mm bore this gave a total swept volume of 2,195cc. Another equally important factor was the larger valve diameters, now 46mm inlet and 40mm exhaust, like the cylinder heads common to all three models. To make better use of the boosted power, clutch diameter was increased by 10mm to

Far left: Le Mans 1970. Rolf Stommelen (centre) in conversation with Ferdinand Porsche (right) and W. Kauhsen (left) in the pits before the race. Car 35 (its number only partly visible) is the Porsche 917 of Vic Elford and Kurt Ahrens.

Left: The Porsche stand at the New York Show in April 1971.

Colourful 911S 2.4 rally car built for the 1970 Tour de France Automobile, where it finished third in the hands of Gérard Larrousse. Note the external fuel filler poking through the bonnet.

215mm, while a limited slip differential was optional on the 911S 2.2.

Referring to the imported 911T 2.2-litre tested in *Autocar*'s 12 March 1970 issue, the road test team were pleasantly surprised by the 911T's performance, at lower speeds at any rate: 'With its relatively low first gear and excellent traction, the 911T steps off the line in a most impressive fashion. Through the gears, changing up at a true 6,400rpm, 0-60mph takes only 8.1 sec, this despite damp track conditions. This is almost the equal of the carburettor-equipped 911S (160bhp DIN) we tested in 1966, which took 8.0 sec.'

Air conditioning first became available in 1969, very welcome in view of the poor fresh-air ventilation of all 911s, even if its output was at first delivered somewhat meanly through small vents each side of the dash. However, there were gradual improvements later.

One of the works team of three 911S coupés sponsored by Sears Roebuck in the 1971 East African Safari Rally. Modifications included extra ground clearance, sump shields, and engines tuned for more torque. Race leader Waldegaard's Porsche went out after a collision with team mate Zasada, who finished fifth.

A 1971–72 911T 2.4 in Stuttgart police livery.

On Safari in Africa

Polish rally driver Sobieslav Zasada, who had run in fifth place in the 1971 East African Safari, asked Porsche if it would supply him with a car for the 1972 event. Porsche's Dr Furhmann, mindful of Zasada's immediate past as European Rally Champion driver, acquiesced to the extent of providing a small back-up team made up of leader Jürgen Barth and two mechanics plus a service vehicle. The ensemble came back with a second place, achieved in Zasada's 1971 car.

The 911S coupé of S. Zasada/M. Bien on the way to second place in the 1972 East African Safari Rally.

Reduced exhaust emissions

For the 1972–73 model years, August 1971 brought the 2.3-litre version of the engine – in fact 2,341cc, which in mild defiance of mathematical practice, was known as the 2.4. The extra 6.7 per cent came from a 4.4mm increase in crankshaft stroke, to 70.4mm. It was required because of two sorts of exhaust emissions worries of the time.

In deference to the American emissions situation, which began to impinge on the 911 for the first time, contemporary technology required that principally because of the tighter oxides of nitrogen

(NOx) limitation required, combustion temperatures had to drop. This in turn meant lowering compression ratios, the last thing any engine designer in search of higher efficiency in both specific power output (PS/litre) and fuel consumption wants. However, there was also the looming prospect in Europe of lower anti-knock lead compound in fuel and reducing the octane value also demanded lower compression. Therefore the only way of maintaining power was to increase engine capacity in compensation.

Thus the Porsche 911 2.4-litre cars ran

on regular (91RM) as opposed to premium (97RM) fuel, the extra capacity doing its job more than well enough to lift all versions' DIN power and torque. The 911T 2.4, still unlike its sister cars on carburettors in the shape of two Zenith 40 TIN triple-choke devices, now had 130PS at 5,600rpm and 107Nm at 4,000rpm at its disposal. The 911E 2.4 managed 165PS at 6,200rpm and 117.6Nm at 4,500rpm, and the 911S 2.4 produced 190PS at 6,500rpm and 117.6Nm at 5,200rpm. Besides a heavier clamp pressure for the diaphragm spring clutch to transmit the added power

Right: Contemporary fashion with a 1973 911S 2.4 coupé as the backdrop.

Below: Black ornamentation and aluminium alloy wheels on a 1973 model 911E 2.4 coupé.

and torque, physical changes to the engines involved a new crankshaft, fully counterbalanced, used in all 911s including the 911T, which benefited noticeably with lower engine noise.

The connecting rods were shortened, reducing the distance between big and little end bearing centres by 2.2mm to 127.8mm. They were normal steel forgings, untreated except in the higher-stressed 911S engine where the previous soft nitriding was changed to the Tenifer process (a form of surface nitriding). Extra piston cooling by oil jets to the crank side of the pistons was controlled directly by oil pressure in the system exceeding 3–4bar and therefore indirectly by oil temperature. Camshafts, and therefore valve opening periods, on all three engines were unchanged, only the 911T and 911E engines having the entire camshaft timing retarded very slightly, by 1° for the 911T, and 2° for the 911E. The 911S's extra oil cooler in the right-hand front wing was changed to a less costly, less effective if still adequate, serpentine pipe cooler that was not so vulnerable to possible stone damage.

Porsche's work on improving the emission control on the 911 paid off in one way, meaning that only the 911T required any serious modification to sell in the US, its engine being uprated by 10PS, giving 140PS at the same 5,600rpm by replacing its carburettors with the Bosch plunger pump mechanical fuel injection system used on the other 911s, which for the US market needed only closer tolerance injection pumps. It was however the 911T whose US version in January 1973 was the first to use the new continuous injection Bosch K-Jetronic system, of which more will be written later.

Above: A 1973 911E 2.4 Targa.

Autocar tests the 911E

For the 911E with the '2.4' engine, *Autocar* for once did not have to wait so long for its first road test of a fuel-injected 911, published in the 25 November 1971 issue. The test team praised the way that Porsche, in defiance of industry pundits who spoke in depressing terms of the ever more pressing advent of anti-pollution equipment on the motor industry, had adopted 91-octane unleaded fuel for all models, (to rationalise European and US-export production) and therefore lower compression ratios. The test commented: '... in terms of bottom- and mid-range performance, the Porsche is, quite simply, one of the fastest cars we have ever tested.' The 6.4sec 0-60mph time was faster than

the Lamborghini Miura (6.7sec) and the Jaguar E-type (6.9sec). Where handling was concerned, there was less enthusiasm. 'The oversteer is still lurking in the background, however, and bears watching. It has been forced to retreat some distance but can still come as a shock to a driver who lifts off in the middle of a corner which he has entered too fast. Provided he is quick-witted and gets some power on again as well as some opposite lock, the situation can be kept in hand: but as we proved to ourselves on the open spaces of the MIRA handling track, there comes a time when one is reduced to sitting there and waiting for the spin to stop.'

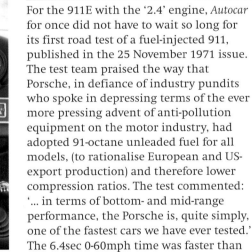

Far left: Driver's view of the 1973 model 911E 2.4 interior. The steering wheel was large by contemporary standards and the pedals were offset. There was a new gear-change pattern with fifth on the right and forward.

Larger torque capacity transmissions

Back in August 1971, ready for the 1972 model year, Porsche introduced the Type 925 Sportomatic semi-automatic transmission (essentially an uprated version of the original Type 905 Sportomatic of four years earlier) needed to cope with the torque of the recently introduced 2,341cc engine. The transmission casing was extensively reinforced with extra ribbing and, inside, the crown wheel and pinion size was

increased, as were the torque converter and clutch, all of which raised the torque capacity by 20.5 per cent to 231Nm.

On the mainstream manual gearbox front, the existing Type 901 transmission was not capable of dealing with the '2.4' engine, so a new box in the shape of the Type 915 was introduced. It owed its beginnings to the Type 916 transmission evolved for Porsche's mid-engined competition cars such as the 1969 Type

908. The production version retained many features of the 916, including the separation of the main casing of the gearbox itself from the differential-cum-clutch housing (done in racing so that ratios could be changed more easily without messing about with drive shaft couplings or clutch). In five-speed versions – a four-speed was also offered – first and fifth ratios were swapped from their positions on the 901 box, now with fifth at

the front, cantilevered into the space covered by the end cover casting. Both end cover and main gearbox were in die-cast magnesium alloy, with aluminium alloy die-castings for the clutch and final drive housings.

First gear was now found immediately behind the front roller bearings of the shafts, on the inner side of fifth, with second, third, and fourth behind in the main casing. Both output or pinion shaft and input shaft ran on roller bearings front and rear, with endways location taken by an additional ball bearing on

the gearbox side of the front end. In the case of the output shaft, this put the thrust ball bearing next to the roller bearing and the pinion itself. Locating the pinion shaft thus meant that the difference between the thermal expansion of the magnesium casing and the steel shaft had far less effect on the mesh clearance between the teeth of the pinion and crown wheel, in contrast to the 901 gearbox's front-end-mounted lengthwise location by the angular contact bearing at the far end of its pinion (output) shaft.

Changes included splash instead of pumped lubrication and a 1mm reduction in input and output shaft spacing, at 76mm, made so to preserve the height of the inboard end of the driveshafts and therefore not to increase the angle at which their constant velocity joints worked. A minor difference noted by Porsche owners familiar with five-speed gearboxes on previous models was the change in gearshift pattern. Previously, reverse was far left and forward; now it was on the right, behind fifth. Torque capacity was designed at 245Nm.

A 1973 911S 2.4 coupé. Note the black 'Porsche' script along the side and the external oil filler to the rear of the door handle.

New front air dam on a 1972 model year 911S 2.4 coupé.

Galvanised body and first 911 air dam

Under the paint of all 911s from 1971 was the beginning of one of the most welcome changes from the customer's viewpoint – an advance in which Porsche was 10 years ahead of any other mass production car makers. That was the adoption of hot-galvanised steel, as distinct from thinner electroplated zinc, for particularly exposed parts of the body.

Bodywork changes included a detail on the 1971 E-series 911 Targa, the sealing of

whose detachable top was improved. More noticeable to the keen eye was that this now 2.4-litre car was the first 911 with an air dam. Formed under the bumper of the 911S, the air dam duly became standard on the F-series, reducing front lift and thus the car's tendency to aquaplane appreciably.

The 1972 Paris Salon heralded the coming of the 2.7-litre engine, first used in the Porsche Carrera RS, a derivative of the 911S. It was inspired by the need in motor racing to boost 911S performance to deal with increasing competition. Regulations designed to keep out 'specials' limited large increases beyond the original production figures and equipment in engine size, bodywork, and aerodynamic aids. However, a specially evolved car – up to 3 litres, with a rear aerofoil and body extensions permitting wider tyres – could be homologated for Group 4 (Special Gran Turismo) provided 500 examples were built.

There was no mistaking this touring car version of the 1972 Carrera RS 2.7 coupé.

The Carrera RSR 2.8 of Georg Loos and Jürgen Barth in the 1973 Nürburgring 1,000km race. The car looked like a normal Carrera RSR 2.8 but was fitted with a 3-litre engine.

Eliminating the iron cylinder liner

Enlarging the 911 engine would be achieved most practically by increasing the cylinder bore but the existing Biral cylinders (a thin iron liner over which was cast a finned aluminium alloy outer) limited how much bore size could be increased within the overall length of the engine. Thinner cylinders were needed. The formidable Porsche 917 sports-racing car of 1971 had posed the same problem,

which was overcome by using Mahle's Nikasil plating process for cylinders made out of aluminium alloy.

It is not possible to run aluminium alloy pistons directly in aluminium alloy cylinders, for obvious wear reasons. The traditional way round this was to make aluminium blocks with cast-in steel or, like the Porsche Biral cylinders, cast-iron liners. Then, in the US in the late 1960s, it was

An October 1974 photograph of the engine compartment of a racing Carrera RS 3.0 Group 3 car.

found that one could eliminate liners by using a very high proportion of silicon in the aluminium – forming a so-called 'hyper-eutectic' alloy – in which not all the silicon is dissolved, so that silicon particles form in the alloy and are dispersed evenly throughout the metal.

Casting an engine block in this, the cylinder bores were then machined. The surfaces of the bores, which were part silicon-aluminium alloy and part pure, hard silicon, were then lightly etched with acid, dissolving some of the surface alloy. This left the islands of silicon exposed as the hard-wearing piston-ring bearing surface, with micro-spaces between to hold some lubricant.

This worked well but at the cost of machine tools with expensive industrial diamond cutters to drill and cut the casting, as required to deal with the silicon.

Thus arose the idea of electro-coating (plating) normal 'eutectic' aluminium alloy cylinder bores with a thin layer of nickel-silicon-carbide. This bore commercial fruit in Mahle's Nikasil process, one of several different companies' similar solutions.

Using Nikasil plating, the necessary thinner cylinders would allow the bore to be increased by a considerable 6mm, to 90mm, which with the 70.4mm stroke brought the swept volume up to 2,687cc. Other power-critical features of the engine remained the same as the 911S: valve sizes, valve timing, the 8.5:1 compression ratio. So it was mainly thanks to the 14.8 per cent increase in capacity above the 2.4-litre engine that the output figures rose (necessitating a heavier clutch pressure) – the power by 10.5 per cent to 210PS at 6,300rpm and the torque by 18.1 per cent to 255.6Nm at 5,100rpm.

'Duck-tail' aerodynamics

The most dramatic aspect of that first Carrera RS was undeniably the addition of the 'duck-tail' rear wing and, only a little less obvious, a more pronounced front air dam than the one first seen on the 1972 911S. Throughout the long, by car model standards, history of the Porsche 911, there have been Porsche customers who were not happy to have the clean curves of the 911 body spoiled, as they saw it, by such ostentatious appendages. That was perhaps understandable and excusable if the unadorned car was always driven quietly and not above, say, 70mph, after which aerodynamic effects could become more noticeable.

Cars generally do not lend themselves well to an ideal aerodynamic shape. The first and fundamental problem is that no car other than a Land Speed Record machine can achieve anything like the high aspect ratio in profile – the ratio of length relative to height – of, for example, an aeroplane fuselage, simply because there is a limit to how long a car may be and how much its roof can be lowered over the occupants. In a relatively short car like the 911, that is all the more obvious.

So the natural thought of the non-aerodynamic artist is to give the sideways profile of this short, box-like object a handsomely tapering pointed nose and tail, distantly reminiscent of a section through a plane's wing. That must surely improve matters by easing the box's forward progress through the air. It does, but wings of planes are there to generate lift, which is just what happens to this shapely car.

The wonderfully pleasing curves, to most people's eyes, of the plain 911 body were innately good lift generators, particularly at the rear. Lift increases the risk of aquaplaning on wet roads, when the tyres ride up slightly on the tiny ramp of water formed perpetually in front of each tyre, breaking their grip on the tarmac. Lift at the back, in the wet or dry, weakens rear grip, which in a tail-heavy car, produces oversteer just when the driver does not want even a hint of it, in a motorway curve taken fast, still possible

Crowded engine compartment of a 1973 Carrera RS 2.7 coupé. The yellow plaques gave servicing information.

The 1972 Carrera RS 2.7 was the first 911 to have different rim widths for front and rear wheels. The 6in rim on this front wheel carried a 185/70 tyre but at the back there was a 7in rim with a 215/70 tyre.

The 'duck-tail' rear wing on a 1972 Carrera RS 2.7 coupé.

and legal on some unlimited German autobahnen. As mentioned earlier, lift also makes a car more sensitive to side-wind effects.

Hence, as on this half sports-racer, road legal 911 Carrera RS, the addition of a front air dam below the nose to reduce front-end aerodynamic lift by denying the underside of some of the airflow underneath the car and of wing-like additions to the engine cover, to counter the lift effects created by the descent of the tail bodywork. On the RS, the front air dam was very obvious, derived as it was from motor racing where its depth provided enough room to accommodate a large oil cooler. Even more blatant was the addition of a 'duck-tail' rear wing. It was also the first 911 with different rim width wheels front (6in) and rear (7in), carrying

respectively 185/70VR-15 and 215/60VR-15 tyres. These necessitated widened rear wheelarches and therefore a wider back end generally, a body modification that was adopted on standard Carrera and SC versions for the next two decades up to 1993.

From the point of view of Porsche salesmen, the Carrera RS – lightened by removing a lot of interior equipment and fittings – was an interesting car. It proved popular enough in spite of its specialist nature to require production to be increased from the homologation minimum of 500 cars to 1,600, two thirds of which were fully lightened cars, the rest having standard 911S trim and kit.

Testing the road-going Carrera RS Touring in its 31 May 1973 issue, *Autocar* was relatively complimentary about the

The 911S Carrera Touring and its rivals

Make and model	Top speed	0–60mph	0–100mph	Standing ¼ mile	Fuel consumption
Aston Martin V8	162mph	6.0sec	14.7sec	14.1sec	12.2mpg
De Tomaso Pantera	159mph	6.2sec	15.3sec	14.4sec	13.0mpg
Ferrari 365 GTB/4 Daytona	174mph	5.4sec	12.6sec	13.7sec	12.4mpg
Lamborghini Miura P400S	172mph	6.7sec	15.1sec	14.5sec	13.4mpg
Porsche 911 Carrera RS Touring	149mph	5.5sec	15.0sec	14.1sec	16.7mpg

Performance figures from *Autocar*

Specifications: 1973 911 Carrera RS Touring

ENGINE

Capacity
2,687cc

Bore and stroke
90.0mm x 70.4mm

Compression ratio
8.5:1

Maximum power
210PS @ 6,300rpm

Maximum torque
256Nm @ 5,100rpm

Fuel system
Bosch mechanical injection

TRANSMISSION

Gearbox
Five-speed manual

BRAKES

Front
Dunlop-ATE ventilated disc, 282mm

Rear
Dunlop-ATE ventilated disc, 290mm

PERFORMANCE
Autocar road test, 31 May 1973

Top speed
149mph

Acceleration
0–60mph	5.5sec
0–100mph	15.0sec

KERB WEIGHT
1,088kg

Above: The 1972 Carrera RS 2.7 was the first 911 to have different rim widths for front and rear wheels. The 6in rim on this front wheel carried a 185/70 tyre but at the back there was a 7in rim with a 215/70 tyre.

Right: The front air dam of the 1973 Carrera RS 2.7 coupé helped to reduce front-end aerodynamic lift.

Cabin of the 1973 Carrera RS 2.7 Touring with minimal trim to reduce weight.

car's handling: 'The best way to drive the Porsche round corners on public roads is also the only safe way in any case; assuming one can see that all is clear, enter the bend no faster than is reasonable, begin to apply power in it, and then make the best use of the traction on the exit to accelerate away to great effect.... "Slow, in, fast out" is the maxim. So good is the roadholding of the Carrera RS on these remarkable Pirelli tyres in both dry and wet that very high cross-country averages can be achieved easily. The one and only catch remains. By sensible development – notably the replacement of the very skittish swinging-axle rear suspension with a semi-trailing arm set up – the inherent dangers of the unavoidably imbalanced rear-engine design are largely avoided. The point at which a driver will run into difficulties is pushed so high that, for all normal purposes, the car is perfectly safe. But if, for whatever reason, a driver finds himself attempting a corner at too high a speed, and if he obeys his first instincts, which will probably be to decelerate, then the rear tyres can lose their grip so abruptly that it is difficult to hold the car out of a spin.'

Continuous injection

Returning to the 911T's North American market 2.4-litre engine introduced in January 1973 in response to new stricter exhaust emission demands, it was the first 911 to be fitted with the new Bosch fuel-injection system, Bosch K-Jetronic. The K stood for the German *kontinuierlich* (continuous) referring to the fact that the injectors of this still entirely mechanical fuel injection system operated constantly once the engine was running, as opposed to intermittently according to when the intake part of the four-stroke cycle occurred for each injector's cylinder. Its fuel metering system took account of the fact that continuous injection meant that when the inlet valve in each port was closed during the compression, combustion and exhaust parts of the four-stroke cycle, injected fuel collected behind the valve.

To determine how much fuel should be injected, all fuel-injection systems need some way of measuring the air demanded by the engine according to the load on it and the throttle opening. K-Jetronic's air meter was simple, if not entirely ideal in terms of how easily air could pass into the engine and therefore in volumetric efficiency. It was also not suitable for engines with considerable valve overlap, as blow-back of intake air, which could happen at lower engine speeds, could upset the counterbalanced disc air sensor.

Air entered the engine via a chamber formed by two opposed cones joined at their large ends, on the atmospheric side of the throttle. The entry side of the chamber was partly closed by a flat disc. The disc was supported on a long, largely counterbalanced lever, on which the disc could swing upward into the wider part of its cone, as airflow forced it upwards. Lever movement worked a fuel metering device formed by a plunger progressively opening a fuel port. The port was fed with fuel pressurised by an electric roller-cam pump, backed up by a spring-loaded fuel pressure reservoir. In spite of its comparative simplicity, which made it easier to service, the system was surprisingly accurate, so it lent itself well to the emissions control standards of the mid-1970s.

Thus equipped, and with a slightly raised compression ratio (8.0:1), the US 911T's engine turned out the same 140PS as before, but at a slightly higher speed of 5,700rpm, with a little more torque, 190Nm at 4,000rpm.

Spread of 2.7-litre applications

August 1973 was when the now K-Jetronic-injected 2.7-litre engine and enlarged clutch became mainstream, being adopted for all Porsche 911s in the new G-series range. Porsche seized the opportunity to rationalise the range mildly, eliminating the 911T with its role being taken over by the base 911 2.7, while the 911S became the mid-range offering, with the 911 Carrera as top model. At first, the engine used the same Nikasil-plated aluminium alloy cylinders as on the Carrera RS but soon the 911 and 911S 2.7s moved over to the less expensive use of hyper-eutectic silicon aluminium alloy cylinders in conjunction with iron-plated pistons.

Valve sizes and camshafts stayed as on the previous models; the 911S 2.7 had an 8.5:1 compression ratio and larger diameter inlet and exhaust ports, commensurate with its 175PS at 5,800rpm and 237.5Nm at 4,000rpm output figures. Figures for the 911 2.7 base model were 150PS at 5,700rpm and 237.5Nm at 3,800rpm. The 2.7's excellent torque delivery encouraged Porsche to offer all three models with four-speed gearboxes, though customers could specify five-speed as an option. Fuel tank capacity was increased to 80 litres.

Bodywork changes to the range brought the first clear evidence of passive safety influences, with shock-absorbing 5mph bumpers fitted for the US market cars, plus passive safety features such as an overtly 'safety' designed steering wheel, seat belts, and integral seat head restraints. The change in nose profile wrought by the American bumpers was not ideal aerodynamically, the drag coefficient of 0.40 increasing five per cent to 0.42. The added weight plus that of steel side-intrusion-resisting beams in the doors, later adopted in 911s for all markets, in due course prompted Porsche to seek some compensating weight reductions, achieved in several ways. Making the fuel tank out of plastic instead of steel had already been done earlier. Now a similar material change was applied to the seat frames (previously steel), the diagonal trailing arms were in aluminium alloy

Porsche's stand at the 1973 Geneva Motor Show with 911s dominating the display.

instead of steel, and the twin batteries were changed to a single one.

All this bore fruit in the G-series 911s with the 2.4-litre engine, introduced in August 1973 for the 1974 model year, which were very little heavier than pre-US-bumper cars. The comparatively sharp edges of that duck-tailed rear wing fitted to the first Carrera RS had aroused official ire in Germany and with bureaucrats in some other places on the grounds of pedestrian safety, so Carrera versions of the G-series had a modified, flatter tray-like wing moulded as part of the engine cover in glass fibre, whose edges were made of flexible polyurethane foam. An incidentally clever detail was that this had the extra effect of improving the airflow over the back lamps, keeping them cleaner. Its aerodynamic effectiveness was good enough to make it necessary to increase the depth of the front air dam – to restore a reasonable balance between front and rear lift – again using a rubber-like polyurethane foam to minimise damage caused by unintended grounding. Tests made on the later H-series Carrera of 1974 proved that this array was very successful, reducing both front and back lift by a factor of 10.

Autocar got its hands on an imported 911S 2.7, road tested in the 3 August 1974 issue, and was immediately an admirer of its performance: '... it is as well to look at how the 911S compares with equivalent models of rival makes.... It will be noted that its maximum speed of 142 mph is bettered only by the Jaguar E-Type, a car having a 12-cylinder engine of almost twice the displacement.... Through-the-gears acceleration times reveal much of the same situation. The 911S and the E-Type are pretty evenly matched, the German car having the edge up to 60 mph, but the Jaguar being the faster over the standing quarter-mile and up to 100 mph.'

The standard 911 2.7, which was the subject of a Test Extra (a two-page mini road test) in the 24 August 1974 issue, was thought remarkable for its relatively good fuel consumption: 'The revelation of this test (as of the 911S tested recently) was the much improved economy conferred by the Bosch K-Jetronic fuel injection. Both cars gave a most creditable 23.2 mpg overall and on a typical journey involving a varied 250 miles, the 911 gave 25.8 mpg. Even in the portion of the test that included the performance testing, the car returned 19.8 mpg, a figure we would hope few drivers are likely to get below.'

The beginnings of 911 motor racing

This book is not concerned with the competition history of Porsche, except where it directly involves the 911. The first such instance was in the spring of 1965, just seven months after the October 1964 start of 911 production. A racing version of the production car engine had been developed alongside the 910/01 (its internal type number), and was experimentally fitted to a sports-racing mid-engined Porsche 904, which ran in the legendary Targa Florio in Sicily, finishing second overall to a Grand-Prix-engined eight-cylinder Porsche.

Structural differences of the Type 901/20 engine (as it was known within Porsche) included magnesium alloy instead of heavier aluminium alloy for some castings, a higher compression ratio, titanium connecting rods, and adjuster-less steel rockers with clearance adjustment by a choice of different thickness valve caps. Items enlarged included ports and valves, intake manifolding, and Weber 46 IDA3 carburettors. In contrast, the cooling fan diameter was smaller, to reduce blade tip cavitation (an aerodynamic phenomenon reducing blade efficiency) at the higher engine speeds of which this engine was capable. Cam timing was changed to typical racing intervals and ignition was twin-plug. This engine developed 210PS at 8,000rpm.

The motor racing history of the Porsche 911 is a mix of Porsche customers racing variously developed versions of the road cars and direct Porsche factory involvement in competition. In 1967 a pair of private owners plus two professionals broke a clutch of world long distance speed records at Monza using an experimentally lightened 911 bodyshell on lowered suspension and powered by that same 130PS engine. Modified production models were the principal source of competition Porsches for much of its sporting career to date, the degree of improvement for racing varying according to the notorious fickleness of sports 'formula' regulations.

The degree of modification was accordingly often remarkable. Weight

The 911S 2.3 coupé of Björn Waldegaard and Lars Helmer on the 1970 Monte Carlo Rally. They started from Oslo, finished first overall, and won their class.

reduction in the body was taken to high, sometimes extraordinary, levels. A good early example was the 911S cars used by Björn Waldegaard and Gérard Larrousse that came first and second in the 1970 Monte Carlo Rally and, in Larrousse's hands, third in the same year's Marathon de la Route, which scaled 789kg, the lightest road-going 911 ever built.

A number of the modifications benefited production cars, such as the replacement of the Biral aluminium alloy-finned cast iron bore cylinders with less heavy aluminium alloy Nikasil electro-coated cylinders. Their thinner walls and therefore bore enlargement possibilities allowed the first steps in the upward climb in capacity of the 911 engine, starting with the 2.7-litre Carrera RS of 1972. That model also introduced a rear wing to reduce the inherent lift at the back of the coupé body and was the first 911 with larger back than front tyres, which its overhung rear engine layout demanded for improved handling and, more obviously, straight-line stability.

The Carrera RS and RSR 2.7 were immensely successful motor sporting 911s in their day, dominating the racing scene with wins in the 1973 Daytona 24-hour race. The same two private entrants/drivers went on to do likewise for the Sebring 12-hour event later that year; a factory-entry won the 1973 Targa Florio.

Above left: The Martini-entered Carrera RSR, seen here with the Martini Racing transporter, carries its number from the 1973 Targa Florio, which it won after leading from lap four to the finish.

Above: Poster advertising the maiden victory of the Carrera RS in the 1973 Daytona 24-hour race. Drivers were P. Gregg and H. Haywood, who averaged 106.27mph.

Left: Poster celebrating Porsche and Martini Racing's success in the 1973 Targa Florio.

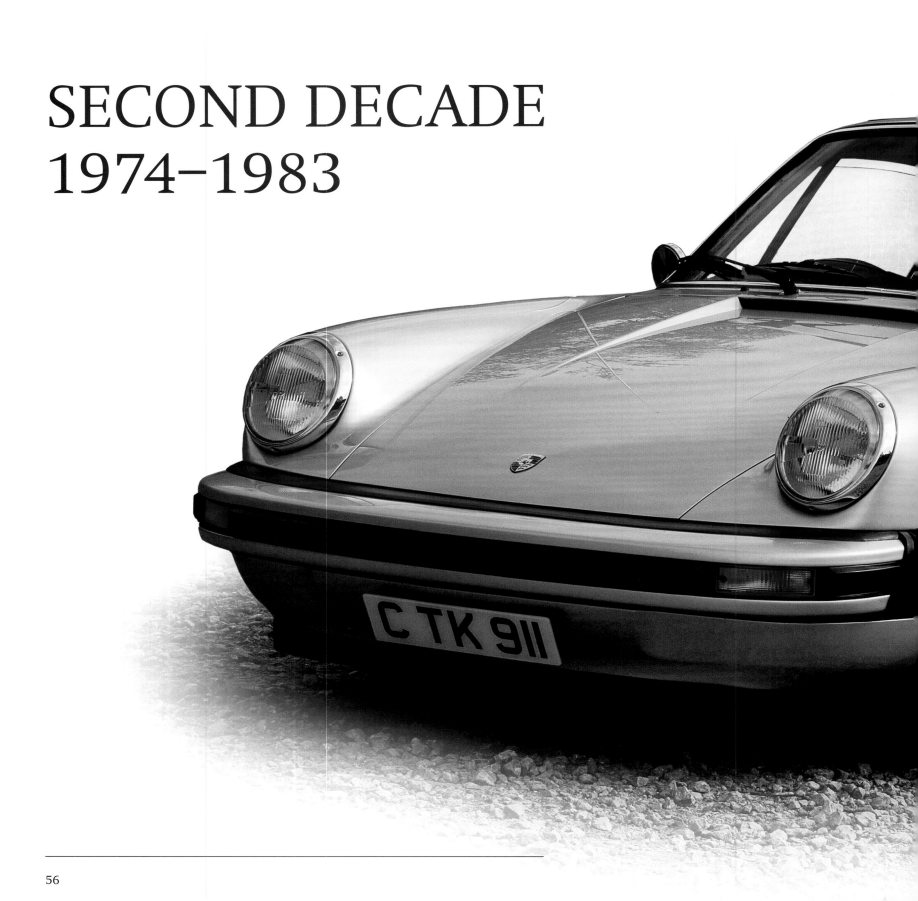

SECOND DECADE
1974–1983

1974–1983
The first 911 Turbo

A landmark year in two ways, 1974 was when engine size was increased yet again, to a nominal 3 litres soon after the introduction of the H-series 911s, and when the world's first turbocharged true sports car, the exhilarating Porsche 911 Turbo, came into being (as opposed to turbo saloons, of which the BMW 2002tii of 1973 was first in Europe). Power increases and other refinements, including improved heating, followed.

Later, plans to replace the 911 with the front-engined 928 stalled development and by 1978 the 911 range was down to just two models. Revival of the 911's fortunes came in 1982 with a Cabriolet model, then an engine size increase to 3.2 litres, and a new five-speed transmission. For the ostentatious there was the option of Turbo Look bodywork on the normally aspirated and slower Carrera 2. Throughout the decade Porsche was actively involved in racing, with numerous successes, and even contested the Safari Rally with specially built 911s.

Right: 1974 Carrera RS 3.0. Note this early example of considerable wheel arch enlargement, to cover 8in front and 9in rear wheels.

The 3-litre engine

As before with a capacity increase, it was the latest version of Carrera RS, aimed at competition as well as road use, in which the first 3-litre 911 engine was installed relatively early in the year. Here was another increase in bore size, to 95mm, which with the same 70.4mm stroke added up to a total swept volume of 2,994cc. This was done as part of Porsche's entry into Group 3 (Production GT cars) racing, homologation for which was possible after building a minimum of 100 cars. Its specification embraced extension of the wings to accommodate 8in and 9in wheel rims, a transmission with a pumped oil cooler, an engine oil cooler set in the front air dam, and brakes taken from the Porsche 917.

The engine broke Porsche's latter-day practice of using 91RM fuel, reverting to 98RM petrol and a 9.8:1 compression ratio, which helped produce 230PS at 6,200rpm and 275Nm at 5,000rpm. This was felt necessary because of the larger frontal area and thus greater aerodynamic drag caused by the increase in tyre and therefore wing size. The engine had Nikasil cylinders with new twin-plug cylinder heads carrying enlarged inlet ports and both inlet and exhaust valves elevated to 49 and 41.5mm head diameters worked by standard 911S camshafts. At first sight a retrograde step, if not to anyone versed in the strength of materials, the magnesium alloy of the crankcase was replaced by stronger aluminium-alloy die castings, for fatigue-resistance reasons.

Left: R. Stenzel's Carrera RSR 3.0 in the Karusell during the 1974 Nürburgring 1,000km race.

Below left: A Carrera RS tackles a slushy bend on the 1974 Heisser Schnee (literally 'hot snows') Rally.

Below: The Carrera RSR Turbo 2.2 of Gijs van Lennep and Herbert Müller finished second overall in the 1974 Le Mans race.

First serious 911 sports-racer

The 3-litre 911 Carrera RS, and its even higher tweaked RSR brother of 1974, was the first 911 racing model in 50 of the 109 examples produced that was designed and built as a competition car from the start, as opposed to a race-modified production car. It used glass fibre bumpers, enlarged wings to suit 60 per cent profile tyres on 8in and 9in forged aluminium alloy rims, and a large rear aerofoil. Bilstein dampers, torsion bars, and the rear anti-roll bar were stiffer. In the engine, cased in aluminium alloy instead of not-so-strong magnesium alloy, the standard crankshaft and connecting rods were polished and crack-tested, and the flywheel lightened. Brakes from the sports-racing Type 917 used a balance-bar for front/rear brake balance adjustment – an expensive change. An oil cooler was added to the transmission, and an extra engine oil cooler. Near invincible in non-factory-backed entrants' hands throughout the 1974–75 seasons, the 3-litre RSR dominated the American IMSA and European GT Championships of both years.

59

*Above: A 1974
2.7 coupé.*

*Above right: A 1974
model year G-series
Carrera 2.7 coupé with
indicators now
integrated into the
front bumpers.*

*Right: The 1974 2.7-litre
model range (left to
right): Targa, 911S
coupé, Carrera coupé.*

The Safari rally beckons again

The second place achieved by Zasada's 911 in the 1972 event prompted the building of a new Safari car. The standard shell was reinforced in some local higher-stressed areas, special bump stops were fitted, suspension members reinforced, and the front stub axle placed lower and the rear torsion bars adjusted to increase ground clearance. Driven by Björn Waldegaard, the works-entered car was leading the 1974 event by 35 minutes when near the finish a driveshaft broke, pulling the car back to second place. Porsche was similarly unlucky with the two further-developed cars in a 1978 attempt, when both proved much faster than the rest but Waldegaard in the leading car suffered suspension trouble, dropping him to fourth place. However, Vic Preston and his similar mount finished second.

Left: Porsche's 25th production anniversary, 10 May 1974, held at the Porsche development centre at Weissach. Ferry Porsche is pictured with family members and employees (from left): Richard Hettman, Franz Xaver Reimspiess, Karl Kirn, Hans Kern, Ferry Porsche, Gustav Wölfle, Herbert Linge, Dorothea Porsche, Ferdinand Alexander Porsche, Brigitte Porsche, and Louise Piëch. In the foreground, sadly only partly visible, is the first vehicle to bear the Porsche name, the Type 356 'Number 1,' a mid-engined design built in Gmünd.

Above: A privately entered Carrera RS on the 1974 East African Safari Rally. Björn Waldegaard came second in a works-entered Carrera RS 2.7.

Right: The Porsche 911SC 3.0 'Safari' team cars for the 1978 East African Safari at rest under a tree. Both cars had increased ground clearance and suffered suspension failures. In the foreground is the car crewed by Nairobi garage owner Vic Preston and J. Lyall. The Björn Waldegaard/N. Thorszelius car (behind) led at one stage but finished fourth.

Turbocharged launch

It was in the autumn of 1974 at the Paris Show that the 911 Turbo (Type 930) made its bow. With the same engine enlargement to 2,994cc, contact-breaker-less capacitor discharge ignition, and an extensively revised gearbox, it had further widened front and rear wings to accommodate the Carrera RS 7in front and 8in rear wheels, which were shod with 205/50VR-15 and 225/50VR-15 tyres and set on a wider track, plus a larger front air dam. The tray-shaped rear wing was more effective even than the 'duck-tail' rear wing used on the Carrera RS 2.7 and first fitted on its successor, the 3-litre version. In spite of the increase in frontal area caused by the bigger body and wider tyres, the power of this compact super-car was enough to propel it to a maximum speed of 156mph, a prodigious figure in 1974.

The turbocharging system was striking in its design effort to overcome the effects of turbo lag – the time taken by the exhaust turbine to regain a useful working speed after slowing during times of low throttle opening. When the throttle was shut after a period of throttle open that had kept the turbine working, the vacuum provoked in the inlet manifold acted on a recirculation valve, opening it so that what would otherwise have been back pressure on the turbine via the supercharger side was negated, air fed to the back of the throttle being allowed to continue doing so by a pipe returning it to the inlet side of the blower. Maximum boost pressure allowed by the usual exhaust wastegate device was 0.8bar above atmospheric.

Much of the engine was Carrera 3.0 RS. The only cylinder head differences were a marginally narrower included angle between the valves and slightly reduced inlet port diameter, to keep gas velocities and therefore combustion quality up at lower throttle openings. However, cam timing was altered and the camshafts ran in four instead of the usual three bearings, cut directly in the aluminium alloy of their housings. In the combustion chamber, each forged piston was near flat-topped as part of the process of lowering the geometrical compression ratio to 6.5:1, necessary as with all supercharged engines to take account of the extra air and fuel forced in above atmospheric pressure, which with a typical unblown-engine compression ratio would result in very serious detonation.

On the inner side of the pistons, oil jets for piston cooling were increased in capacity by 50 per cent, with a similar increase in oil pressure-pump size. Overall cooling of the engine was improved by increasing the fan speed by 28 per cent, to 1.67 times crankshaft speed. For the first time in a proper road-going 911, fully electronic ignition eliminated the potential variability and wear of a contact breaker. Output numbers were considerable, as one might expect. On 96RM fuel, the engine turned out 260PS at 5,500rpm and a whopping 343Nm of torque at 4,000rpm.

The 1975 Turbo 3.0 coupé had a widened track and wings to accommodate larger tyres. The front air dam was deeper too.

The 1975 Turbo 3.0 coupé was capable of over 150mph.

Autocar tries the Turbo

The combination of 260PS performance with improved 911 handling had the *Autocar* testers in the 20 September 1975 issue impressed: 'The steering is heavier than on previous Porsches, partly because of the steering wheel size, and partly because of tyre size and suspension layout. It is delightfully accurate however, and less prone to kick-back. Straight stability is much better than we remember, and the car is not as twitchy as before.... Understeer is prominent the more power is applied, thanks to the tremendous grip of the back end; but if you then decelerate sharply, and the cornering speed is high enough, the back end will break away.... The transition isn't nearly as sharp as on previous Porsches, and re-accelerating hard whilst quickly correcting will sort everything out, and send you streaking away up the straight, thanks to the excellent traction – most exhilarating.'

Specifications: 1975 911 Turbo

ENGINE

Capacity
2,994cc

Bore and stroke
95.0mm x 70.4mm

Compression ratio
6.5:1

Maximum power
260PS @ 5,500rpm

Maximum torque
343Nm @ 4,000rpm

Fuel system
Bosch K-Jetronic mechanical injection

TRANSMISSION

Gearbox
Four-speed manual

BRAKES

Front
Ventilated disc, 282mm

Rear
Ventilated disc, 290mm

PERFORMANCE
Autocar road test, 20 September 1975

Top speed
153mph

Acceleration
0–60mph	6.1sec
0–100mph	14.5sec

KERB WEIGHT
1,140kg

The tray-shaped rear wing of the 1975 Turbo 3.0 coupé proved very effective and was an instant recognition point.

Uprated transmission

The Turbo's considerable maximum torque was too much for the existing Type 915 transmission, so a major development of it, with the same 930 type number as the Turbo project, was necessary. Entirely cased in heavily extra-ribbed aluminium alloy, the gear ratios were kept to four – easily suited to the wide engine and power range of the blown 3-litre engine and allowing the use of wider, and therefore stronger, gears. With bigger diameter input and pinion shafts plus a bigger clutch (increased from 225mm to 240mm), the Type 930 transmission was well reinforced. Other changes included modified synchromesh, the option of an 80 per cent limited slip system for the four-star-wheel differential, and a choice of two final drive ratios (4.0 or 4.22:1) to suit tyre size variations.

Two years later, in 1977 for the 1978 model year, the irritation of gearbox chatter at low speeds was addressed with the fitting of a heavier clutch pressure plate and a Porsche-designed cushioned hub, of which more detail is given later. Not applied to the standard 911s however was the simultaneous move from aluminium alloy to cast steel for the Turbo's clutch housing, at the same time making the housing 30mm deeper to accommodate the hub.

Turbocharging enters racing

In circuit racing proper, changes in CSI rules for GT racing for the mid-1970s meant that production cars had to be the basis of competition ones. The opposition in the prototype class – Gulf-Ford V8s, Alfa Romeo, and 12-cylinder Matras – were larger-engined and sleeker than the 911 Carrera, so the obvious way was turbocharging. However, the 1.4 times swept volume equivalence requirement meant that to compete within the 3-litre limit, a turbo Carrera would have to be reduced to a maximum of 2,142.8cc.

Porsche's development of the 911 Carrera is a good example of the lengths to which the company would go to evolve the 911 into the right car for the job. With a suitably crack-tested crankshaft from the original

66mm stroke 2-litre and 83mm Nikasil cylinder bores, a capacity of 2,142.6cc was achieved. New con rods in titanium, a die-cast magnesium-alloy crankcase, and twin-plug cylinder heads from former racing engines, plus sodium-cooled larger valves and contact-breaker-less ignition, made up the core of the engine. A single KKK turbocharger blowing at up to 1.4bar through an air-to-air intercooler ensured an excellent output by the end of the 1974 season of 490PS at 7,600rpm and 450Nm.

Weight reduction was essential, done by replacing much of the unstressed bodywork with thin glass fibre. Major changes at the back included swapping the torsion bar and its hefty enclosing tube for coil-spring

suspension, while the rear chassis was totally changed by using an aluminium alloy tube subframe, in both cases with far lighter suspension members, still with basically the same strut front, semi-trailing arm rear geometry. No spare wheel or front fuel tank allowed better ducting of air to the brakes as well as some weight saving. Moving the tank back to the right-hand back 'seat', (behind a new safety bulkhead) close to the car's centre of gravity, meant that fuel level variations to the car's handling were avoided. The rigidity added by integrating an aluminium alloy safety cage into the structure permitted the transverse beam formed by the part behind, which carried the instrument panel, to be redesigned much lighter.

More changes in 1975 and 1976

Modifications to the heating system exhaust heat exchangers, now with the passage of exhaust through them made more efficient, were introduced in 1975. The same year saw the coming of 6in rimmed cast aluminium alloy wheels to the standard 911.

At the other end of the price/power scale, 1975 saw the revival, six years after the original had ceased production, of the 912 name. Dubbed 912E, it was powered not by the long dead VW-based 1.6-litre engine but the 1,971cc 90PS opposed-four-cylinder pushrod engine of the base model VW-Porsche 914 mid-engined sports car. This was for export markets only and was not sold in Europe.

On the transmission front, a further up-rating of the semi-automatic Sportomatic, labelled Type 925/10, had been required to match the further development of the 2.7-litre engine. First used on American export 911s, it became essential for the 3-litre range. The major difference was a cut in ratios to three, allowed by the relatively wider power range of the larger engines, and simultaneously contributing to the uprating with wider gears. The previous 7/27 crown wheel and pinion was changed to an 8/27 tooth gear set that, in spite of the extra pinion tooth, was designed to be stronger.

In 1976 Porsche introduced the 3-litre engine in the standard 911 Carrera, in

Above: Manual version of 1976 US export model 2.7 coupé with revised instruments. Note the warning lamp for the exhaust gas recirculation system between rev counter and speedometer and the red seat belt reminder to the right of the clock.

Left: The 1975 Carrera 2.7 Targa with removable roof panel was the nearest Porsche came to open-air motoring.

coupé and Targa forms, now with K-Jetronic injection and offering 200PS. This car began with a four-speed gearbox as standard, five-speed or Sportomatic being optional; the following year all three transmissions were available as standard. At the same time, reflecting the combined influences of a 911 getting heavier, and probably too the number of women buyers of Porsches, the brakes became servo-assisted.

The fundamental irritation of heat for cabin warming being variable according to engine load remained. The need for the controls to be perpetually adjusted brought the eventual realisation that this could be done far more conveniently by a handful of sensors and servo motors under automatic electronic control. Such a system was first seen in the 1976 911 Carrera 3 litre and the Turbo.

The coming of full zinc anti-corrosion

The partial galvanising that Porsche had adopted in 1971 (see 1963–73 chapter) was from 1976 applied to all body parts of both the 911 and the newly introduced Porsche-VW 924. The use of a covering of zinc had been proved as an excellent way of avoiding destruction of steel by rust long before car body construction. However, it is important to emphasise that the use of hot-dipping in molten zinc – how zinc had been applied to steel traditionally – must be kept distinct from the less expensive method of galvanising on mass production cars introduced first by Fiat on the Tipo hatchback in 1988.

Electro-plating zinc on to steel is an excellent protection against corrosion, but the thickness of the zinc coating is

Opposite: A trio of 1975 models (left to right): Carrera 2.7 Targa, 911S 2.7 coupé, and 2.7 coupé.

Below: The 2.7-litre power unit of a 1976 American export model on the engine assembly line.

Above: A pair of 1976 model Turbo 3.0 coupés in equine company.

Right: This 1976 US export 2.7 coupé's 5mph bumpers stand out from this angle.

considerably less than that provided by hot-metal galvanising, where the steel is passed through molten zinc. The Audi plant at Neckarsulm, through the long-lived connection between Porsche and what was now the Volkswagen group, had won the contract to use the Thyssen process to make the Porsche bodies. In this procedure, after the pre-galvanised sheet had been pressed and formed and spot-welded into bodyshells, the complete shell was then passed through molten zinc, to repair any places where the coating had been damaged in any of the production processes, particularly including welding.

This had the incidental and structurally valuable advantage that the molten zinc would enter any joints, in effect 'soldering' or, to misuse the name of the joining process, brazing and thus uniting the joints much more thoroughly than spot-welding. Porsche could therefore optimise the number of spot welds to take advantage of this gain. A small indicator of the amount of zinc coating on a 911 body is given by the total weight of zinc added, no less than 10kg.

Anyone lucky enough to secure an invitation to visit Porsche's Weissach design, research and development centre today does not have to penetrate the security of the site very deeply before seeing the most convincing, continuing and indeed spectacular demonstration of the longevity and total corrosion-protection of a 911 galvanised body in the still glistening, silvery-looking shape of an unprimed, unpainted, windowless zinc-covered shell sitting out on display, naked to the elements, as it has been for many years already.

Above: The famous naked Targa 2.7 bodyshell in its fully hot-dip galvanised state photographed in 1984, eight years after its 1976 introduction. The bodyshell stands outside the entrance to Porsche's Weissach design and research centre, where it remains, uncorrupted by rust, to this day.

Racing in Groups 4 and 5

The next motor racing application of the 911 was prepared in 1975 for the 1976 season, when the 911 Turbo (Type 930) was the basis for two different derivatives to meet the challenges posed by the new Group 4 GT and Group 5 (modified production cars) categories. Group 4 demanded a minimum production of 400 cars built over not more than two years, a capacity-related minimum weight, limits on tyre and wheel width and wheel-arch width, and no replacement of drivetrain and suspension parts, which could be modified, however. In Group 5 a similar minimum weight and body width applied but more modification was allowed of parts, which had to originate from the production car. Detail suspension parts could be changed but not the principle. Engines could be bored or sleeved but had to use the original production part. Extra aerodynamic aids were on, if limited in size.

The RSR racing version label was no longer used, so the cars were named 934 and 935 – the numbers came, of course, from 930 and the Groups. The production Turbo basis gave each model a good start, an ideal road car for such development.

The 934 for Group 4

In the 934, torsion bar suspension had to stay, if supplemented by added coil helper springs, which provided a means of overall spring rate adjustment, and needle-roller bearings replaced rubber bushes in rear suspension pivots. A racing-style safety bag tank replaced the standard steel fuel container. An aluminium alloy tube bridged the front suspension strut towers, and there were diagonal braces across what had been the luggage compartment.

Engine modifications included K-Jetronic injection, larger ports, higher lift camshafts differently timed, a larger turbocharger blowing at 1.4bar through water-cooled intercoolers, one to each side – the first use of water for any cooling purpose in any Porsche. The output figures

Left: A 934 passing through the Karusell in the 1976 Nürburgring 1,000km race.

were again impressive: 485PS at 7,000rpm and 589Nm at 5,400rpm. Finding itself, thanks to the turbo equivalence factor, in the unblown 4-litre to 4½-litre class with a correspondingly high minimum weight, Porsche deliberately lightened the car overall. It was brought up to the required limit with 40kg of ballast in the nose, to lower the centre of gravity and improve the weight distribution, if not the polar moment of inertia. The 934's ensuing success included a fourth European GT Championship and in the US providing the mount for the Trans-Am champion, both in 1976.

The 935 in Group 5

The 935 was much closer than the 934 to the 911 Turbo original. Some suspension changes were allowed, so the standard torsion bars were replaced by less heavy titanium coil springs with height-adjusting abutments and front suspension arms were lightened by using tubes in front. Anti-roll bar rate could be varied from a cockpit control and Bowden cable, ingeniously through the use of blade-shaped spring steel torsion bar levers that, when rotated, changed in beam stiffness. As on the 934, in the chassis itself, the nose section was braced with aluminium alloy tubing. Front bodywork, rendered in a single glass fibre moulding readily removable for access, achieved a two-fold gain from a single piece of design: re-shaping the front wings (wheel covers) with flatter upper surfaces and a longer forward slope increased front aerodynamic downforce and minimised the loss of such force in a side wind, which is much greater on the standard 911 nose with its pronounced curved-top wings that shield airflow over the bonnet.

Porsche took sensible advantage of the freedom allowed to reduce engine size, by using a 92.8mm bore in place of the standard 95, dropping the swept volume to 2,857cc, which multiplied by the 1.4 turbo equivalence factor gave 3,999.8cc, fractionally inside the 4-litre limit. This allowed a lower minimum weight of 970kg, which the car's designers knew could be achieved easily. With 1.4bar of boost, the engine was claimed to turn out 590PS at 7,900rpm and 589Nm at 5,400rpm, giving a one-up laden power-to-weight ratio of 563PS/tonne – formidable.

The 935 went through a number of variants. After a success-filled first season, Group 5 rules were relaxed in several ways for 1977, so the Porsche 935/77 was conceived. In the engine department, two smaller blowers were substituted for the previous single KKK turbocharger (in what was now called the 935/76) to improve throttle response, giving the same boost and a power output as established at the end of the previous season, when it had increased to 630PS at 8,000rpm and 320Nm at the same engine speed. The most obvious change visually was to the bodywork, with a new glass fibre shell at the rear complete with the aerofoil, lowering the drag coefficient usefully. Suspension changes included replacing the essentially standard front with a cocktail of light alloy parts, the moving of the cockpit-adjustable anti-roll bar to the front and raising the track control member pivots to minimise camber variations. Two cars were enough to secure a fourth World Championship of Makes in that year.

A Martini Racing 935 in action at Watkins Glen in 1976.

Left: Cabin of the 1977 Turbo 3.0 coupé with turbo boost gauge in the bottom segment of the rev counter.

'Baby' Porsche with 370PS

Next variant was the 935/2, nicknamed the 'Baby' because its engine was downsized to the smallest capacity it ever saw, 1.4 litres. This arose from a striking example of – justifiable – boardroom pique. Circumstances too complex to recount here found Porsche dominating the World Championship of Makes, with little competition, while the German National Championship 2-litre class was fought out between BMW and Ford. This drew ungenerous press comment suggesting Porsche was afraid to join the 2-litre battle, disregarding Porsche's lack of a suitable car. When German TV opted to broadcast the 2-litre race at the Norisring in preference to the over 2-litre race in which Porsche was running, this stung chairman Dr Fuhrmann into ordering the building of a turbo 1.4 to contest the 2-litre class.

That meant some severe weight reduction to take advantage of the 725kg minimum weight, which entailed replacing the standard 911 steel chassis/body at the ends of the centre cell with aluminium alloy tube frames, along with the rear suspension semi-trailing arms re-fabricated in aluminium sheet. For the engine, a 2-litre 911 was linered down to 71mm bore and a 60mm throw crankshaft fitted, giving the required 1,425cc (equivalent under the formula to 1,995cc). A smaller intercooler housed in the engine compartment was ingeniously cooled by use of an exhaust venturi on the end of the tailpipe, saving the weight of the radiators needed for the water-cooled intercoolers. The result was 370PS at 8,000rpm, but at the cost of too narrow a power band, denying the car victory in its first race in 1977. After this was remedied, Jacky Ickx took the 'Baby' to a half-lap-ahead win at the next race at Hockenheim.

3.3-litre Turbo

The 911 Turbo received its first engine size increase with the replacement of the original 3-litre with the 3.3-litre unit in September 1977 ready for the 1978 model year and the first fitting of an air-to-air intercooler. The added capacity – now 3,299cc – was achieved for the first time by increasing both bore and stroke sizes. The cylinder bore went up by 2mm to 97mm, again made feasible by the use of Nikasil-plated cylinder bores, though the air-cooling fins had to be redesigned smaller where clearance mattered, which was also where the fan's output was high, and larger on the opposite side, in an effort to balance the cooling on each side.

Increasing the stroke by 4mm to the same 74.4mm used earlier in the 2.4- and 2.7-litre engines required multiple changes. As before, shortening the connecting rods would avoid the problem of weakening the crankcase to clear the sideways swing of the rods, so the centre to

Above: Quite a lot of visual differences between the 1977 Turbo 3.0 coupé (left) and the Carrera 3.0 coupé.

Above: The wide wheelarches of this 1978 911 Turbo 3.3 coupé required additional protection from flying stones. Pressure headlamp washers are fitted on top of the front bumper.

Right: A 1978–79 Turbo 3.3 engine to North American specification on the assembly line.

centre distance between big and little ends was reduced by 1.8mm to 127mm. Webs of the new crankshaft, its counter weights adjusted to suit the different reciprocating weight, were thickened and bearing journal diameters swollen by 3mm, taking big ends to 55mm and main bearings to 60mm to compensate for the slight reduction in bearing width of the thicker webs.

Despite turbocharged cylinders working at a high brake mean effective pressure of 15.7bar, this engine used no cylinder head gasket, head to cylinder faces being machined well enough to seal simply by being clamped together. Lubrication was reinforced, the previously aluminium-alloy-housed gear pump being redesigned in cast iron to reduce expansion losses (iron expanding much less with temperature increase than aluminium), and the gears in

the pressure pump were widened by 18.6 per cent to 51mm and on the scavenge side by 37.9 per cent to 80mm.

Power output increased considerably, from the 3-litre Turbo's 260PS to 300PS at the same 5,500rpm, and the torque was boosted from 343Nm to 431Nm, also at 4,000rpm as on the 3-litre. Compression was raised to 7.0:1, largely made possible by the fitting of an air-to-air intercooler mounted under the rear aerofoil. Airflow through it was kept above a good working minimum by its position in the intake of the faster-running engine cooling fan. The intercooler was claimed to reduce the temperature of the air compressed by between 50°C and 60°C.

Another vital factor was the re-engineered turbocharger itself, which used a larger diameter compressor driven by an unaltered exhaust turbine and blew at a maximum of 0.8bar. A perhaps surprising further boost to performance, if not a huge one, was provided by the addition of an exhaust air pump (part of the emissions control system long used on US market cars) to help burn any excess hydrocarbons (HC) which escaped from the engine. To work, this pump had to be positioned where the exhaust was hottest, just outside the exhaust ports, and therefore upstream of the turbine. This meant that exhaust gas temperature was raised by as much as 80°C, a useful improvement to the thermal efficiency of the turbo at lower engine speeds.

More fresh air

Another attempt to overcome a long-standing irritation of the 911's interior heating and ventilation system was made in 1977. As well as the variability of heat, fresh air supply in hot weather was not satisfactory either. Matters were made worse when, in the first primitive attempts to overcome the 911's vulnerability, too often exploited by criminals, to break-in and steal the car, the swivelling front quarter lights were deleted. In some customers' view, too long after that, in 1977, the central position of the loudspeaker was changed, making room for good-sized fresh air vents.

The Turbo's performance

Autocar did not see a 3.3-litre 911 Turbo until its 30 April 1983 road test, which was understandably dominated by the way the car went. There is too much in the section to quote under the performance heading – suffice it to say that, as the following snippet demonstrates, the magazine's test team was impressed: 'On the road it is the car's amazing mid-range acceleration that is so thrilling.... Squeeze the throttle "half open" at around 80 mph [this test was done mostly on German autobahnen] and the car rushes from the front of one motorway queue to the rear of the next. Drop a gear, and it catapults forward. The overtaken car instantly becomes a tiny mirror image. Few – if any – cars combine such a handy overall size with anything like this performance.'

Quietening the chattering gearbox

It was on the 3.3-litre Turbo that Porsche introduced a cure for the long-standing problem of low-speed gearbox chatter which had plagued previous cars virtually since the birth of the 911. The answer was a rubber-damped clutch hub, which allowed 34° of movement either way, limited by steel abutments to prevent over-stressing the rubber – nearly 14 times the original movement permitted by the clutch centre plate springs. To this was added a change in the clutch body material from aluminium alloy to steel and using a heavier centre plate to make a complementary difference to the resonant frequency of the assembly. The combination did the job but at the cost of the damper hub's not inconsiderable width effect on the gearbox casting, which had to be lengthened in the bell-housing area, forcing the engine further back by 30mm – not ideal from the handling point of view. On that last point, the 16in Fuchs forged aluminium alloy wheels were made standard, now in 7in and 8in front/rear rim widths carrying 205/55 front and 225/50 rear VR tyres.

Left: Cockpit of a 1977 model Turbo 3.3 coupé with much enlarged fresh air vents in the facia.

Front-engine favouritism

In March 1977, the year of the 911 Turbo 3.3's appearance, Porsche had announced the 928, the big front-engined, rear-transmission, rear-drive GT coupé. It had been preceded at the other end of the Porsche price scale by another front-engined rear-drive coupé 18 months before, in the shape of the Porsche 924. These were both practical manifestations of the thinking led by Porsche's chairman and technical supremo, Professor Ernst Fuhrmann, who had earlier worked as technical director, designing the 356 Carrera engine. He had then left but returned in 1971, becoming chairman from 1972, and favoured the new front-engined cars over the 911.

Fuhrmann's return was one of the results of a quite long-running but mostly polite struggle within the Porsche and Piëch families over control of the Porsche company. The politics of this were fairly involved and not directly or entirely part of the 911 story, except to explain that in the autumn of 1970 the family decided that all family members should in due course leave, to allow in qualified professionals.

Two years later, in 1972, a joint holding limited liability company, Porsche GmbH, was formed, with offices in Robert Bosch Strasse in Stuttgart. It was headed by two leading family members. One was the son of the late father of the clan, and father of the 911, Ferry Porsche. The other was his five-years-older sister, Louise Piëch, married to

Opposite: US market 1978 models: 911SC 3.0 coupé, with 911SC 3.0 Targa and 3.3 Turbo coupé behind.

Left: The 1978 Porsche range, in orange (front to back): 911SC coupé 3.0, 911 Turbo 3.3, 924 coupé, and 928.

Anton Piëch, father of Ferdinand Piëch. Porsche GmbH saw to the overall financial control of Porsche KG in Stuttgart, the part-owned VW-Porsche company in Ludvigsburg, and Porsche Konstruktionem KG in Salzburg. A new management team was appointed to look after the main company, Porsche KG, which was where Professor Fuhrmann came in as technical chief and chairman.

911 evolution temporarily stifled

Most remarkably and heretically in the eyes of 911 enthusiasts, the 928 was conceived as the eventual replacement of the 911. All of this, compounded by declining American market sales largely due to the rise in value of the Deutschmark against most currencies including the dollar, resulted in severe rationalisation – and a slowing of the evolution – of the 911 range, from the four models of the 1977 model year to two in 1978.

Of the 1977 model year line-up – 911, 912E (sold only in the US), Carrera, and Turbo – the 2.7-litre 911 and 3-litre Carrera were combined in a new L-series 911, the 911SC. This was to sit alongside the 911 Turbo as the first pair of the slimmed two-model 911 range for the next decade. Offered in coupé and Targa forms, the 911SC was a 3-litre 911 based on the Carrera including its suspension, 15in diameter 7in- and 8in-rimmed wheels and tyres, and therefore wider rear wheel-arches. Fuchs forged aluminium alloy 16in wheels were optional in the same rim widths. A minor detail for the SC coupé was the adoption of fixed rear quarter windows.

Left: A 1978 model 911SC 3.0 Targa in the closed position.

Right: Light tan trim makes the interior of a 911SC 3.0 Targa appear more spacious.

Far right: Lack of rear legroom in this 1978 911SC 3.0 Targa, like all 911s, restricted the usefulness of the back seats for passengers.

Far right: Partly built 911SC 3.0 flat six on the engine assembly line in the 1978–81 period. The red fan shrouding directed cooling air over the engine.

Below: Crowded engine compartment of a 1978 model 911SC 3.0.

Structurally, the 911SC engine was something of a hybrid of its immediate antecedents. It used the 3.3 Turbo crankcase and main bearing diameters, with a new crankshaft with thinner webs but smaller (53mm) big end bearing journals. One small modification to suit the new air injection pump aside, cylinder heads were from the Carrera, as were the compression ratio, valve and port sizes. The fan returned to the quieter if a little less effective 11-blade design, while a first for an unblown 911 engine was the use of the Turbo's solid state ignition system. Though using Carrera 3-litre camshafts advanced by 6°, the engine had maximum power reduced from the Carrera 3-litre's 200PS to 180PS at 5,500rpm but more torque, up by 3.9 per cent to 265Nm at 4,100rpm.

In terms of 911 development, perhaps the most significant change during 1979 to 1982 was the fitting of the electronically controlled automatic heater system (first seen on the 1976 Carrera 3.0 and Turbo) as standard on all 911s. Otherwise this time was relatively uneventful, despite Professor Fuhrmann resigning late in 1980, a year before his contract had expired, due to

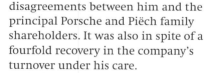

disagreements between him and the principal Porsche and Piëch family shareholders. It was also in spite of a fourfold recovery in the company's turnover under his care.

In the 1980 model year, the engine of the 911SC had its compression ratio raised very marginally to 8.6:1, which did not readily explain the new maximum power rating of 188PS at the same 5,500rpm, with unaltered maximum torque. Interestingly, rumour at the time suggested that the original 180PS was conservative – to ensure that the 911SC did not match or exceed the maximum of the larger and more costly 928. The following year, a change from 91 to 98RM fuel allowed a 9.8:1 compression ratio with appropriate adjustments to ignition timing and injection and what were claimed to be improvements to the combustion chamber brought about by greater piston 'squish' generation – in

Left: Jean-Pierre Nicholas takes his rented Carrera 3.0 round a snowy hairpin bend on his way to winning the 1978 Monte Carlo Rally, the first truly private entrant to win a World Championship event.

Below: The winning Porsche (driven by Klaus Ludwig, Hans Heyer and Toine Hezemans) in the 1978 Nürburgring 1,000km race.

other words, mixture-improving turbulent swirl of the mixture produced by squeezing it into a tight space. The net results were new output figures of 204PS at 5,900rpm and the same 265Nm of torque developed 800rpm higher, at 4,900rpm.

Road testing the 911SC

Porsche traction has its disadvantage as well as advantages, which *Autocar* had to battle with during performance testing of the 180PS 911SC Sport 3-litre in its 17 December 1977 road test: 'A familiar problem reared its head when timing acceleration from rest. The 7in.-wide rear wheels shod with 225 width P7s accentuate the already inherently great traction of the car. Weight transfer to the rear on an already rear-heavy car under acceleration couples with these wide tyres to make the

Sport very hard to unstick from the line. All the recent performance Porsches have posed similar problems to their testers.'

In case any reader is tempted to point to the possibility that magazine road testers are not necessarily skilled enough to master the difficulties of driving some 911s, it is worth mentioning that when one member of such a team was ex-Grand Prix driver and later ride-and-handling consultant engineer John Miles – as it was for the test of the 911SC with higher-tuned 3-litre engine in *Autocar*'s 31 January 1981 issue – there was still some criticism: 'The rear-engined Porsche's greatest attribute, yet, one might argue, also its greatest failing is that it sometimes requires considerable skill to master. In wet and windy conditions it could even be argued that one can make better progress (with more peace of mind) in one of the more stable front-engined sports or a high performance saloon car.'

Right: The Martini Porsche 935/78 'Moby Dick' of Rolf Stommelen and Manfred Schurt at Le Mans in 1978. They finished eighth.

The Le Mans 935

In 1978 the grown-up 935 was upgraded with four-valve water-cooled heads for its otherwise air-cooled engine, with the individual cylinder head castings electron-beam-welded to their cylinders, which saved the potential vulnerability of a gasket, always higher in a seriously supercharged cylinder. Reliability was also sought through the better cooling of the design. In 3.2-litre form – the engine was also built in 2.1- and 2.65-litre versions for other racing purposes – the compression ratio was increased to 7.1:1, with boost also raised to 1.5bar, good enough for no less than 750PS at 8,200rpm.

The body of the 935/78 built to use this engine was the most altered 911 shell ever, with advantage taken of a Le Mans Group 5 rule which permitted the floor to be raised to sill level. The standard 911 floorpan was therefore cut out entirely, replaced by an accordingly higher glass fibre floor, supported by further aluminium alloy tubework made part of the roll cage. A similar amount was taken off the height of the cabin relative to the floor, further slimming the shape and lowering projected frontal area aerodynamically.

Particularly in Martini Team Racing colours, with thin stripes following the elegant sweep of the body's lines, tapering in the slim, sleek profile to the long slender tail with its sail-fish-like fin supports for the rear aerofoil, the 935/78 had a somewhat piscine grace, so it was all the more puzzling that it acquired the nickname 'Moby Dick' – anything less like the blunt front of a whale is hard to imagine.

Large titanium drive shafts, linked by rubber doughnut couplings to provide accommodation for endways movement were fitted. From lessons learnt the hard way in the previous year, and with the lowered state of the car in mind, the transmission was mounted upside down. This lifted the inboard ends of the shafts nearer to the 19in wheel hub end height, minimising the working angle for the universal joints. This was not as straightforward as it may sound, as new castings were needed for both the transmission and clutch bellhousing.

Previously, the rear suspension semi-trailing arm on these racing models had been a hybrid of steel and light alloy arms. Now, a new single semi-trailing member combining the functions of the two was made, all aluminium alloy, and forked. They were arranged to provide some anti-squat under acceleration. Brakes were further upgraded, with four-piston calipers acting on massive 332mm diameter 32mm thick ventilated perforated discs. Thanks to its lower profile and better drag coefficient, this most advanced of all 911 progeny was the fastest 911 derivative ever built, timed at 227mph on the Le Mans Mulsanne straight.

Below: A driver change in the pits for the winning 935 of Klaus Ludwig and the Whittington brothers at Le Mans in 1979.

911 development restored: launch of the Cabriolet

Professor Fuhrmann was replaced in January 1981 by an interesting outsider, Peter W. Schutz, a qualified engineer and a German-born, German-speaking American. With previous experience of large diesel engines with the Caterpillar company, he was not the obvious man at first sight but, along with Ferry Porsche, he believed in the 911 and its potential, as did Porsche development chiefs Helmuth Bott and Ferdinand Piëch.

First fruit of the Schutz enthusiasm was an open cabriolet version of the current 911, something raised earlier but damped down under the Fuhrmann regime. Approval for the project was given in March 1981 and a concept turbocharged four-wheel-drive version appeared at the Frankfurt Show in the September. The 1982 Geneva Show saw the launch of the final rear-drive prototype, which went into production as a convertible version of the 911SC that September.

Aerodynamically, it was for the time impressive, just bettering the 0.400 drag coefficient of the 911SC coupé with a Cd of 0.395 (even if this did predictably shoot up to 0.487 with the top down). Some of the depth of the occasional rear seat was lost

in the Cabriolet form of 911, so that the rearward lean of the seat backs had to be reduced to nearer upright. In the soft-top itself, the entire rear panel containing the window could be unzipped, making it easy to replace if the vinyl of the window was damaged. The only equipment differences between a Cabriolet body and a coupé were the replacement of the automatic heater control with a manual system and the option of replacing the rear seats with lockers. These were standard on US and Australian market cars because the rear seats were in effect outlawed by those countries' requirement to have seat belts fitted to those seats, something that was not structurally practical.

Lowering the top on the 911SC 3.0 Cabriolet.

The 3.2-litre 911 arrives

In August 1983 Porsche introduced the 3.2-litre version of the engine, together with a brand new five-speed transmission. In its leading dimensions it was a marriage of the 3-litre engine's 95mm bore and the Turbo 3.3's 74.4mm stroke, giving a swept volume of 3,164cc. The hallmark of its design was best possible efficiency, with the proviso, however, that its torque did

not exceed the capacity of the existing Type 915 five-speed gearbox. In the search for high efficiency, destined for a revival of the 911 Carrera, it ran a high compression ratio of 10.3:1.

Once again, to achieve the 95mm bore without having to enlarge the cylinder spacing, Nikasil liner-less bores were used. Pistons were forged aluminium alloy, as

When the Cabriolet's hood was down it was concealed by a neat fitted cover. This is a 1983 model 911SC 3.0.

Right: The dashboard of the 1980 model Turbo 3.3 coupé follows the usual 911 pattern but with a 300kph speedometer and the addition of a turbo boost gauge in the bottom segment of the rev counter.

Far right: A 1980 US export model 911SC 3.0 showing the rear space as a luggage carrying area, the only sensible use of it anyway, with small suitcases. The rear seat belts were mandatory.

A 1981 model Turbo 3.3 coupé with the drilled brake discs visible within the five-spoke wheels.

always fitted to Turbo engines. As on the 3.3-litre Turbo engine, accurate machining and careful design allowed a gasket-less seal to the head/block joints. Valve sizes were those of the previous 3-litre engine, albeit in larger ports and with a lower back-pressure exhaust system, made so by improved interior heater heat exchangers, double-skinned to reduce heat losses, and a larger silencer.

Camshaft drive chain tensioning, up to 1983, had been done by a jockey sprocket pressuring each chain with a spring-loaded plunger. This was supposedly kept oil tight and both lubricated and damped by its own fill of lubricant. However, this proved to create a long-standing problem of leakage in the plunger past its containing cylinder wall, which could let air in, reducing the damping effect. That in turn could allow the plunger to vibrate, slackening tension on the chain, which

could be disastrous, of course. To eliminate this, oil pressure and damping were combined in a feed from the engine's lubrication pump. Another detail improvement, made necessary by the steady advance in the electrical demand from added equipment, was an increase in alternator output.

Autocar's test of the 911 Carrera 3.2-litre in the 24 December 1983 issue was inevitably written under the shadow of the 911 Turbo tested the previous April, so it was remarkable that the new (unblown) engine gave the Carrera performance that was not so far off that of the Turbo. A maximum speed of 150mph (2mph lower than the factory's

claimed figure because of tyre scrub losses on the Millbrook 100mph hands-off-speed banking) was only 12mph below and the 0–60mph time of 5.4sec only 0.3sec slower. The handling provoked the usual unease: 'Like all other 911s we have driven, the Carrera has a nervous feel about it.... The Carrera may be less demanding to drive but it still calls for care at high speeds; the rule, as usual, is not to get caught cornering on a trailing throttle, or dithering on and off the power, because even well below the limit of adhesion this usually causes a rear end wriggle that could develop into a pendulous tail slide or spin.'

First sequential injection

A useful advance in fuelling was made, thanks to the adoption of Bosch LE-Jetronic injection and ignition. A sequential injection system, it fired each injector only when each cylinder was on its induction stroke. An interesting kind of 'dead reckoning' was used to programme the electronic management system with a detailed map of the matrix of injection and ignition requirements according to engine load, speed, and emissions demands, previously established on an engine dynamometer. However, the indications from the map were modified in each car by readings from sensors of atmospheric pressure, coolant, and air temperature – but not by any form of knock detection, which was not then widely available. Amongst other things, the system was accurate enough to allow an idling speed of only 800rpm. It provided fuel cut-off if, on a trailing throttle, the engine speed dropped below the 1,100rpm setting for restoration of supply. At the other end of the scale, the system also allowed electronic control of maximum permitted engine speed by cutting injection from 6,500rpm, replacing the previous less accurate system of ignition cut-off set by a centrifugal device.

The new 3.2-litre engine produced an impressive 231PS at 5,900rpm and 281Nm at 4,800rpm. The peak power figure corresponded to a specific power output of 73PS/litre and the maximum torque to a brake mean effective pressure of 11.1bar, both good for a production engine of that time.

Gearbox advances

The new transmission, known internally as the Type G50, made and supplied as usual by Getrag (manufacturers of the previous gearbox for the 911), provided a potentially higher maximum torque capability to cope with the planned new 3.2-litre 911 Turbo due to appear, as it in fact did, in 1989. In normal 911 Carreras its design eliminated the need for a separate oil cooler and pump. Moulds for the cast aluminium alloy casing were designed so that, if necessary, they could be poured from lighter magnesium alloy. The distance between shaft centres, which influences gear size and therefore torque capacity, was increased from the 76mm of the previous Type 915 gearbox to 85mm, so that the latter went up by 22 per cent to 300Nm. Where both input and output shafts carrying the gearbox gears in the Type 915 were cantilevered as far as first and reverse gears were positioned, the G50 input shaft had an extra ball bearing supporting the front end of the input shaft.

To ensure that this new transmission fitted the body without having to alter it, the plain spiral bevel final drive gears of the previous transmission were replaced by a 9/34 teeth (3.444:1) hypoid bevel final drive, which had two advantages. In contrast to a spiral bevel, a hypoid pinion is offset from

the centreline of the crown wheel gear, which makes it potentially a little more compact in length – useful here to keep overall box length within bounds. The offset, countering the 9mm increase in gearbox shaft centre distance, was used to preserve the final drive axis height above road level unchanged, important to avoid needlessly larger driveshaft joint angles.

An interesting detail was the dropping of Porsche's famous own-design synchromesh system in favour of Borg-Warner-type synchromesh, of which the company had acquired experience in the Audi-based transmission of the front-engine, rear-drive 924 and 944. The Porsche system had proved durable and reliable,

A 1980 911 Turbo 3.3 coupé resplendent in silver with black detailing.

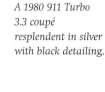

Milled ventilation slots in the brake disc of a 1982 911SC.

Right: Family gathering in 1979 in the garden of the Porsche villa to celebrate the 70th birthday of Ferry Porsche (1909–98), seated at the front with Dorothea Porsche (1911–85). Standing (left to right) are his sons Gerhard, Hans-Peter, Ferdinand Alexander (Butzi), and Wolfgang.

but demanded higher gear-change effort than the Borg-Warner design. There was also a change in the gear-change pattern, with an added longways plane on the left for reverse, instead of putting it opposite the fifth dog leg.

A higher capacity clutch to match the new gearbox, the 240mm diameter disc design first used in the contemporary 911 Turbo since 1978, was installed, its cushioned hub dealing with the previous low-speed gear chatter. In place of cable operation, Porsche fitted a more driver-friendly hydraulic release, which made it easier to reduce pedal effort with a better mechanical advantage. The introduction of the larger G50 meant a re-design of the rear chassis cross-member to suit.

The considerable activity on the manual transmission front obscured the fate of Porsche's now 16-year-old Sportomatic semi-automatic gearboxes, sales of which had declined. It was dropped on the arrival of the 3.2-litre engine in August 1983, ready for the 1984 model year.

'Turbo Look', if not really a Turbo...

Considering how ostentatious cars can be, particularly sports cars of genuinely high performance like any Porsche 911, even when they are clean of overtly show-off additions like wings and spoilers, it is perhaps remarkable how many buyers admire and seek out the wilder sorts of display, whether or not these have a functional purpose. The first appearance of the 930-series 911 Turbo in 1974, with its enlarged wheelarches and big rear wing, aroused the attention of such buyers. A small but healthy market grew for such additions to less powerful 911s, supplied by specialist bodybuilders, so much so that the attention of the manufacturer's sales department was roused, and so was born the idea of the 'Turbo Look', first offered optionally for the 1983 model year Carrera 2 coupé.

The slightly mocking pseudo-sounding name was both appropriate and perhaps reflected the underlying feelings of the creators of such an exemplarily honest car in its shape and style – not least because putting a wider-wheelarched, be-winged body on to a car with not so much power as a Turbo did nothing to improve its performance. It in fact slowed it, taking around 3mph off the top speed thanks to the increased aerodynamic drag of the larger projected frontal area, and adding no less than 40kg in weight, which affected acceleration. In addition, not that most Porsche buyers would care much, there was increased fuel consumption.

Besides improved high-speed cornering and stability however, the only functional improvement of 'Turbo Look' was that it also brought with it the Turbo's bigger brakes.

Above: Large front air dam and rear wheel-arch cooling intakes were a feature of the 1982 model Turbo 3.3.

Right: A 911SC 3.0 coupé finished in the orange paintwork very fashionable in and around 1983.

Far right: A 1981 model 911SC 3.0 Targa with the roof panel removed. The Targa hoop is now finished in black.

The Group B racers

For the 1982 season new FISA rules were introduced: Group A for production touring cars, Group B for small production (200-off) GTs, and Group C for relatively 'free' prototypes, limited mainly by setting a maximum amount of fuel which could be used in any race. The 956 was – from Porsche's viewpoint – tolerably on top in Group C; it was a Group B car that Porsche customers would want, for which the 911 Turbo was the obvious base.

Body modifications to make a Group B racer out of a standard car were limited to a 100-litre safety bag fuel tank in the front 'boot', to which also was added the dry sump oil tank. Structural changes involved just a roll cage and a cross-bracing strut bridging the tops of the front suspension strut towers. The 1,235kg minimum weight applied to turbocharged Group B cars meant that the Porsche had to carry ballast, which the racing department made the best of by installing it as far forward as possible in the passenger-side footwell to improve weight distribution. Suspension changes permitted did not allow supplementary springs so, to stiffen the car

High speed express: a Turbo 3.3 coupé on an autobahn in 1983.

suitably, front and rear torsion bar diameters were increased, as was that of the front anti-roll bars, the standard size rear one incorporating that ingenious rate-adjustment system.

Engine improvements were similarly restricted, with a bigger intercooler, valve timing with more overlap, a 0.1bar increase in boost pressure gained by wastegate adjustment, and stronger head gaskets. Power increased to 364PS at 5,500rpm and

no less than 501Nm of torque at 4,500rpm. This required a 935 sintered metal lined clutch, transmitting the power through the gearbox (standard apart from the addition of external oil cooling) with either a limited slip final drive or – remarkably – a locked diff, something Porsche had used on most 935s. Of the six entered in the 1983 Le Mans, four of these Group B 911 Turbos finished, winning the class, with one ending up 11th in overall race order.

Returning from a day's sailing to the waiting 911SC 3.0 Targa and coupé (1983 models).

Specifications: 1983 Carrera

ENGINE

Capacity
3,164cc

Bore and stroke
95.0mm x 74.4mm

Compression ratio
10.3:1

Maximum power
231PS @ 5,900rpm

Maximum torque
285Nm @ 4,800rpm

Fuel system
Bosch DME injection

TRANSMISSION

Gearbox
Five-speed manual

BRAKES

Front
Ventilated disc, 282mm

Rear
Ventilated disc, 290mm

PERFORMANCE
Autocar road test, 24 December 1983

Top speed
150mph

Acceleration
0–60mph	5.4sec
0–100mph	14.1sec

KERB WEIGHT
1,165kg

THIRD DECADE
1984–1993

1984–1993
Turbo and all-wheel-drive era

The limited-production 959 of 1987 was Porsche's first essay at a four-wheel-drive vehicle and also introduced twin turbochargers (with a sophisticated control system) and double wishbone suspension – features that were to appear on the 911 itself in due course. The 1989 Carrera 4 was the first manifestation of a mainstream production four-wheel-drive 911, although it retained the semi-swing-axle rear suspension. Aerodynamic issues concerning high speed stability and the avoidance of lift were tackled in this decade, with the addition of front spoilers and rear wing aerofoils for the Type 964. An additional model for 1989 was the Speedster, the nearest the 911 came to an open sports car.

The 911 Turbo, now with a 3.3-litre engine giving 320PS, and Tiptronic transmission, in a later ZF four-speed form, both made a comeback in 1990. On the sporting front, the lightweight Carrera RS brought a 3.6-litre engine and Porsche took part in its own racing series with the 911 Cup models.

911 Carrera arrives

The 911SC of 1978 was replaced in 1984 by the freshly named 911 Carrera with coupé, Targa and the newly introduced Cabriolet bodies, the 3.2-litre engine providing 231PS or with catalytic converter 207PS. Bodywork changes included front air dam fog lamps, an optional lower air dam and rear tray wing, and Turbo-style appearance for the catalyst-fitted coupé. In the following year, a first was power seat adjustment, and the Turbo body additions were available for the Targa and Cabriolet in addition to the coupé. *Autocar*'s testers examined a 'Turbo Look'-equipped Carrera

This 1987 model Turbo 3.3 Cabriolet now has a power-operated soft-top.

SE in the 8 January 1986 issue and established a 148mph maximum speed and a 0–60mph time of 5.6sec. They liked some if not all aspects of the suspension: 'The excellent ride quality has not been achieved at the cost of overall handling either, which remains impressive, if a little quirky, on the limit.

As ever, one has to treat this latest version of the 911 with a certain amount of respect bearing in mind the extreme rearward weight bias.' An extra 10PS arrived for the catalytic converter engine in 1986 and a new five-speed gearbox,

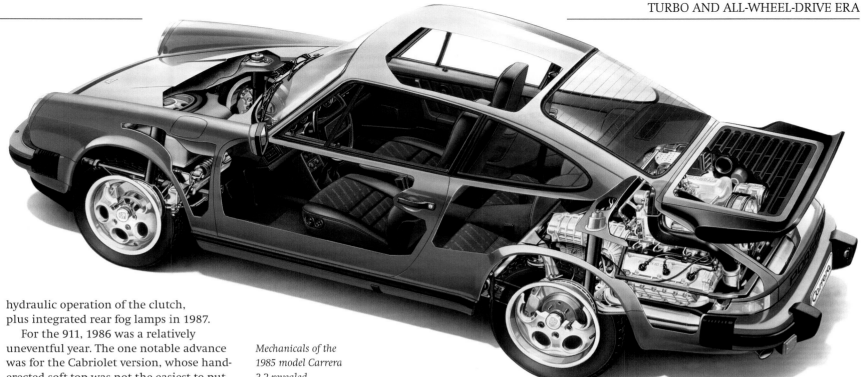

hydraulic operation of the clutch, plus integrated rear fog lamps in 1987.

For the 911, 1986 was a relatively uneventful year. The one notable advance was for the Cabriolet version, whose hand-erected soft-top was not the easiest to put up or take down. Locking the top when up required the use of two removable – and therefore potentially losable – locking handles; the top was heavy when tugging it down into place and within reach of the locks. Salvation came in 1986 with the introduction of the G-series 911s and a power system for the Cabriolet roof.

Mechanicals of the 1985 model Carrera 3.2 revealed.

The Targa, with fog lamps inset in the front air dam, was one of the new Carrera 3.2 range for 1984.

Above: A tray rear wing was an option on the 1984 Carrera 3.2 coupé.

Below right: Driver's view of the controls of a 1985 model Carrera 3.2.

Below: The large air cleaner dominates the engine of this 1986 model 911 Turbo 3.3 coupé.

Above: A 1986 model year Carrera 3.2 coupé engine, which now had 217PS when fitted with a catalytic converter.

Below: A 1985 Carrera 3.2 Cabriolet with 'Turbo Look' bodywork.

Above: The 1984 Carrera 3.2 Cabriolet with 'ruff' formed by the folded soft-top.

Above: The 1987 model
Targa (left) and Cabriolet
Turbo 3.3s have the
integrated rear fog lamps.

Below: A 1984 Turbo 3.3
engine with intercooler and
clearly visible exhaust-
driven KKK turbocharger.

Right: A US 1986 model
Turbo 3.3 coupé. The tray
rear wing lifts up with
the engine cover,
revealing the large oil
cooler. The much larger
American-market
bumpers are fitted.

Far left: The seats of this 1986 model Turbo 3.3 coupé, shown in the reclined position, featured power adjustment.

Middle left: Rear 'seating', with one carpeted seat back folded down, on a 1986 Turbo 3.3.

Left: There was limited luggage capacity for suitcases in the front 'boot' of the 1986 Turbo 3.3 coupé.

Below: Muscular wheelarches of the 1986 Turbo 3.3 coupé were complemented by a twin-pipe exhaust.

Ultimate 911? – the 959

Porsche were persuaded by Jacky Ickx, sponsored by Rothmans, to enter the tough 1984 Paris–Dakar Rally, and built three four-wheel-drive Carrera 3.2s (Type 953, based on the 1978 Safari car) for the event. René Metge and Dominique Lamoyne won for Porsche, with the Ickx/Brasseur car sixth and Kassmaul/Lerner in the third Carrera in 26th place.

The highly interesting Porsche 959, a limited production development exercise cum show car based on the 911 to show and test a possible way forward for future road-going Porsches, was launched in 1987. Shown first as a 'Group B Studie' two Frankfurt shows back (1983), it was radical for the Stuttgart company in several ways: an engine cooled with a hybrid system, a new swept volume, four hydraulic-tappet-actuated valves per cylinder, a very interesting use of two turbochargers, a four-wheel-drive chassis with an electronically controlled torque split, and a six-speed transmission. The unequal-length wishbone and coil spring suspension also had variable height; the

ride height varied automatically according to road speed.

The engine owed its beginnings to the Type 935/76 Group C unit of the 956 competition cars based on the 911 and 930 engines of the standard 911. However, it differed considerably from standard in many respects. While the cylinder barrels remained air cooled, the cylinder heads were separately cooled by liquid. Bore and stroke was 95 x 67mm, giving a total capacity of 2,849cc, specially chosen with Group B's turbo equivalence factor in mind, where the swept volume of any blown engine was

multiplied by 1.4. This put the 959 in the 4-litre unsupercharged class, which carried a minimum weight requirement just attainable with a car stripped for racing. A forged crankshaft of nitrided chrome-molybdenum steel worked titanium forged connecting rods and forged pistons.

The cylinder heads, sealed to the cylinder barrels by ring gaskets, each carried hydraulically-tensioned duplex chain-driven double overhead camshafts operating four valves to each cylinder, set at 28° included angle. Inlets were 35mm diameter and the 32mm exhaust valves were sodium filled to improve their cooling. Valves were returned by double springs, and any clearance lash taken up by hydraulic tappets capable of working at more than the engine's maximum crankshaft speed. Single 12mm sparking plugs (instead of the standard 14mm) were made necessary by the valve head sizes.

Lubrication was looked after comprehensively: the dry-sump system used one pressure pump as normal but, not so usually, no less than five scavenge pumps feeding oil back to an oil tank hidden below the right-hand B-pillar of the body, to guarantee against the slightest possibility of oil starvation during high fore and aft or sideways forces. This apparently profligate number of scavenge pumps was made so by the addition of two extra, one to each turbocharger bearing. Also doubled were the

oil coolers. Bosch Motronic-controlled injection was through racing-style double injectors to each cylinder. Motronic also looked after the ignition, its timing feedback-controlled by knock sensors on each bank. The usual sensors fed temperature and pressure information to the electronics and added an overrun cut-off, which perhaps incongruously in such a high performance car, helped economy in town driving.

Two turbochargers reduce lag

The turbocharger set-up was the most remarkable feature of the 959's engine. Its relative complexity was all about overcoming, or at any rate minimising, the notorious turbo lag of that time. This occurred when the accelerator was opened abruptly from low engine speed or, even in

Porsche 961, Le Mans practice, 1987.

This 1985 picture shows how different visually the 959 (centre) was from the 911. On the left is a Carrera 3.2 Cabriolet, with a Turbo 3.3 coupé on the right.

some very poor cases, during an upward gear change. The exhaust manifold of each bank of cylinders carried its own KKK K26 water-cooled turbo, the compressors of both turbochargers being fed to a common throttle body. A pipe running across the engine connected the two exhaust manifolds just downstream of each manifold's three exhaust port tracts.

Without a diagram to help, it will make understanding the system simpler if we label the right-hand turbocharger turbo A and the left-hand one turbo B. There was a slightly more complex set of pipes on the compressor side. What was called the recirculating pipe ran between the by-pass valve on the exit side of turbo A to the entry side of turbo B. The by-pass valve was also connected to a shorter pipe plugged

into the upstream side of turbo A, just downstream from another valve set in the exit from turbo A's compressor. Turbo B also had a recirculation pipe connecting the inlet and outlet sides of its compressor controlled by a valve.

At lower engine speeds, when the flow of exhaust gas was relatively slight, the exit from turbo A's exhaust turbine was shut, so that exhaust gas from its side was forced through the cross-pipe to join and double the flow from turbo B. This ensured both a rapid response and adequate supercharging. To encourage turbo A to keep windmilling while deprived of its exhaust, so that it would speed up more rapidly when required, the recirculation valve was closed and the by-pass valve set so that compressor air could recirculate

through turbo A. The recirculation circuit on turbo B was normally kept shut, except when the throttle was closed, when it opened for the same reason.

At around middling engine speeds and load, when turbine B was still not working at its maximum, the exhaust block to turbo A was progressively but not fully released, as was the valve blocking the compressor outlet, so that turbo A began to work, adding its increasing output to that of turbo B. Flat out, all by-passes closed, the system turned into a simple twin turbocharger set up, each turbo blowing into its own cylinders, providing a maximum intercooled boost of 0.9bar above atmospheric, which on an 8.3:1 compression ratio and 95RM fuel, turned out 450PS at 6,500rpm and 500Nm at 5,500rpm.

The 959's four-wheel-drive system used electro-hydraulic control.

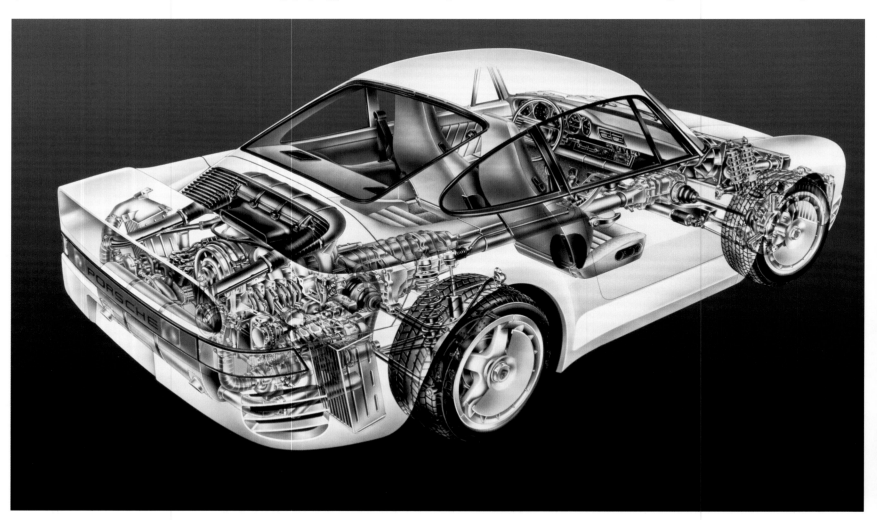

One form of all-wheel drive

Handling the 959's prodigious output was Porsche's first try at all-wheel drive. Although the heaviest 911 yet, weighing around 1,650kg fully equipped for the road (roughly 100kg less in stripped competition form), such power corresponded to between 274 and 289PS/tonne, which demanded traction even better than the 911 layout could provide. In any case, four-wheel drive had come into rallying in a big way at the time, which was an added driver of the decision.

The company's engineers had by now learnt the primary challenge of four-wheel drive in competition – or simply sporting – driving. Compared to rear drive, where in a corner taken quickly the front tyres have only steering duties, putting power through the front increases the dynamic loads on the outside tyre and therefore its slip angle – the angular difference between where the wheel is pointed and where it actually runs. In a nutshell, all-wheel drive in a powerful car driven hard produces understeer, denying the enthusiastic and capable driver the means to vary the car's balance and cornering attitude with power, as happens for much of the same reason in a front-wheel-drive car.

One way to minimise four-wheel-drive understeer is to vary the proportion of engine power that goes through the front wheels, minimising it during cornering, returning it to a higher proportion, as required by traction without wheel-spin, during straight-line acceleration. That is why the 959 had what looked at first sight like an exceptionally simple four-wheel-drive transmission, lacking even a centre differential, with the propeller shaft to the front enclosed in what used to be called a torque tube linking the front end of the gearbox to the front differential case.

Closer inspection showed that instead of a centre differential, there was a hydraulically-operated multi-plate wet clutch in the casing before the front diff, whose clamping pressure and therefore slip could be varied between unlocked and fully locked. Another similar clutch in the rear differential performed the function of a variable differential lock.

Setting the front clutch coupling to slip slightly varied the proportion of power transmitted to the front and also permitted the speed of front and back wheels to differ as they have to during cornering. Tyre/wheel combinations were chosen so that the rolling diameter of the front tyres was slightly larger than at the rear, to ensure that some slip of the clutch was sustained. This made certain that in straight running, controlled variation of the clutch slip had some effect in providing variation of the front/rear torque split.

Electro-hydraulic control (worked from sensors of gearbox ratio, engine speed and load) looked after the system, providing anything from full locking of both clutches for extracting the car from deep snow or mud, via 40/60 front/rear for ice and snow driving, varying this split in rain, to 20/80 in full-power acceleration. The various modes were selectable from a steering column stalk. At parking speeds, both clutches were fully freed to minimise tyre loads and steering effort. There was a dedicated engine-driven hydraulic pump and pressure accumulator to power the clutches.

Double wishbone début

Turning to the 959 chassis, it was realised that to minimise potential torque-steer – that tiresome interference in steering familiar to anyone who has driven some more powerful front-drive cars enterprisingly – front wheel offset would need to be kept well down. (Offset here means any difference in length sideways between the theoretical centre of the tyre's contact patch and where the steering axis intersects the road – zero offset is when the two points are coincident.)

With very wide tyres, it is virtually impossible to achieve very low offset with a strut type of suspension. So Porsche decided to use an unequal length double wishbone suspension at the front, where the outer ends of the wishbones, and therefore the king-pin or steering axis, can be contained within part of the wheel, something not possible with a strut. A similar system was applied to the rear, replacing the standard 911 semi-trailing arm, whose various weaknesses (especially toe-in change during longer suspension movements) could not be tolerated in such

The 959 front tyre rolling radius was, unusually, slightly larger than the rear's, to ensure some constant slip of 4wd system clutch, in order to allow controlled variation of clutch slip for effectively varying front/rear torque split.

Production versions of Porsche's radical and forward-looking 959 were limited to just 220 for wealthy customers.

a high performance machine – particularly when a competition version was used in a rally. Both were coil-sprung instead of torsion bar-suspended, allowing a small weight saving.

To avoid the necessarily firm damping the road car version needed at high speed ruining ride quality at lower speeds, each wheel's damper was paired with a second damper combined with a hydraulic ram. Between them, each provided automatic or manual adjustment of damper firmness and ride height. Ride height could be varied manually between 120, 150 and 180mm according to road conditions, but the system automatically set it to 150mm from 50mph and to the lowest height from 100mph onwards, for the sake of stability and, at the higher speed, less drag. Brakes were ventilated discs (322mm diameter by 32mm thick in front and 308mm by 28mm at the rear), whose aluminium alloy four-piston calipers were powered by an engine-driven hydraulic pump backed up by pressure accumulators through twin diagonal hydraulic circuits. A major departure was the fitting of a Wabco anti-lock system.

Wheels were 17in diameter with 8in front width and 10in rear, carrying 235/45VR front and 255/40VR tyres. Finding tyres capable of standing up to the over 200mph maximum speed of the 959 with run-flat capability, as Porsche wanted, was not straightforward. Dunlop was approached to develop suitable rubber on its Denloc run-flat design but, although the firm managed the task later,

Desert rally development

Not surprisingly, evolution and development of the 959 took longer than originally expected, around two years, not least because Porsche rightly demanded that, especially with such a radically different and in many ways advanced car, it had to be tested and proved well. Prototypes being allowed, the company therefore entered three cars in each of three consecutive annual Paris–Dakar desert rallies.

These were development prototypes, which evolved closer during this period, and in the light of what it taught, to the final production 959. The first event, in

Bridgestone beat it to the job, providing the first tyres for the car. Punctures in such low profile, short-sidewall height tyres are not always immediately obvious to the less experienced, so tyre safety was backed up further by fitting an early form of tyre pressure monitoring. This used membrane pressure switches on each rim and a cockpit audio warning plus display to signal which tyre had lost pressure.

1984, was a mixed success: one car winning, the other two finishing sixth and 26th overall, a good result in terms of reliability. But 1985 was a disaster with none finishing even though one led for a while. However, 1986, with cars close to the final specification, was a huge success, the 959s achieving first, second and fifth places. Finally, one car entered the Le Mans 24-hour race, winning its class and coming seventh overall. Demand from those that could afford the (very expensive) production car, 200 of which had to be made to satisfy Group C requirements, was so great that 220 were finally built.

Far left: Helmuth Bott in the Porsche styling studio with a 911 scale model. He worked for Porsche for 36 years, rising from plant assistant to board member responsible for research and development by his retirement in 1988.

Left: A 1988 model Turbo 3.3 built to US Federal Safety Standards with high-back seats, which had power adjustment and heating operated by the seat switches seen in the foreground.

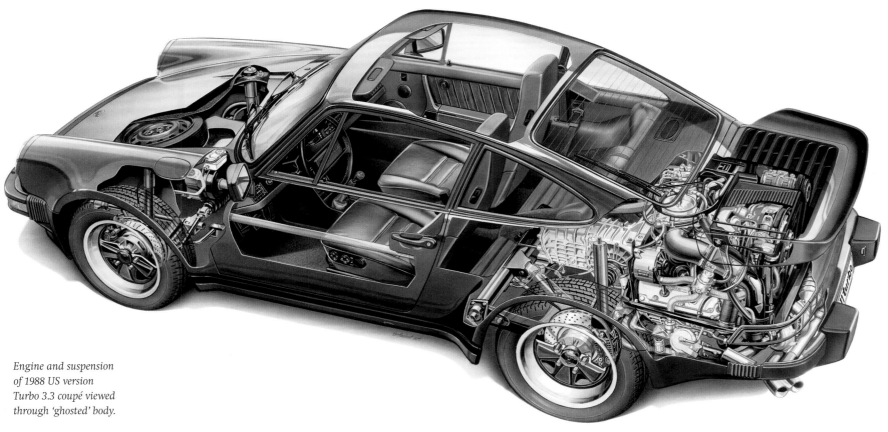

Engine and suspension of 1988 US version Turbo 3.3 coupé viewed through 'ghosted' body.

First production four-wheel drive: Carrera 4

The most obvious 911 presaged by the 959 was the Carrera 4 of 1989, Porsche's first production essay into the sporting all-wheel-drive field (heralded by Britain's Jensen FF of 1966 and extended 14 years later in 1980 by the Audi Quattro, brainchild of Ferdinand Piëch, former Porsche development chief and nephew of Ferdinand Porsche). It followed a number of the Porsche precedents established by the 959: for the first time on the 911 there was coil spring instead of torsion bar suspension, power-assisted steering and anti-lock braking. The steering was still rack and pinion but, in contrast to early 911s, an asymmetric design as on the 959, with the pinion on the steering column side to keep the rubber-mounted assembly no wider than before with the addition of the hydraulic assistance piston and cylinder. This was the first 911 with power-assisted steering and also the first example of the new Type 964 generation of 911.

Isolating from noise

The isolation aspect – the ability of the suspension to insulate the occupants of the car from road bumps and tyre noise – is interesting. When the wheel of a car hits a bump, as well as the upward force acting on the wheel, there is simultaneously also a backward force. This becomes more obvious if one considers a wheel falling into and coming out of a sizeable pothole. To achieve a reasonable ride and also quiet running in any car, the suspension has to be arranged so that it will absorb some of that horizontal component of the bump force, as well as the much more obvious vertical component absorbed by the suspension spring. This is usually done by providing suspension pivot bushes that are aligned parallel to the car's longways axis with what engineering jargon calls 'longitudinal compliance' – meaning fore-and-aft springiness in addition to the obvious sideways rubberiness of such pivots.

Because Porsche, unlike Alec Issigonis when designing the humble Morris Minor,

Suspension differences from before were not the sea change in 911 wheel location seen five model years later in the wishbone-geometry rear suspension Type 993 but they were an improvement. The only disadvantages of the engineering elegance of torsion bar suspension in a road-going car are structural and, with transverse bars, isolationist. The suspension arm pivoting about the torsion spring carries its corner's share of the load of the car directly, in bending, becoming a cantilevered beam, with a necessarily stout root at the suspension arm pivot cum torsion bar end. This means that, for the same permitted working stress in it and in the same material, it tends to be inherently heavier than an equivalent lateral suspension member in a compression-spring system where the (usually) coil spring acts directly on the hub carrier.

had used transverse torsion bars, that made it next to impossible to provide longitudinal compliance in the 911, unless its designers had somehow provided parallel rearward compliance in the torsion bar mounting. It had to be parallel so that even when only one side had struck a bump, both left and right sides moved back the same amount, to avoid unwanted steer effects. This was impractical and potentially expensive.

It was far simpler to adopt a compression springing system of some sort. Porsche went for the conventionally obvious, a coil spring surrounding and part-located by a damper strut, with fore-and-aft compliance in the pivot bushes of the lateral bottom wishbone, which located each front wheel sideways and longways. For equally obvious reasons, the 964 version of the Carrera 4 would require a front suspension that did not obstruct its front drive shafts, so ideally the suspension would be designed to ensure that it could be used in both two- and four-wheel-drive models.

Offset influences

Another aspect of the previous front suspension was that by the late 1980s, due to the adoption of 7in wide wheel rims, the positive offset of the steering had increased to 52.4mm. What is meant by offset in discussing front suspension and steering should be explained briefly. In a strut front suspension, when the wheel is steered, it turns 'vertically' – the word must be used approximately because of the strut's inclination – about the longways axis of the strut. Looking at an engineering scale drawing of the suspension in section from in front, if one continues the line of that axis downwards until it meets the road, its optimal position relative to the centre of the front tyre contact patch on the road would seem to be that the steering pivot line should go through the road surface at the same place as does the centre of the contact patch. This ensures that the tyre undergoes the least 'scrubbing' movement when steered. If, however, the steering pivot line meets the road surface on the inboard side of the contact patch area, it is said to be offset positively. If it does so on the outboard side, it is offset negatively.

This business of ground offset had become critical with the adoption of anti-lock brakes. Anyone who has driven any car so equipped and who has tried braking too hard, stimulating the anti-lock system into working, will remember that a vibration is felt, as the system alternately applies the brake, then releases it when it starts locking the wheel, then re-applying the brake, and so on, at a quite high frequency. Especially if anti-lock action occurs only on one front wheel, which has found itself on a less grippy surface than the other side, a suspension system with a notable amount of ground offset will pull intermittently to one side, playing havoc with the steering – exactly what anti-lock is designed to avoid. Certainly, the over 2in offset of pre-964 models would not permit the use of ABS (from the German for anti-lock brakes, *Antiblockier system*).

Keeping the front anti-roll bar out of the way was simply a matter of mounting it high enough. The larger challenge was

Opposite: 1990 model year Carrera 4 3.6 coupé.

Targa version of the 1990 model Carrera 4 3.6.

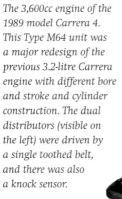

The 3,600cc engine of the 1989 model Carrera 4. This Type M64 unit was a major redesign of the previous 3.2-litre Carrera engine with different bore and stroke and cylinder construction. The dual distributors (visible on the left) were driven by a single toothed belt, and there was also a knock sensor.

doing something similar with the spring-strut, normally placed in line with the wheel hub axis, to reduce the ground offset. However, in this case its bottom end connection was pushed back to the rear of the axle line, with the top end positioned so that the strut leant back to provide a small amount of caster angle (4.17° initially, later increased to 4.67°) and no ground offset, so that ABS could now be applied. The track control member or wishbone at the bottom was displaced forward, with the centre of the radially stiff rear pivot bush on the axle line, so that most of the sideways load when cornering was taken mostly by that bush. This ensured that any deflection of it which could move the wheel rearwards and cause unwanted steering effects was minimised.

Harnessed compliance

In the now coil-sprung semi-swing-axle (as all semi-trailing-arm suspensions are) rear suspension, the car's designers were interested in an extra way of using suspension pivot bush compliance. As a semi-swing-axle-located wheel moves upward in bump or (more relevantly) roll, depending how much the swinging arm pivot axis is angled off either zero (pure swing-axle) or at 90° (pure trailing arm) to the car's longways axis, it turns a little outward in the steering sense, producing oversteer – exactly what is not wanted in a rear-heavy car.

Pivot bush compliance to counter this oversteer effect was done ingeniously in the Type 964 rear suspension. The swinging arm was cast in aluminium alloy with its front pivot made of a flexible bush, which was stiff radially but allowed some axial movement. However, the arm did not extend inwards as far as the rear pivot, its inner end instead having another example of Porsche suspension's spring blade arm. This was aligned on its side to allow the rearward movement of the entire suspension member permitted by the front bush.

The clever part about this was two-fold. It had the minor advantage of allowing a simple flexible bush to be used as rear pivot. However, this pivot was arranged with its axis 30° outwards, thus converting the rearward movement provided by the front pivot bush during roll into a small outward movement of the back end of the arm, turning the wheel fractionally inwards, in the understeering direction. This countered both the inherent oversteer of semi-swing-axle geometry and the combined effects of radial compliance in the pivot bushes and tyre slip angle increase, which otherwise have the same oversteer tendency effect on the car overall.

The power for the conventionally

assisted steering was provided by an engine-driven vane pump worked by a toothed belt. Control of assistance was derived from a piston valve on the rack casing, later (in 1992) changed for a less expensive rotary valve. With a steering ratio of 18.5:1 in LHD 911s and 17.5:1 in RHD, the box itself was flexibly mounted with elastomeric-pivot bushes for the steering arms as well.

Knock control

On the outside of each bank of cylinders, a bridge piece spanning the cylinders carried a knock sensor; ingeniously, by noting crankshaft angle, the engine management computer could work out which cylinder was suffering from knock and retard its spark timing accordingly. The air intake system was a novelty, each cylinder trio feeding from a plenum chamber, the two chambers joined by two different diameter passages. Air entered the larger passage via the throttle control but also fed the smaller passage, which could be cut out of the system by its own electrically controlled valve. Opposing cylinders breathed alternately from these plenums, setting up pressure waves whose frequency was dependent on the volume of the passages. This effect was exploited by the engine management system, which opened access to the second passage from 5,500rpm onwards.

Subtly different engine

The engine of the new car, Type M64, was a considerable redesign of the 3.2-litre found in 911 Carrera 2s since 1987, and the basis of the 3.3-litre power units for the unblown 964 model 911s. Both bore and stroke changed, from 95mm x 74.4mm to 100mm x 76.4mm, giving a total capacity of exactly 3,600cc. Although the engine was built on the same bore centre spacing, the 5mm larger bore conflicted with the previous positions of the four studs holding each barrel and the cylinder head common to each trio of cylinders. So they had to be replaced further out, which required some re-design of the crankcase and its reinforcement in the area. Cylinders were unusual in being machined with progressively very slightly larger bores nearer the bottom of the cylinder, to allow for the greater expansion at the hotter top of the stroke. An even more unusual feature was the fitting of ceramic liners to the exhaust ports, whose fundamentally poorer heat conduction reduced cylinder head

temperatures usefully – enough to make the expense of sodium-filled exhaust valves unnecessary.

The cylinder heads carried two sparking plugs per pot, fed by an unusual dual distributor running off a single drive via a miniature toothed belt. Doubling sparking plugs ensures faster burning of the mixture and this was proved by the ability to retard ignition advance, compared to the previous 3.2-litre engine, and to increase the compression ratio by a whole number to 11.3:1. The necessarily new crankshaft – 76.4mm was the largest stroke up to that time in a 911 engine – was in fact a little less heavy, by 2.2kg, and fitted with a vibration damper doubling as a vee-belt pulley to drive a pump when air conditioning was specified. Gudgeon pins were offset slightly more, from 0.5 to 0.9mm, to counter some of the sideways force with which pistons act on the cylinder during the power stroke.

A new 12-blade cooling fan, whose shaft carried the alternator driven off the other end of the crank opposite to the vibration damper, ran at 1.6 times engine speed. The oil cooling system was simplified, eliminating the engine-mounted cooler and relying only on a larger version of the previous front wing-mounted heat exchanger.

A new timing chain drive for the camshafts did away with sprocket hydraulic chain tensioners in favour of simpler polyamid-coated shoes, which improved engine quietness. The deletion of sodium-filling of the 42.5mm exhaust valves has been mentioned; unconventionally, the stems of the particularly

The 1990 model Cabriolet carrying 'Carrera 4' badging on the engine cover.

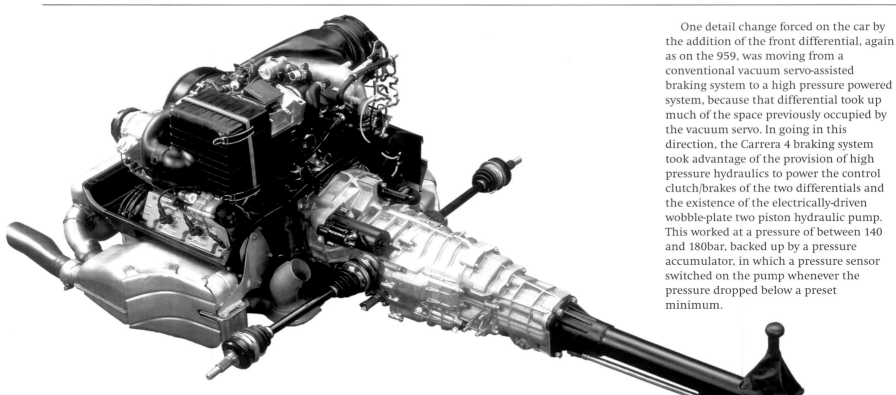

One detail change forced on the car by the addition of the front differential, again as on the 959, was moving from a conventional vacuum servo-assisted braking system to a high pressure powered system, because that differential took up much of the space previously occupied by the vacuum servo. In going in this direction, the Carrera 4 braking system took advantage of the provision of high pressure hydraulics to power the control clutch/brakes of the two differentials and the existence of the electrically-driven wobble-plate two piston hydraulic pump. This worked at a pressure of between 140 and 180bar, backed up by a pressure accumulator, in which a pressure sensor switched on the pump whenever the pressure dropped below a preset minimum.

Entire drive train (front final drive, torque tube, transmission, engine) of a 1989 model Carrera 4 3.6.

large-headed 49mm inlet valves were hollowed and sodium-filled to reduce their weight. Upstream of the inlets, the Bosch Motronic fuel injection system used a hot wire air mass sensor, improving volumetric efficiency thanks to the minimal obstruction to airflow, especially compared to Bosch's earlier K-Jetronic swinging disc system. In a similar field, the engine's catalytic converter used a metal foil matrix as distinct from the usual ceramic brick, reducing exhaust back pressure usefully, so that the output of this engine, which met all main world market emissions requirements for the first time in a Porsche, was the same whether or not a catalyst had to be used. What was known properly as the M64/01 engine turned out 250PS at 6,100rpm and 310Nm at 4,800rpm.

All-wheel-drive in production form

The car was available in all three body styles and its road behaviour set a new standard for the 911, the all-wheel-drive system largely taming the notorious on-limit trickiness of 911 handling superbly.

The transmission needed to turn the 911 into an all-wheel-drive car was an extensive modification of the standard rear-drive gearbox. What was known internally as the G64/00 had a considerable space where normally the end cover space was found, to make room for an extension of the gearbox output or pinion shaft forwards through the centre differential ('centre' in the strategic as opposed to simply geographic sense) and thence out to the front differential via a long shaft within an enclosing torque tube – thus far like the 959. Where the Carrera 4 differed was in a centre differential providing a front-rear torque split of 31 per cent front and 69 per cent rear. However, 959 practice came back in the use of a multi-plate clutch built in unit with the differential, electro-electronically controlled, so that if wheel-spin was detected by the control system via the anti-lock brake wheel speed sensors, drive was automatically redistributed to the unaffected axle. A similar arrangement applied in the rear differential, so that electronic control of either rear wheel was possible.

Anti-lock details

The control ability of electronics is immensely valuable and has been the major reason for much of the advance in the civilisation of the internal combustion engine over the past 50 years. A good example was provided in the first four-wheel-drive production 911, in the anti-lock system for the brakes.

Besides preventing locking of wheels during extreme braking, the essence of anti-lock braking is preserving the stability of the car under such conditions. So the system in the Carrera 4 ensured that if one rear wheel started to lock, operating pressure to both rear wheels was released, to avoid the car pulling to one side and consequently becoming unstable. On the other hand, anti-lock requires that each brake and wheel is controlled individually, which is clearly incompatible with a system of differential locking. However, the diff locks on the Carrera 4 were not the basic mechanical automatic type, using some form of speed-difference dependent device within the differential but controlled externally. The electro-hydraulic system controlling the differential restraints was made to free the differentials immediately the brakes were used.

Returning to the mechanical elements of the system, all brake discs were 299mm diameter ventilated internally, 28mm thick in front, 24mm rear, arrested by four-piston aluminium alloy calipers. In the Bosch anti-lock braking system, the pressure applied by the brake pedal acting on the tandem master cylinder was further magnified by a hydraulic servo to the tune of 4.8 times.

The front differential, final drive and viscous coupling seen through the sectioned case of a 1989 model Carrera 4 3.6.

Unprecedented 911 stability

During the press launch of the first Carrera 4, I recall being driven by one of Porsche's accomplished test drivers at high speed round the Weissach test circuit, part of which runs round a corner through an intimidating concrete-walled gully under a bridge. The car was near its cornering limit, so I was alarmed when the driver deliberately lifted off the accelerator as we tore through the turn. Instead of the disastrous sharply initiated oversteer, which long *Autocar* road test experience had taught would inevitably have occurred, the car simply twitched almost imperceptibly and ran securely on, its grip and stability undisturbed. One extra reason for this remarkable and wonderful insensitivity to clumsy or deliberately provocative use of the throttle was that the electronic control of the differential brakes was used above certain speed to keep the rear differential lock applied, which countered potential oversteer.

Part-time lift spoiling

The issue of aerodynamics had also to be addressed. By this time, an increasing number of cars had been designed with an eye to reducing aerodynamic drag. In the view of several manufacturers, a lower drag coefficient (Cd) bordered on a sales point. The 911 looked like a slippery-enough shape but the 0.42 drag coefficient of the body with American-style 5mph bumpers was way behind what more and more less-sporting cars were claiming. In competition driving, the lessons of the evils of lift generation had been appreciated for a fair time. Hence the coming of air dams in front and impressive wings above the tail of the car, which had started with the Carrera RS 2.7 seven years earlier.

However, a proportion of 911 customers did not care for such devices, requesting examples without the rear wing and so on. Their clamour had grown loud enough for the company to offer all the range except the Turbo in 'clean' wingless form. The objectors had grown enough for Porsche to look seriously at how to meet their point and preserve high speed stability, while at the same time improving the drag coefficient without adding excrescences like great aerofoils. Wind tunnel work on the shape – which Porsche knew its customers did not want lost – showed that

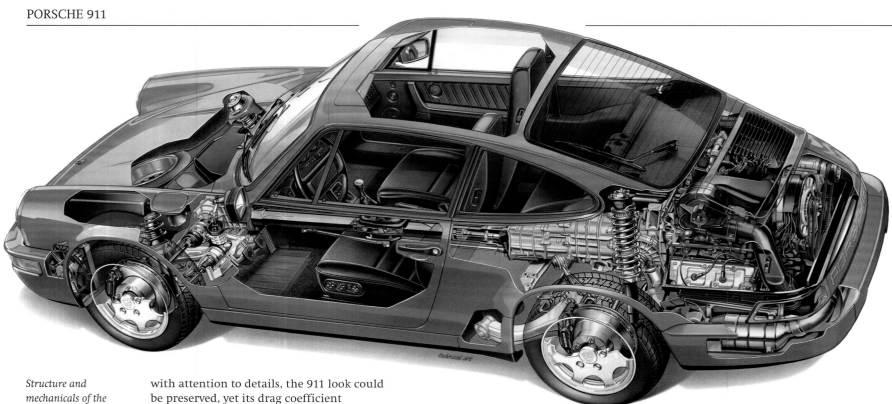

Structure and mechanicals of the four-wheel-drive Carrera 4 3.6 coupé. This is a 1991 model.

with attention to details, the 911 look could be preserved, yet its drag coefficient reduced usefully.

One of the major – and normally effectively unseen – ways was to make the underside of the car aerodynamically smooth. In fact, the car's designers went a little further, borrowing from contemporary sports-racing cars the idea of using the underside to generate some downforce. This was nowhere near the full scale half-venturis of racing, limiting the principle to a small increase in ground clearance towards the back of the underbody, which was all that the engine position would allow. Just applying underbody downforce to counter top-body lift may reduce overall lift but is counter-productive, increasing the drag coefficient

and therefore the overall drag of the car. Far better to reduce lift generated by the upper profile of the body behind the highest point of the cabin roof as well, maximising the gain in both lift and drag.

So the 964 design met objections to overt aerodynamic add-ons pragmatically, by introducing the 911's first self-erecting rear spoiler that, powered by an electric motor, came up at 80kph and retracted again once the speed dropped back to a few mph. The retracting spoiler was supposed to get over the clean-body fans by ensuring that the car was not seen by its driver with the spoiler up. Porsche took advantage of its presence

in and on the engine cover by using the opening, now under positive aerodynamic pressure, to force more cooling air through the engine compartment.

Drag-reduction on a car body is as much as anything a matter of close attention to detail. Work on this Porsche included reducing the inset of the windscreen and windows to reduce local turbulence, merging the thermoplastic bumpers into the nose, and adding plastic wheelarch guards to smooth the interior of the wings as well as improve protection against stone damage. The result was a very worthwhile 20 per cent drop in drag coefficient to 0.32.

The Carrera 2 and its rivals

Make and model	Top speed	0–60mph	0–100mph	Standing ¼ mile	Fuel consumption
Ferrari 348	*171mph	5.6sec	13.3sec	13.8sec	18.4mpg
JaguarSport XJR-S	150mph	7.1sec	17.7sec	15.5sec	15.4mpg
Lotus Esprit Turbo SE	159mph	4.9sec	12.4sec	13.5sec	23.5mpg
Porsche 911 Carrera 2	158mph	5.1sec	12.7sec	13.6sec	20.4mpg
Renault GTA Turbo	149mph	6.3sec	17.3sec	15.3sec	20.5mpg

*Manufacturer's claimed figure. Other performance figures from *Autocar & Motor*

Safety considerations

The bumpers, now made of a deformable thermoplastic resilient enough to cope with small bumps and recover their profile, were based on an aluminium alloy cross beam underneath the plastic. American export examples as before had absorber struts to provide impact resistance at up to 5mph without damage; in cars built for what motor industry jargon calls 'ROW' (the rest of the world), the bumper beams front and back sat on the ends of crushable, and relatively easily replaceable, longerons. There wasn't at first sight much difference made to the 911 shape in the 964 remodelling of the car, but under the outside there were a number of improvements. To deal with more serious collisions, as increasingly demanded by this time, the passive safety of the car was raised considerably. The new body structure was made capable of a high standard of impact absorption and strength, where each mattered, at the ends of the car and its cabin respectively.

Inside, the steering remained non-adjustable for reach and height but raised slightly. Also raised a little was the height of the central tunnel through the cockpit. Instruments remained in the same simple logical layout as ever, although the dials were filled now by completely new occupants, with far better night-time legibility thanks to backlighting. Various warning indicators were provided for minor but important points which the driver might overlook or not be immediately aware of, such as a handbrake left on, or brake pads that had worn to the point of needing replacement.

Specifications: 1989 Carrera 2

ENGINE

Capacity
3,600cc

Bore and stroke
100.0mm x 76.4mm

Compression ratio
11.3:1

Maximum power
250PS @ 6,100rpm

Maximum torque
184Nm @ 4,800

Fuel system
Bosch L-Jetronic DME injection

TRANSMISSION

Gearbox
Five-speed manual

BRAKES

Front
Ventilated disc, 298mm

Rear
Ventilated disc, 299mm

PERFORMANCE
Autocar & Motor road test,
6 December 1989

Top speed
158mph

Acceleration
0–60mph	5.1sec
0–100mph	12.7sec

KERB WEIGHT
1,380kg

Below left: Revised interior of the 1989 model Carrera 4 3.6. The steering wheel level was raised, but it remained non-adjustable.

Below: Rear 'seating' of 1989 model 911 Carrera 4 3.6. The transmission tunnel carrying the drive to the front wheels intruded more into the cabin.

Better fuel-level sensing

An interesting detail was the sensor used to drive the fuel contents gauge, the accuracy of which is always a debatable point in any car, especially a sporting one. Fuel level is no guide to how much is left, because the variability of level in a car subject to relatively violent accelerations forward, backwards and sideways is highly dubious. The practice of using relatively shallow, wide tanks (demanded in modern cars for packaging reasons) also means that the level, even if the car was idling when stationary, would vary very little for a comparatively large consumption of fuel. The only reliable method would seem therefore to be to measure the weight of fuel, or exactly how much is used at any given moment. In the 964, Porsche tried to improve tank contents indication by using the temperature of an electric conductor immersed in the tank, which varied according to how much of its length was cooled by contact with fuel. To achieve some sort of indicated average of what would obviously be a variety of readings due to vehicle disturbance over any period, the system's electronic controller in effect scanned a series of measurements every so often.

Heating addressed

In the 964, heating and ventilation engineers in Porsche's design department had got to work on the always somewhat parlous exhaust heat-exchanger system, to try to overcome some of its long-held weaknesses. To overcome the irritation of heat from the propeller of warmed airflow (the engine cooling fan) that diminished with falling engine speed, an electric fan was installed before the heat exchangers. This had the dual purpose of increasing flow at low engine rpm and inhibiting it to an acceptable level during higher engine speeds, to keep the supply of heat more nearly consistent. The reduction in windscreen and window inset to improve surface drag aerodynamically on the 964 had the unwanted consequence of depriving the cabin of an exhaust for stale air. On the new car, it was instead let out through hidden vents in each door that led it forward to outlets in the front wheelarches. Understandably, because of the possibility of changes in pressure trying to reverse flow, flexible one-way flap-valves were fitted in the vents.

Speedster reborn

In 1989 there was a re-creation of the Porsche Speedster name, first heard of 34 years earlier as the handle for a lightened, basic form of open sports car. This time the original 911 SC-based Speedster had started life some time before the 1987 Frankfurt Show, along similar lines. It was aimed at markets with guaranteed good weather, having a simplified design involving no top of any sort, a low wind-deflector screen *sans* wipers, and removable side windows. Although the prototype was ready very quickly, in time to be shown at that Frankfurt Show, for a variety of reasons unconnected with the Speedster itself, this entertaining-looking machine's launch was stalled for some while. So by the time it did enter production as a 1989 model year car, dreary legislation had slightly diluted the concept. Some markets required screen wipers, so a larger windscreen – still removable – had to be adopted, with a simple soft-top. This was unlined so that it stowed away less obtrusively than on the Cabriolet, folding under a rigid plastic cover. The car also acquired wind-up side windows.

Carrera 3.2 Speedster with 'Turbo Look' bodywork in 1989.

Racy lines of a 1990 model Carrera 4 3.6 speedster.

Five-speed Turbo

The 911 Turbo was modified in 1989 to accept a suitably strengthened variant of the G50 transmission first introduced in 1984, but with five instead of four gears. In a transmission, engine torque acting on the gears generates forces trying to bend the shafts they run on, of which there is an axial longways component generated by the helix angle of the teeth, which in final drive bevel gears is considerable. The considerable torque of the supercharged engine thus demanded stiffening of the differential housing and end cover of the gearbox itself. For similar reasons, the crown wheel and pinion size was increased by 25mm, but not the number of teeth (9/31). This and the thicker end cover moved the engine 30mm further rearwards compared to the 911 Carrera.

Ferry Porsche in a Speedster 3.2 'Turbo Look'. The 1989 model year saw two versions of the 911 Speedster, with either the standard width Carrera style or the wider Turbo bodywork.

Above: Dashboard of a 1989 right-hand-drive Turbo 3.3 coupé with 170mph speedometer and rectangular ventilation outlets.

Above right: Detail view of the drilled ventilated front disc brake of a 1989 Turbo 3.3.

Below: A 1989 model Turbo 3.3 coupé.

Tiptronic-ing to proper automaticity

The re-introduction of two-pedal driving to the 911 came in 1990. This time it took the form of Tiptronic, a relatively conventional ZF epicyclic four-speed automatic transmission with Bosch-developed and supplied electronic control for the Type 964 911 Carrera 2. A lock-up torque converter (a fluid coupling whose fluidity and therefore slip was cut out mechanically by a clutch inside the converter once past a pre-set minimum engine speed) did the job of a conventional clutch in a manual box. Mechanically the assembly was interesting, being a real departure from what had become Porsche's traditional gearbox layout. The gearbox part bolted to the front of the torque converter bellhousing – clutches and epicyclics in a tightly enclosing cylindrical housing typical of automatic transmissions – ended on its front end in a three-pinion helical gear set. This allowed the output to side-step the gearbox in order to turn a short shaft running forward to the final drive built partly underneath the gearbox. After passing through a pair of longitudinally-locating opposed taper roller bearings, the shaft ended in the final drive pinion.

In the spirit of sporting driving, the user was able to operate this new automatic offering a fair simulacrum of full manual control if required. This was achieved either by moving the transmission selector lever to the right of the main PRND321 slot into a slot marked '+' or '–' (plus or minus) for upward or downward sequential gear changing, or by operating the box via fingertip control of steering-wheel switches. The electronics provided five different control regimes, selected automatically according to how the car was being driven.

A key difference from contemporary convention was that a rapid deceleration while accelerating did not cause the box to change up but held it in the gear in which the car was accelerating immediately prior to the lift-off of throttle. In a further provision in the same vein, a lateral g sensor was part of the control system, so that the system knew that the car was being cornered. If the cornering rate was above 0.5g, the system did not allow automatic upward changes. Both control features were there to prevent instability in fast cornering due to abrupt reversals of drive, something to which all cars are variously subject, but to which all 911s prior to the Type 993 of 1994 were especially sensitive.

An important development to the M64/01 engine and drivetrain, introduced in the first Carrera 4 the year before, was the elimination of the previous rubber hub to the clutch centre plate used to overcome the long-established irritation of gearbox chatter. This job was now done reportedly better by a Freudenberg dual mass flywheel, thanks to its greater rotational mass.

The 1990 model year ZF Tiptronic transmission for the Carrera 2. The three-pinion helical gear set at the rear of the gearbox (on right) transfers the output to the final drive alongside.

Right: Interior of a 1992 Carrera 2 3.6 fitted with Tiptronic transmission. The slot to the right of the gear lever allowed manual upward or downward changes to be made.

Far right: A 1991 Carrera 4 3.6 coupé.

More powerful Turbo

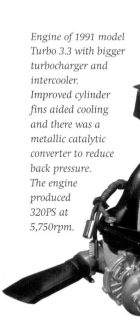

Engine of 1991 model Turbo 3.3 with bigger turbocharger and intercooler. Improved cylinder fins aided cooling and there was a metallic catalytic converter to reduce back pressure. The engine produced 320PS at 5,750rpm.

Economic circumstances – certainly the fall in value of the American dollar against the German mark – had conspired to reduce Porsche sales in the late 1980s. In a hurried attempt to rescue the situation, at the end of 1990 Porsche reintroduced the 911 Turbo, which had last been sold in mid-1989. Based on the Type 964 Carrera 2,

the pressures of time encouraged the further development of the previous Turbo engine. Power was boosted with a bigger turbocharger and intercooler, plus a metallic (rather than ceramic-brick) catalytic converter to reduce exhaust back pressure. Cylinder fins were improved to increase cooling, and the clutch made integral with the twin mass flywheel used to reduce crankshaft vibration.

There was also a new programmed electronically controlled ignition system to control spark timing more accurately. The engine was designed to work on 98-octane fuel, but if the owner wanted or had to use 95RON petrol, it was possible to switch the system to less advanced timing. As before, Bosch KE-Jetronic fuel injection provided fuelling. All this combined to help the 3.3-litre engine produce 320PS at 5,750rpm and maximum torque of 450Nm at 4,500rpm. The car was fitted with power-assisted steering and 17in wheels.

However, its performance did not satisfy the sterner of 911 enthusiasts, which is why the much

more costly 911 Turbo S model came into being. Although a true road-going machine, it was the brainchild of the racing department, despite a major part of its role usually being the other way round, turning standard road-complying 911s into racers. The engine was boosted with 0.9bar (instead of 0.8bar) turbocharging, polished inlets and ports, with different camshaft timing. A second oil cooler, mounted where normally the condenser for the air conditioning was housed, improved reliability.

Integrating the sidelamps with the headlamps allowed the holes left in the air dam in front to act as intakes for brake cooling. Intakes in the rear wings ahead of the wheel arches helped cool the engine compartment better. Ride height was lowered, 18in wheels with wider tyres making room for larger brake calipers. The now usual cross-strut between front suspension strut towers was added, the strut mounting stiffness being increased. Only 81 examples of this entertaining car were built, although lessons learnt from it did help development of the later 3.6-litre Turbo production car.

In 1991 some minor changes to what had become the G50/03 gearbox were made, including swapping the spring-loaded pin used to locate the gear selector shaft for a spring-loaded ball, giving a sweeter gear change. Also introduced was a variant of the G50 transmission for the Turbo, in the form of its unusual limited slip differential. This provided only 20 per cent differential locking during acceleration forwards, but 100 per cent on the overrun under full engine braking, to try to reduce rear-end sliding if the driver lifted off the accelerator when cornering. On the M64 engine, a small but useful weight-reducing development was the replacement of the aluminium alloy intake manifold with a glass fibre-reinforced plastic manifold.

The next 964 variant of the 911 was of course a rear-wheel-drive version of the Carrera 4, the Carrera 2, again available in all three body types – coupé, Targa, and Cabriolet.

Above left: The revised Type 964 styling of the 1991 Turbo 3.3 with integrated bumpers is evident here. The large tray rear wing remained a feature.

Above: A 1991 model Turbo 3.3 with 17in alloy wheels and power-assisted steering.

Far left: Dashboard and front interior of 1991 model Turbo 3.3 showing the new style instruments and the airbag four-spoke steering wheel.

Bottom left: A 1990 model Carrera 2 3.6 Targa.

Left: 'Turbo Look' bodywork on a 1992 Carrera 2 3.6 Cabriolet, showing the curved glass of the side windows.

Structure and mechanicals of the 1991 Carrera 2 3.6 coupé.

Carrera RS brings biggest engine

The 911 Carrera RS, a lightweight super-sport variant of the Carrera 2 in coupé form only, with 260PS and 17in wheels, arrived in 1992. Its immediate descendant of 1993, the Carrera RS 3.8 (as it was called somewhat inaccurately) was an historic landmark. This greatest enlargement of the

original 2-litre engine had been won by combining the 76.4mm stroke with a 102mm bore, the sum of all the six 624.29cc cylinders adding up to 3,746cc, which did not quite round up to 3.8 litres. That change represented the ultimate stretch of the original flat-six engine

conceived and produced 30 years earlier; in 1963 it had been thought capable of stretching to 2.7 litres. To any observer unfamiliar with Porsche engineering caution, stretching the bore by so much (27.5 per cent from its original 80mm) may have looked like engineering brinkmanship. In so doing, the engineers lifted the bore-to-stroke ratio to a very over-square 1.34 – though making more room for bigger valves, this does no good to inertia loading of the crankshaft, connecting rods and pistons at maximum power speeds. However, this was not carried out irresponsibly or with the thought that road car longevity did not matter, as its primary purpose was for motor sport.

Other engine changes included a higher compression ratio of 11.6:1 and an extra oil cooler was provided in the left front wing. There were larger valves – intakes increased from the 3.6 Carrera RS's 49mm to 51.5mm and exhausts from 42.5 to 43.5mm – with racing-style individual throttle butterflies, one to each intake tract. In road form, the engine's 300PS was turned out at 6,500rpm and peak torque was 360Nm at 5,250rpm.

A 1992 special edition 911 Carrera RS 3.6 homologation model pictured on delivery in September 1990. Just 2,000 examples were built for Group N of the GT class.

The five-speed gearbox was unchanged from that in the 3.6 Carrera RS, except for the substitution of steel synchroniser cones.

The uprated engine proved its reliability most convincingly, taking home the GT class trophies for Le Mans and the Spa 24-hour races in 1993. The same privately entered car won the following year's GT class at Le Mans.

Although conceived for racing, it was made in a fully road-legal, emissions-compliant form. Doors were pressed from aluminium alloy, power assistance for the steering was deleted, and it used 911 Turbo S brakes. The engine cover was moulded in plastic in unit with the considerable rear aerofoil. There were enlarged wings to make room for 18in wheels with 9J front and 11J rear rims carrying 235/40ZR and 285/35ZR tyres.

A more nearly pure racing version, the Carrera 3.8 RSR, was developed. It had all trim removed, a roll cage, fire extinguisher system, race seats with harness, suspension pivots almost all ball-jointed, racing cam timings for the engine, a sintered lined racing clutch, and a range of different wheel/tyre combinations to suit the now different regulations bedevilling GT racing.

Above far left: The Carrera RS 3.6 had racing-type bucket seats with apertures for fixing a four-point racing seat belt harness.

Above: Simple script on the tail of the 1992 Carrera RS 3.6 replaced the previous colourful graphics.

Above left: Carrera RS 3.6 in action with Dieter Roscheisen at the wheel.

Left: The 1992 Carrera RS 3.6 was produced only with a coupé body.

Right: Enlarged wings on the 1993 model Carrera RS 3.8 accommodated 18in wheels with 9J and 11J rims and ultra low profile tyres.

Far right: A fast brace of Porsches: 1993 911 Carrera RS 3.8 (in foreground) and 968 Turbo S.

Above: Engine cover and rear aerofoil wing on the 1993 Carrera RS 3.8 were made from moulded plastic.

Far right: Dashboard and interior of a 1993 Turbo 3.6 coupé. A pollen filter was now fitted.

The 3.6-litre Turbo

Although it may seem in retrospect to be something of a makeshift, the 3.3-litre Turbo was comparatively short-lived, its production ceasing after only two years, to be supplanted by the 911 Turbo 3.6 in early 1993. The larger power unit was based on the Type M64 3.6-litre engine, with relatively modest modifications, such as thinner cooling fins, new camshafts, a heavier crankshaft torsional vibration damper, and different pistons to provide a 7.5:1 compression ratio. With a stronger wastegate spring, maximum boost

pressure was raised by 0.1bar to 0.92bar, accompanied by increases in airflow meter size and injector volume. All of which added up to a 12.5 per cent power boost to 360PS at 5,500rpm and 15.5 per cent more torque at 520Nm, endowing the car with a 180mph maximum speed and 0–100mph acceleration in 9.5sec.

Running gear changes were limited to the fitting of 18in wheels with 8 and 10J rims and 225/40ZR and 265/35ZR tyres front and rear. This 911 was the first not to be fitted with Fuchs-supplied aluminium

alloy forged wheels, which were only available with too much offset for either anti-lock or in the case of the Carrera 4, all-wheel-drive. Their place was taken by new cast seven-spoke aluminium alloy wheels developed by Porsche. In the unblown cars, the amount of isolating rubber in the steering system at the track rod ends was reduced, and the gearing ratio of the rack and pinion itself brought down to 16.5:1, both to improve precision and response.

In 1993 a further development of the engine cooling-fan-driven cabin heating system (when fitted with air conditioning) was to run the latter on tetrafluoroethene instead of the much more environmentally toxic freon refrigerant traditionally used. This involved some redesign of the system with materials not affected by the new coolant. Pollen filtration was added, as on many cars of the period, and the different exhaust system layout meant that excess hot air was now vented to atmosphere behind the engine instead of into the rear wheel-arches.

One-make 911 racing

In 1986 came the start of an enterprising idea from Porsche, when it organised a series of Porsche one-make races to provide something nearer that always highly elusive ideal, motor racing which was less expensive for the driver and entrant. To add spice, one car driven by an established professional was supposed to provide a gauge of driving skill for the punters. The fact that not a few of said punters were

competent enough to win more often than the pro says something for the standard of racing.

The cars provided were initially mildly changed 911 Turbos, in 1990 becoming machines rooted on the 911 Carrera 2. Built at Porsche's Weissach racing cum research and development establishment outside Stuttgart, the Cup models were lightly modified, stripped of unnecessary

items, with a roll protection cage, manual window winders and a cable door release. The front 'bonnet' was remade in aluminium alloy and thin glass was fitted to all windows but the windscreen, resulting overall in a 200kg weight saving.

Engines were improved only by 'blueprinting' (specially careful assembly to ensure optimum fits, bearing clearances and so on) and a less restrictive air cleaner.

Above: Wide track and tyres of the 1993 911 Turbo 3.6 coupé are evident in this rear view.

Below: The powerful 1993 Turbo 3.6 coupé was ideal for storming mountains.

A quintet of 1993 911 competition cars. Front row: Turbo IMSA Super Car (right) and Turbo S Le Mans GT. Back row (left to right): Carrera RSR 3.8, 968 Turbo RS, and Carrera 2 Cup model.

Rubber was taken out of the front and rear suspension. Much stiffer springs and anti-roll bars (the latter made adjustable), Bilstein dampers, and a lower ride height changed the ride and handling to racing standard. Steering was changed to non-assisted. Weight saving was limited to replacing the aluminium alloy intake system with an even lighter plastic one (the cost of moulds etc being justified by incorporation of the same change in

production cars later). Transmission improvements included higher gearing for first and second, steel synchro rings modified, and a lightened flywheel to make gear changes faster, a limited slip differential, a better clutch, and stiffer engine mounts.

The fruit of these modifications was four years, from 1990 to 1993, of highly successful racing, untroubled for most competitors, with excellent reliability. In

1992 the Type 964 911 Carrera RS, a road-legal edition of the Cup cars for those customers keen to run a near racing version on public roads, was available. It was only produced for that year.

Near racing road-going versions of standard production cars could be more readily made into full competition cars, of course – good examples of this were the 3.3- and 3.6-litre Turbo competition variants of the briefly-produced 911 Turbo S offered in

1990 (described earlier in this chapter). The IMSA series stimulated the evolution of the Turbo S into the lightly varied cars used by Hans Stuck, Walter Rohrl and Hurley Haywood in those events in 1992 and 1993, in which championship wins went the Porsche's way for three consecutive years, racing against stiff opposition from Nissan, BMW, Lotus, Pontiac and Chevrolet. Turbo S rear intakes were not allowed but suspension strut mounts could be changed to ball type as distinct from rubber-bushed.

Le Mans-class 911 Turbo

There was also a special turbo 911 in 1993, the 911 LM Turbo, developed for the Le Mans and Sebring events. Another case of a highly dedicated racing model taken even further, with carbon-fibre for all non-structural bodywork, Perspex substituted for glass in all side and rear windows, fully ball-jointed suspension, and four-piston-caliper racing brakes devoid of any servo assistance. It was powered by a twin-KKK-turbo intercooled air-cooled 3,164cc engine close to that fitted in

3.8-litre 993-series Cup racer

Planning for a second series of 911 Cup races began in 1993 based on the new 993-series 911 with 3.8-litre engine. With the motor of the previous 964 Carrera RS 3.8 in mind, this later edition was developed enough to deliver more power (315PS at 6,200rpm and 370Nm at 5,500rpm) in spite of having a catalytic converter in its exhaust. The geometrically proper wishbone rear suspension made the new

the IMSA sports prototype class 962. Regulations called for 32mm restrictors in the intakes, limiting power to 505PS – 29.9 per cent short of what the unfettered engine could achieve. The car won its first race, the Sebring 12-hours, and proved fast enough at the 1993 Le Mans, but a small accident with another car put it out of the race. Later it achieved a string of wins in four-hour GT races at circuits in countries ranging from France to Japan.

car more nearly ideal for racing, particularly as the Cup cars were given eccentric-mounted, mostly ball joint pivots front and rear that allowed adjustment of toe-in, camber, and caster. The usual hard springing and damping were applied, anti-roll bars were adjustable, and ride height lowered. Centre-lock composite 18in wheels with 8.5 and 10in rims were shod with 235/165 and 285/645 Pirelli tyres. Doors were aluminium alloy panelled, and thin glass was used in the usual way in all but the front window. Deleting the handbrake was a further weight saving, the sum total of which resulted in an all-up weight of 1,100kg without fuel. The base of the large rear aerofoil incorporated air intakes to help cool the engine area. The usual sintered plate clutch handled power on its way to the six-speed gearbox with its steel synchro cones. Brakes were ex-911 Turbo 3.6, worked by a high pressure pumped supply.

Celebrating 30 years of Porsche production in 1993, Ferry Porsche (right) and his eldest son, Ferdinand Alexander (Butzi) pose with a 1964 911 and a 1993 Carrera 4 coupé. Ferdinand Alexander Porsche was the leader of the Porsche KG styling studios from 1961 and was responsible for the 911's shape. With the reorganisation of the family-owned firm in 1972 into a limited company, the styling department was set up as an independent operation. In 1975 Porsche Design GmbH moved to new premises in Zell am See in Austria.

FOURTH DECADE
1994–2005

1994–2005
Proper location and proper cooling

Here was the next major step in 911 evolution, with the coming of the Type 993 911, announced in the autumn of 1993. The truly big news was at the back end of the new model. As well as a major (by Porsche standards) face-lift of the body, the important and valuable move was to brand new multi-link (unequal length wishbone geometry) rear suspension. By controlling wheel camber, caster and toe-angle, changes in these three parameters – vital for good handling as well as roadholding – were kept to a sensible minimum.

This was a huge, and to critics of 911 handling, long overdue improvement over the previous semi-swing axle, let alone the original Porsche system. The difference this made to the ease of handling of the 911 was vast. No longer did the 911 driver have to tread quite so very carefully on or near the car's cornering limit; its power and huge grip could now be exploited more confidently. Although the undesirable inertia effects of that overhung rear mass of engine remained, they were mostly undetected by the majority of drivers, who did not extend the car to its now even more elevated cornering limits.

Subtleties of good location

That Porsche was aware of the deficiencies of the long used semi-trailing link rear suspension, which introduces both undesirable camber and caster (toe-in) changes as the suspension moves up or down, is proved by the use of a proper unequal length double wishbone rear suspension on many of its competition cars and most notably on the 959. However, the one virtue of a semi-swing axle is that it intrudes relatively little into the chassis and body. At a time when sales had sunk, the considerable re-design of the rear end of the chassis to accommodate the notably larger intrusion into the body of any sort of double wishbone linkage for the 911 was not deemed affordable.

However, the company had rather more than toyed with the idea of going into the four-door sports saloon market, until the (by

Specifications: 1993 Carrera (Type 993 – double wishbone IRS)

ENGINE

Capacity
3,600cc

Bore and stroke
100.0mm x 76.4mm

Compression ratio
11.3:1

Maximum power
272PS @ 6,100rpm

Maximum torque
342Nm @ 5,200rpm

Fuel system
Sequential injection

TRANSMISSION

Gearbox
Six-speed manual

*Manufacturer's claimed figure

BRAKES

Front
Ventilated disc, 304mm

Rear
Ventilated disc, 304mm

PERFORMANCE

Autocar road test, 6 October 1993

Top speed
168mph*

Acceleration
0–60mph	5.2sec
0–100mph	13.2sec

KERB WEIGHT
1,370kg

then expensive) project had been abandoned in 1992. Its design had involved a double wishbone suspension system, which the new management under Dr Wendelin Wiedeking decided could be used on the next 911.

As seen on the Type 993, this involved a four-part cast aluminium alloy subframe, cross-braced by an elegant cast Warren-girder-like hoop over the transmission space formed by two halves joined at the top centre point. The subframe anchorages to the chassis were elastomeric supports designed to allow some fore-and-aft movement – as required to help minimise the transmission of the longitudinal component of tyres striking a road deformity – but little sideways movement, to ensure handling precision. The actual wheel-locating members on each side, all aluminium alloy castings, consisted of upper and lower wishbones and, if one counted the one-piece lower wishbone as two links, a fifth lateral link behind the hub carrier to control toe-in. The upper pair of links, forming the more approximate top wishbone, were attached not to a common

Above: A 1994 model-year collection of 911 (Type 964) models. Left to right: Speedster Carrera 2 3.6, Carrera 4 3.6 coupé, and Carrera 2 3.6 Cabriolet. Behind is a Turbo 3.6.

Opposite: Restyled 1994 model Carrera 3.6 coupé (Type 993).

Right: Front suspension assembly of a 1994 model Carrera 3.6.

Below: The most important and valuable advance in 911 history up to 1994 and after: the new double wishbone geometry five-link rear suspension assembly, showing the aluminium alloy subframes, conferring considerably improved road behaviour and road holding.

axis at either end but two different ones, one above the other.

To counter the inevitable oversteer-generating effect of rear tyre slip angle during cornering, the system was designed to provide a pre-designated amount of toe-in on the outside wheel. This was done in the usual way by endowing the rear inner pivot of the bottom wishbone with a rubber bush having a radially lower rate than the front pivot, so that lateral force, compressing the rear pivot bush, induced a rearward movement of the outer end of the wishbone and therefore of the hub carrier. This rearward movement was translated into toe-in by the action of the rear lateral link running behind the wishbone to an inward extension of the hub carrier. Braking reaction forces had the same effect on both rear wheels, adding to stability.

Front suspension remained largely the same as the preceding coil-sprung strut

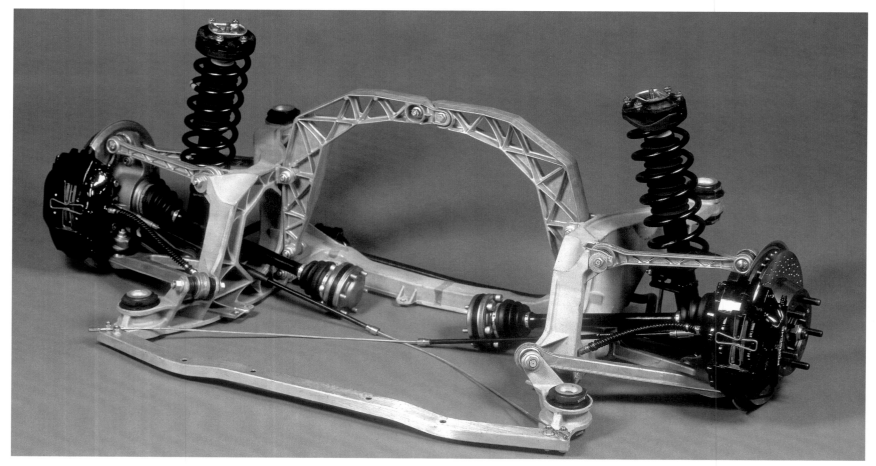

The 911 Carrera (Type 993) and its rivals

Make and model	Top speed	0–60mph	0–100mph	Standing ¼ mile	Fuel consumption
BMW M3	162mph	5.4sec	13.1sec	13.9sec	26.2mpg
Ferrari 348tb	163mph	5.6sec	13.3sec	13.8sec	18.4mpg
Honda NSX	159mph	5.8sec	13.7sec	14.2sec	19.6mpg
Lotus Esprit S4	161mph	5.0sec	12.7sec	13.4sec	16.0mpg
Porsche 911 Carrera	*168mph	5.2sec	13.2sec	13.8sec	19.8mpg

*Manufacturer's claimed figure. Other performance figures from *Autocar & Motor*

front end system on the Type 964 911. The only major difference was a 25mm increase in front track on the standard issue 16in wheels, from 1,380mm to 1,405mm; similarly, at the rear, track was increased by 70mm, from 1,374mm to 1,444mm. There were anti-roll bars front (18mm diameter) and rear (21mm) and the standard tyres were 205/55ZR-16 front on 6J rims and 225/50ZR-16 rear on 8J rims.

Viscous-coupled four-wheel drive

The Type 993 version of the 911 Carrera 4 appeared in August 1994. It sported a higher geared rack and pinion – formerly 18.48:1 (17.47 for RHD models) changing to 16.5:1 – with less flexible steering link ball-joint mountings to recover steering precision.

Under the engine cover there was a revised version of the Type G50 transmission, the G50/21, with six instead of five speeds. Modifications began at the front of the unchanged main gearbox casing with the end cover. It was fitted with a roller bearing to support the end of the pinion shaft as well as the roller bearing that had supported the front end of the clutch shaft since the original G50,

Far left and above: The revised bonnet shape of the 1994 Carrera 3.6 is seen in these two views of the Cabriolet.

Left: The Turbo 3.6 IMSA Super Car racing at Sebring in 1994.

Tyre sizes on the 1995 model Carrera 4 3.6 coupé were chosen carefully to avoid excessive understeer in hard cornering.

both of which were extended to carry the sixth gear, selector-cum-synchromesh ring, and fifth gear. An additional detail end cover change was the inclusion in the new casting of a housing for the front drive unit mounting bush. The clutch housing now included a duct to direct cooling air to the clutch centre, while openings in the clutch cover plate ensured the heated air was exhausted centrifugally.

Experience with the original Carrera 4's handling had raised the familiar criticism of all-wheel-drive when used in sporting cars – excessive understeer in hard cornering on high-grip surfaces. That first system had distributed 31 per cent of the engine's torque to the front. Porsche interestingly used the variability of a

viscous coupling between the gearbox and front differential to counter this. Tyre sizes front and rear were again deliberately chosen to provide slightly larger rolling radii at the front than the back, so that the front tyres rotated slightly slower than the rear ones. This meant that the viscous coupling was permanently effective to a mild extent – delivering between five and 15 per cent of the half of engine torque available to the front depending on rear wheel slip on a good road surface. The amount of rear wheel-spin likely on a good surface in appropriate circumstances could provide up to 40 per cent of that half to the front wheels; on a loose or slippery track, rear wheel-spin could be high enough for the coupling to transmit 100 per cent, or 50/50 front/rear for the whole car.

Electronic brake control

The automatic variability of a viscous coupling was one major part of how the Type 993 Carrera 4 all-wheel drive was a blessedly simpler – and usefully less heavy – system than previously. Another was the deletion of the manually selected lock for both rear and centre differential. This was compounded delightfully ingeniously with

electronic control of either rear wheel brake, applying it enough to slow a wheel spinning on one side, so that torque to the rear differential was redistributed to the other, non-spinning side wheel – ideal in very slippery conditions. However, Porsche did not depend entirely on this ABD (*Automatische Brems-Differential*), as the

engineers retained the previously fitted asymmetric conventional limited slip differential at the back, which provided 40 per cent slip limitation on overrun (to mitigate any potential instability if the driver decelerated abruptly in a corner on good surfaces), and 25 per cent on drive.

The operation of the individual rear brakes was triggered by signals from the anti-lock brake wheel-speed sensors, interpreted by additional ABD circuitry added to the anti-lock brake control. Actuation of each brake was driven by an electrically powered hydraulic pump via control valves. Simplifying the system thus, plus the progressive action of the viscous coupling, allowed weight savings of over 50kg through less stiff, and therefore less heavy, transmission parts.

Additionally, Porsche claimed that losses in the overall transmission, thanks partly to the deletion of the previous hydraulic pump, were reduced considerably. Independent contemporary observations suggested that handling was, as Porsche had intended, much more like the two-wheel-drive cars.

Engine improvements

Some work was also done on the M64 3.6-litre engine used in the 1994 cars. What was called the M64/05 (to go with the manual box) or M64/06 (Tiptronic) adopted hydraulic valve lash take-up. Hydraulic adjusters in the cast rockers were fed via drillings of the rockers to take oil pressure from the lubrication

system. The oil supply on the intake side rockers, which otherwise tended to lose oil when the engine was stopped, was backed up with small oil reservoirs. Inlet port size was enlarged by 1.5mm to 43mm, and both valves had their stem diameters reduced by 1mm to 6mm, saving 10g in reciprocating weight, valuable with these comparatively large-headed valves. Their covers changed from aluminium alloy to less heavy polyamid.

There was a new crankshaft, its vibration damper deleted thanks to reinforcement of the shaft with thicker webs and correspondingly small reductions in crankpin width, down by 3mm to 19mm. Bearing diameters stayed unchanged at 55mm and 60mm for crankpins and main bearings. Connecting

The 1995 model Carrera 4 3.6 coupé showing the new bonnet profile.

The M64 3.6-litre engine of a 1995 Carrera 3.6 showing the totally new exhaust system.

rods obviously had to follow suit, their width reduced, saving 8.2 per cent in weight. A totally new exhaust system offered reduced back pressure, thanks to a bigger volume silencer and catalytic converters. The Bosch Motronic hot wire air mass measurement sensor was updated to the later Bosch hot film design, where the same principle (measuring the heat taken away by air passing an electrically heated element) was applied to thin film resistances. These were contained on a ceramic substrate, which protected them from any risk of damage by anything carried in by the airflow past the air cleaner.

A number of these changes added up to improved efficiency, confirmed in the new power figures of 272PS at 6,100rpm and 330Nm at 5,000rpm on 98RM fuel – all from a 6kg lighter engine.

Right: From this angle the smoother blending of the Carrera 4 3.6 coupé's tail with the bumper can be seen. The rear window glass was bonded to the bodyshell.

Aerodynamic changes

Bodywork changes, in contrast to the previous 964 generation, were much more to the outside. Bonding of the front and back window glass strengthened the shell usefully, and the recession of the windscreen was reduced by 3mm and of the side glass by 7mm to get nearer to the aerodynamic ideal of totally flush windows. The noticeable profile change was to slope the front bonnet less, enough to increase boot space by nearly one third, its front end blending smoothly with the top of the bumper. Something very similar was done to the join between the tail and back bumper, while the rear itself was made wider, as were the front wings.

Other detail work included improvements to the ease with which headlamp bulb changing could be

Left: The 1995 Carrera 3.6 Cabriolet received the same styling changes as the coupé below the waistline.

Below: A 1995 line-up of three 911s (left to right): Carrera 4 3.6 coupé, Carrera 3.6 coupé, Carrera 3.6 Cabriolet.

Above: The 1996 range of 911s. Front row (left to right) Turbo 3.6, Carrera 4S 3.6, Targa 3.6 with glass roof panel. Back row (left to right) Carrera 3.6 Cabriolet, Carrera 3.6 coupé, Carrera RS 3.8.

Right: Revised dashboard of a 1994 Carrera 3.6 Tiptronic S with new steering wheel, in this case with switches for the Tiptronic gearbox. The floor-mounted selector was an alternative means of gear changing.

performed, and twin halogen bulbs in place of single ones for headlamps, which combined with different reflectors, gave a much better dipped beam. Better positioning of the windscreen wiper pivot points, very much closer to each other, improved the swept area of glass. Inside the cabin, the design of the airbag-equipped steering wheel changed, a passenger-side airbag was fitted, and dashboard switches were different. In spite of the aerodynamic-biased work, the drag coefficient rose by 3.1 per cent to 0.33 and, because of the widening of the body, the product of drag coefficient and projected frontal area (CdA) rose by 1.7 per cent. Gas discharge headlamps were fitted on the Turbo and became optional on other 911 models.

Above: Rear wings contrasted in 1995: a Carrera RS 3.8 with its Clubsport version behind.

Left: A 1995 Carrera RS 3.8 coupé.

The 400PS two-wheel-drive border

By 1995 figures like 400PS were not so rare, prompting Porsche to set a new policy. This dictated that its road cars with more than that power figure would put it through all wheels, not just two. After all, the company had been building four-wheel-drive 911s in two versions for nearly six years, since the first 3.6-litre Carrera 4 of 1989, so there was no lack of either experience of all-wheel drive or the hardware to achieve it in a 911. The first practical road-car application of this rule was in the spring of 1995, at the Geneva Show, when the most powerful 911 Turbo yet arrived. A twin turbocharger set-up extracted 408PS at 5,750rpm from 3.6 litres and 540Nm at 4,500rpm, respectively 13.2 and 3.8 per cent improvements. Set in the Type 993 shell, the engine was extensively modified to provide and cope with these output figures.

Performance-improving measures included: a higher 8.0:1 compression ratio (7.5:1 previously), new pistons, intake valves with 11.6mm lift and exhausts with 10.5mm, and, most importantly of all, maximum boost raised to 0.94bar at 3,500rpm. Porsche had used two turbos on

Top: Cockpit of a 1996 model Carrera 3.6 Cabriolet. The central rev counter is easily readable through the new-style airbag steering wheel, which partially obscures the speedometer.

Above: A 1996 model Targa coupé 3.6 with glass roof panel.

Right: The 1995 Carrera RS 3.8 Clubsport complete with racing roll cage and finned rear aerofoil.

The powerful 1997 model Turbo 3.6 coupé with 408PS delivered through all four wheels.

Below: Cockpit of a 1997 Turbo 3.6. Hydraulic servo assistance was provided for the clutch.

the 959 eight years earlier, but that engine had a complex control system (see 'Two turbochargers reduce lag' in the 1984–1993 chapter). Turbo design had advanced somewhat since then, so the 1995 911 Turbo simply used two intercooled KKK K16 turbochargers, one per bank. These were smaller than in the 959, which had the advantage that their lower turbine inertia should keep turbo lag within limits. Remarkably, this was confirmed in practice, the far simpler 1995 system having half the throttle response time of the 959.

To cope with the power and torque, there were several interesting features. One of the most striking was to machine the cylinder heads so that each cylinder bore extended into the combustion chamber and the piston reached top dead centre 5mm into the head. This reduced slightly the peak combustion pressures and heat acting on the joint between head and block. A conventional gasket was replaced by a

spring steel ring recessed in the head face. To improve cooling, cylinder fins were made thinner, the cooling fan speed increased, from the standard 1.6 to 1.8 times crankshaft speed, and exhaust valves were sodium-filled. Lubrication of the turbo bearings was via a feed from the timing chain tensioner supply, scavenged from a catch tank by a gear pump that was part of the air conditioning compressor. Connecting rods had reinforced big ends, a feature eventually carried over to the standard engine.

To be capable of transmitting the huge torque of the engine against the resistance to torque-relieving wheel-spin of the all-wheel-drive system, the pressure on the clutch plate had to be increased appreciably, which in turn meant a heavier clutch release load demanded via the pedal of the driver. For this reason, a Kongsberg hydraulic servo system was fitted to the release.

Mechanicals of a 1997 Turbo 3.6, showing the new six-speed gearbox and the drive to the front wheels.

On Board Diagnosis

Fuel injection and ignition were provided and controlled by a Motronic M5.2 system, the first use of this particular Bosch system on a 911 Turbo and, according to Porsche, the first world-market application of the American On Board Diagnosis Phase 2 (OBD II) system. Fuel demand was sensed as usual by measuring airflow in the intake, the hot-film air mass sensor used being more accurate and not obstructing airflow nearly so much as the previous K-Jetronic's swinging disc airflow sensor.

Air mass sensing also had the advantage that through measuring mass, as opposed to flow, the measurement of air temperature and atmospheric pressure became redundant, as mass changes according to those parameters. Relying on acoustic knock sensors in each bank of cylinders, the system could drive ignition timing close to the actual knock limit of the fuel running through the injectors, taking automatic account of any variations in the petrol, therefore providing automatic retiming to suit 98 or 95RM petrol.

Six-speed gearbox arrives

The coming of the 993 breed of Porsche 911 brought with it a six-speed version of the G50 transmission, the G50/21. The 911 Turbo had begun life with four speeds but there had been a demand for more ratios, which the huge range of road speed of which the latest Turbo was capable made all the more important. Accordingly, the 993 twin-turbo was fitted with a six-speed gearbox.

The design of the basic G50 had been uprated in 1989, for the introduction of the first – and, many felt, long overdue – replacement of the four-speed gearbox of the then current Turbo with five speeds. To deal with its power and, more important, torque, a larger diameter crown wheel and pinion of unchanged ratio was fitted and the casing was strengthened in the final drive area, as was the end cover, which located the pinion and took the end thrust generated by its hypoid bevel layout. Later adding the sixth ratio to form the G50/21 was not done by cramming the extra pair of gears within the main gearbox, which would have meant reducing the width and therefore the strength of the other five gears, but by placing the extra pair on the front of the box, thus preserving the torque capacity.

Therefore the only changes needed to adapt the G50 transmission to provide drive to the front wheels were lengthening the pinion shaft to take the viscous coupling placed between it and the shaft to the front differential, and adding an extra chamber in front of the standard end cover to house the additions, as on the then contemporary Carrera 4. The following year, to comply with new drive-by noise regulations, overall gearing was raised.

Purposeful stance of the 1997 Turbo 3.6.

Varioram variable intake

A further development in 1996 of the 3.6-litre engine was the introduction of Porsche's Varioram three-mode variable resonance intake system. This greatly widened the area of good torque, meaning a better spread of mid-range as well as high-end power – 285PS at 6,100rpm and 340Nm of torque at 5,250rpm, with a still very healthy 330Nm at only 4,000rpm. Varioram was made up of an intake manifold with three entry tracts into the intake ports, linked by cross-pipes at the front and back ends of the manifold. On top of this was saddled what looked like a second manifold, the exit pipe 'legs' of which, three per side, could move telescopically into the lower manifold, powered by a vacuum servo. Air from the air filter was fed to the centre entries in one of the cross-pipes of the upper and lower manifolds; the entry of each was controlled by a solenoid-operated butterfly valve.

At low engine speeds, below 5,000rpm, air only passed through the upper manifold, whose 'legs' were moved down to blank off the lower manifold, and fed straight into the inlet ports. That way, each inlet tract was longest, ideal for low speed resonant ram effects to occur. At what (for an unsupercharged Porsche engine) were

middling engine speeds, above 5,000rpm, the 'legs' of the upper manifold were raised clear of the port entries, so that air from both manifolds, whose butterfly valves were both open, was inhaled. This setting maximised the airflow passages, yet with both running relatively short, higher-frequency ram tracts.

A third butterfly valve sat in the middle of the under manifold's other cross-pipe, which in the two modes described so far remained shut. At high engine speeds, from 5,800rpm upwards, it was opened, along with both the entry butterfly valves to each manifold. Keeping both the latter open and also with the upper manifold 'legs' raised, again provided easiest flow

through short tracts into the engine, but with the added effect of higher frequency resonant effects, generated by the now open other cross-pipe combined with the alternating inhalation of the engine's six cylinders. This most interesting system was a major reason for the wider spread of power developed.

This engine, type M64/21 in manual gearbox form or M64/22 with Tiptronic transmission, went into the Carrera and Carrera 4. The four-wheel-drive model could be obtained with the Turbo wheels, tyres and extended bodywork, in which case, contrary to Porsche practice of a decade earlier, it now had a formal model name – Carrera 4S.

Racing 911s: the GT trio

Returning to real racing itself, it is easy for anyone not fully versed in sports-racing classes who looks at the Porsches introduced in the 1990s to be mildly confused by some 911 derivatives, which do not appear in the chronological order suggested by their names. The names concerned, in order of their first appearance, were 911 GT2 (introduced in 1994), 911 GT1 (1996), and 911 GT3 (1999). The explanation is simple. All the GT parts

refer to the sports-racing class for which the car concerned was designed and built. GT1 and GT2 were Le Mans categories: GT1 embracing highly modified cars with engines restricted to produce around 600PS, GT2 being for less modified production cars whose intake restrictors, sized according to engine size and type, and car weight, were designed to ensure outputs of around 450PS, in both cases to try to ensure closer racing.

A sliding glass panel in the roof of the 1997 Targa 3.6 allowed sunshine and fresh air into the cabin.

911 GT2

The GT1 and GT3 are the subjects of later parts of this chapter; being the first of this trio to appear, the 911 GT2 is worth a closer look. The basis of the car was the 993-series Porsche 911 Turbo, planned at the time of the GT2's gestation in the winter of 1994/5, and due to launch later in 1995.

That Turbo, properly called twin-Turbo as it followed the Porsche 995 of 1987 in using two turbochargers, albeit in a different way, was four-wheel drive. Since the 911 GT2 was intended to be a lightweight machine, and in any case four-wheel drive was and is not favoured in racing circles, the new car stuck to rear drive. Brakes were 380mm perforated and ventilated discs in front and similar 322mm discs at the rear, with deliberately wide calipers to take thicker pads for long-distance races. This car did have power-assisted steering, and its 993 suspension shared much in its differences from the road version with the 3.8-litre Cup cars,

with the exception of the centre-lock 18in wheels which had 10in and 11in rim widths.

Only slightly modified for racing, the M64/81 engine was close to the Turbo 3.6 litre except for a higher boost pressure of 2.1bar absolute with no catalyst to hinder the exhaust. The standard Bosch engine management system was replaced by a TAG racing one. The hydraulic tappet valve gear was changed to a solid mechanical system, using various thickness valve caps for play adjustment. With Le Mans regulation restrictors in the intakes, the engine developed 465PS at 5,700rpm and 670Nm at 5,000rpm. With a weight of 1,105kg, that worked out as a respectable one-up laden power-to-weight ratio of a 394PS/tonne.

This exciting car spawned some derivatives. There was a road version, trimmed and tyred for the purpose, at a third less cost to the buyer, and a little later a 911 GT2 Evolution model to enable customers to enter the GT1 class. That

Opposite: The 1997 Porsche model range of five 911s and one Boxster. Front row (left to right): Targa 3.6, Carrera S 3.6, and Type 986 Boxster 2.5 roadster. Back row (left to right): Carrera 3.6 coupé, Carrera 3.6 Cabriolet, and Turbo 3.6.

Mid-engined 911: the GT1

Now we come to what was probably the racing 911 with the least connection with the road car – the 911 GT1 of 1996. It was conceived as an answer to the challenge at Le Mans and in other variously related sports-racing formulae of cars like the McLaren F1 GTR, not least because, within those racing classes, the limit to which Porsche might go in modifying the 911 to match more expensively developed special cars was obvious.

In such an extreme frame of mind, it was perhaps not surprising that the Porsche racing department at Weissach should design the new car – for new is what it was, nearly from stem to stern – with the only 911 parts beside the transaxle to be found in the GT1's front-end understructure, from nose to the A-pillars. Most remarkable of all – given how 911 was part of its name and the overhung rear engine was and remains the core of 911-ness – the Porsche 911 GT1 was a mid-engined car. The 3.4-litre engine sat in front of the transaxle behind the cockpit and between cockpit and rear axle line.

The GT1's wheelbase makes the point very effectively about the space efficiency of rear engine versus mid engine (referred to in the Design and Development chapter). To accommodate the engine's bulk inside (instead of outside) the axle lines of this strictly two-seater car, the wheelbase had to be lengthened from the 2.35m of the latter-day Type 996 911 (due to launch the following autumn at the 1997 Frankfurt Show) to 2.5m, an increase of 150mm. To be fair to its designers, there was a handling motive to such a large difference. The standard 911's comparatively short wheelbase – even the 996 figure, the longest for any production 911, was 5mm shorter than that for an Opel/Vauxhall Corsa supermini of the time – was not ideal for optimum handling, regardless of rear engine difficulties. So the choice of the much longer figure, particularly when matched with the inherently kinder reduction in polar moment of inertia of a mid-engined layout, would potentially give the GT1 optimum cornering behaviour.

The glass-roofed 1997 Targa 3.6.

meant its engine could be let loose to the extent of 600PS at 7,000rpm and 720Nm at 5,000rpm, thanks to a totally unrestricted exhaust, larger diameter intake restrictors, bigger blowers working at 2.3bar absolute, and a better intercooler. To withstand the higher output, the crankshaft and con rods were upgraded further. More extensive bodywork lightening took the form of most remaining metal parts of the body being re-made mostly in Kevlar. Other outward changes included lifting the back window enough to make it flush with the frame, for better aerodynamic flow.

One *Autocar* test team member, Andrew Frankel, contributed driving impressions of a road version of the 911 GT2 in the 17 May 1995 issue. He clearly enjoyed the performance: 'By 4,000rpm, power is being poured into the rear wheels in raging torrents. Eyes flicker from road to revs and back again. Power delivery is far from linear: those extra horsepower are crammed into the last 1,000rpm of the rev range and as you close on the 5,750rpm

power peak, your speed changes from startling to genuinely alarming.' However, the handling had to be respected: 'Remember all those wise words you've read about how tame and forgiving the 911 is these days? They don't apply. This is a 911 with a savage temper, menacingly calm as you gently push your luck, lashing out at you when you go too far. How far is that? It decides.'

In and around 1996, Japan had its own near-production car sports-racing class called GT3, entirely unconnected with any European category not least because it was specifically for unsupercharged cars. Porsche therefore developed a suitable 911, closely derived from the European 911 3.8 Cup car in terms of all but its engine. This was further tuned with an 11.5:1 compression ratio and higher lift camshafts, ran without any catalytic converter, and used six separate throttle valves plus a variable volume resonance intake system. It produced 340PS at 7,000rpm and 380Nm at 5,500rpm.

To further ensure that ideal, wheel location was classic racing car with unequal length double wishbone geometry at the rear – as on the new 996 production 911. There were no strut compromises in front suspension, which (unlike the 911 to this day) followed the same pattern as the rear. Spring/damper units acting directly on the uprights replaced the struts pivoting from the suspension domes in front, but at the back they were placed near horizontally, working through bell-cranks and pushrods as on most pure racing single-seaters; anti-roll bars were adjustable at each end of the car.

Built to competition rules

The original steel 911 unitary chassis used ahead of the screen pillars was not echoed behind the steel-floored cockpit, where there was a steel tube spaceframe. The floor itself remained flat between the wheels as demanded by Le Mans rules, but rose under the tail, with side fences to improve the generation of downforce at speed. That Porsche was conscious of the tenuousness of the GT1's links with the 911 was confirmed cosmetically by using doors the same shape as the production ones and with headlamps and rear lamps from the same source.

Steering was conventionally assisted rack and pinion, and there were high-pressure pump-powered brakes, backed for Le Mans only with a Bosch anti-lock system. The brakes used the same size front and back ventilated carbon racing discs, 380mm diameter by 37mm thick.

The engine remained in 911 flat-six format, and its bore and stroke figures were those of the Porsche 962 (95mm x 74.4mm) giving a 3,164cc swept volume. Water-cooled cylinder heads had four valves (37mm intake and 32mm exhaust) worked via bucket tappets and double overhead camshafts that were chain-, not gear-, driven. Beside the chain timing drives, another production connection was the connecting rods with the same distance between centres, 127.8mm as on the 962 and some normal 911 engines.

The lubrication system was also similar to old Porsche practice, dry sump with an oil/water heat exchanger. Twin KKK turbochargers blowing at absolute pressures of either 2.1bar for Le Mans or 1.79bar for the FIA GT Championship did so into a geometrical compression ratio of 9.3:1, so that the engine in Le Mans trim produced 640PS at 7,200rpm and 650Nm at 5,500rpm. In Le Mans state, the 1,050kg minimum weight with that power figure gave a one-up laden power-to-weight figure of 567PS/tonne.

The usual racing sintered metal lined single-plate clutch fed this power to the G96 six-speed synchromesh gearbox – a production car part but with steel synchro cones, an oil pump built in to spray the gear pairs, and with an oil/water heat exchanger in the circuit. The disc limited slip diff applied 50–60 per cent locking on power and 80–90 per cent on overrun. Centre-lock BBS 18in wheels, 11.5in rimmed in front and 13in rear, sat 1.60m apart in front and 1.568m at the back, compared to 1.465/1.530m for the 911.

In profile the different roofline of the 1997 Targa 3.6 is apparent. Note the rear quarterlight's pointed, instead of rounded, rear corner.

The winning 911 GT1 (driven by Laurent Aiello, Allan McNish, and Stéphane Ortelli) coming through the Le Mans chicane in 1998.

Successes at Le Mans

To preserve the usual homologation fiction about originating from a road production car – something Porsche had always observed more or less scrupulously – the prototype GT1 was a road-legal car, as dictated by race organisers. Later it was properly developed for road application, at a projected price in Germany's pre-Euro currency of 1.5 million Deutschmarks. But how did this revolutionary 911 racer do in the competition that it was really designed to overwhelm?

In its first Le Mans, it took the top two places in the GT class, finishing second and fourth overall, behind the winning Porsche-engined open sports-racer. In the second half of the 1996 season, works GT1s totally dominated three BPR series events, to the unavailing protests of their outclassed rivals. A year later in the 1997 Sarthe 24 hours, two works-entered 911 GT1s, with a year's further development behind them, led from the start until one crashed in the 16th hour and the other was sidelined two hours before the finish by a burst oil cooler and the ensuing fire.

Autocar's test team got its hands on one of the few examples of the road-going version of the GT1 in the road test of 4 June 1997. This is notable for totally approving notes on the car's handling: '... on the right road, say a fast dual carriageway with some high-speed sweeps

Opposite: Le Mans, 1996. Both 911 GT1s finished, in second and third places overall. Here the two mid-engined GT1s are in front of the pack shortly after the start of the race.

and twists in it, the GT1 is pure magic.' As for its performance: '... once the GT1 gets into its stride, and the power can be properly deployed, it piles on the acceleration with a ferocity that verges on the surreal.'

Even before the 911 GT1's Le Mans victory in 1998, it was obvious to Porsche that open sports prototypes stood the better chance of Le Mans glory – and the invaluable publicity of an overall win there – than GT prototypes. A planned unblown 5.5-litre V10 example of such a car got as far as initial testing with the 1999 24-hour race in its sights, but there wasn't enough time to do the job properly and the idea was dropped. Later it was reincarnated in the ravishingly handsome mid-engined 5.7-litre carbon-fibre bodied Carrera GT road car – not 911 Carrera GT – previewed at various motor shows and in limited production now. A major contributor to that original thumbs-down was the commitment, financial, in development effort, and in setting up a new Leipzig-based plant to build what became the Porsche Cayenne high performance 4x4. There was also work to be done in adding a Turbo 996 and a Cabriolet, so that there were no engineers left unoccupied to work on competition cars, even developments of the 996 generation of the 911 for racing.

Birth of the Type 996

There was commonality of components between these 1998 Porsche models. Front to back: 911 Carrera 3.4 Cabriolet, Boxster 2.5 roadster (Type 986), and 911 Carrera 3.4 coupé.

At the Frankfurt Show in the autumn of 1997, Porsche displayed the most radically improved 911 of the car's now long life – the Type 996. To those uninterested in what was under the skin, the changes were only obvious to the observant; the same observer might know that moving to a radically different form of engine

cooling was a big deal for Porsche, which it was. However, the Type 996's differences were on more than just a plain engineering level.

Thoughts of the next 911 generation started near the end of 1991, a time when the Porsche company was doing badly enough financially for its future as an

independent manufacturer of cars to be questioned. Immensely successful in sales and the all-important profits during the 1980s, largely because of the high proportion of sales to the large North American market, Porsche had suffered badly when the value of the dollar against the German mark dropped, forcing 911 prices up and sales down. Also, the front-engined 928, intended at the time of its inception to be the ultimate replacement for the 911, had not sold nearly well enough. Similarly, the 944 and 968 had not done as well as they might – and the three models' production lines shared very little in common except for some engine parts used in both the 928 and 944/968, making production costs higher than necessary.

At the same time, the company realised that it could not depend on the sales of just one model line, particularly when the model concerned, the 911, was a top-end, relatively expensive machine. A step up to the 911 was important, some sort of lower-priced sports car for the aspiring but not so well-off Porsche buyer. This was how the Boxster was originally conceived and came about, Porsche's first re-entry into the mid-engined rear-drive production sports car field since the 914 of 22 years earlier. It was exhibited as a concept car at the 1993 Detroit Show, to very great interest from both the press and public; the production Boxster went on sale three years later and was an immediate success.

All of this had concentrated minds in Stuttgart and in Porsche's research and development centre outside Stuttgart, near the village of Weissach. Yes, the two radically different cars ought to be produced, but only if production costs were lowered considerably – and the first principle of such a reduction is to reduce the total parts list for the two models. The new 911 took design priority, in that its engineering requirements came first but at the same time, if a part could be used on both 911 and Boxster (internally numbered Types 996 and 986 respectively), so much the better. Thanks to a big effort by the engineering department, just such commonality of components was achieved, to an extent unprecedented in Porsche car production history, combined with better production methods. The result of this great and thorough effort on the part of the design team was a dramatic cutting of costs, while evolving two outstandingly good sports cars, life-saving for the company and benefiting the Porsche customer too.

Another change for the better: water cooling

The engine for the Type 996 (code-named M96/01), though still an opposed six-cylinder, was a brand new design, for the first time entirely liquid-cooled. This eliminated the power loss and noise generated by an effective fan, simplified engine construction, and had other incidental advantages like reducing engine height (by 120mm) – permitting the novelty of a rear parcels shelf in a 911 – making heater design simpler and more controllable, and providing a possible reduction in the radiation of engine noise.

Development work had proved that cooling four-valve cylinder heads with air was more difficult than for two-valve heads. The only disadvantage of liquid cooling, specific to the comparative sprawl of a flat six compared to an in-line or vee engine, was the relatively large length of water passages and pipes needed, plus, of course, the additional length of water piping from the tail-mounted engine to the necessarily front-mounted heat exchangers

(so often incorrectly called radiators). All this meant the addition of a total liquid content weighing 22.5kg.

The usual over-square bore and stroke dimensions remained but with new figures – 96mm x 78mm, giving a total swept volume of 3,387cc. Only the 118mm spacing between the centres of the cylinder bores of the old generation of engines remained in the new one. Previous 911 engines had separate cylinder heads on cylinders spigotted into either of each crankcase half. The 996 engine used conventional cylinder blocks and cylinder heads of three cylinders on each side of the usual Porsche vertically split crankcase. The head castings were held by long studs screwed, not into the crankcase but into each half of the vertically split main bearing block. This put the block castings in compression between head and bearing block – an innately simpler design thanks to the single cylinder block and head on each side. This was structurally sound,

The 3,386cc flat-six engine of the 1998 model Carrera 3.4 was completely new and broke with Porsche tradition in being water-cooled.

making use of the same principle of exploiting the compressive strength of aluminium and the tensile strength of steel as in all previous Porsche engines.

One striking example of the adoption of a modern production process, first used by Ford in America some years earlier, was the adoption of fracture-jointed big end caps for the connecting rods, which were 145mm between centres. The connecting rod was forged integral with its entire big end but with weakening nicks on either side of the big end eye. The cap half was then broken off, which it did without any bending, so forming two perfectly mating complex joint surfaces. As well as providing a perfect key to unite the joint over its entire face – structurally ideal – this method has the production advantage that each cap will only mate with its own rod end, eliminating the need for any assembly line identification method.

Besides the studs, bolts, nuts and so on, plus the forged nitro-carbon-treated fully counterweighted seven-bearing steel crankshaft, the other notable ferrous parts were the cast iron supports, cast in the cylinder blocks for main crankshaft bearing shells. An example of the considerable thought that went into minimising production costs was in the cylinder blocks, heads, and cam containers, which were made interchangeable, avoiding any sort of handed aspect of their design. Blocks, heads and crankcase were of course aluminium alloy, which has a considerably higher coefficient of thermal expansion than cast iron; the choice of cast iron for the main bearing supports therefore minimised the increase in bearing clearance with engine temperature rise, keeping down bearing rumble and oil pressure loss at high temperatures.

Another route to aluminium bores

A modern feature, whose advantages lie as much in weight reduction as reducing parts count and production cost, was the adoption of the Kolbenschmidt aluminium casting company's Lokasil process for the cylinder blocks.

Porsche used Nikasil bores first in the 2.7-litre engine launched in the 1972 Carrera RS, then a little later after the first 2.7-litre 911 and 911S engines had been in production, the company switched to the hyper-eutectic silicon-aluminium alloy technique (used under licence from Reynolds Aluminium by Kolbenschmidt) for aluminium cylinders. Now Porsche changed again and adopted Kolbenschmidt's own Lokasil system for the 996 engine, partly because it avoided one of the problems of the Nikasil plating process. This was its sensitivity in some cases to deterioration when high sulphur fuel was used and the major disadvantage of casting entire cylinders in hyper-eutectic alloy, which required expensive tooling to cope with the nodular silicon.

Lokasil centres round the creation of a mesh liner of silicon set in place in the cylinder block casting die, into which normal aluminium alloy is then high-pressure injected. The alloy mixes with the silicon, forming a highly wear-resistant hyper-eutectic bore but leaving the rest of the block in normal, conventionally machinable alloy – an ideal compromise steel-linerless cylinder block.

As in other high-specific-power engines, the M96/01 unit had oil jets in the main bearing block pointed at the pistons' 'undersides' (not the ideal word for the con rod side of a piston in a horizontal cylinder) to provide cooling. The pistons themselves (as usual in such cylinders) were iron-coated to improve their compatibility with the silicon.

Valves (37.1mm inlets and 32.5mm exhausts inclined at an included 30.5°) were worked through travels of 10.5mm and 10mm (inlet/exhaust) via inverted bucket hydraulic zero-lash tappets.

This cutaway view of the 2001 Carrera 3.4 engine shows the chain driven camshafts and inverted bucket hydraulic tappets operating four valves per cylinder.

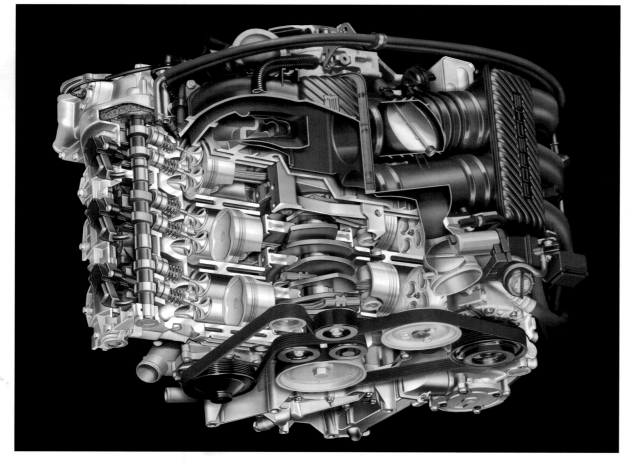

Operated by two through-drilled camshafts, the entire valve assembly was housed in separate cam boxes bolted to the heads. Camshafts were chain driven, with a total of five chains: one down from the crankshaft to an intermediate shaft, two long chains from that shaft out sideways to each cylinder bank's exhaust camshaft, and one more on each cylinder head, linking the camshafts. The two long duplex timing chains to drive each cylinder bank's camshaft pair were at either end of the engine, in that the chain for the left bank was placed at the front of the engine and that for the right at the back. The clever point about this was that in an opposed (or, for that matter, vee) cylinder engine, one bank of cylinders has to be offset along the crankshaft axis relative to the other – cleverly placing each chain drive at the inset end saved some 70mm in overall length.

Variable position chain tensioner alters cam timing

A casual glance at the short single-row chain between each cam box's exhaust camshaft and inlet camshaft might at first sight have provoked puzzlement over the somewhat over-long loop of this chain. This length was in fact a key feature of the Porsche Variocam variable inlet valve timing mechanism introduced on this engine. Clearly, to keep the chain tight on its sprockets, a chain tensioner was required. This was provided by a spring-loaded expanding plunger placed between the upper and lower runs of the chain – so far, so conventional. If, however, the tensioner body was moved upwards, pushing the chain so that the upper run had to loop over the tensioner pad, this rotated the inlet camshaft relative to the exhaust in one direction; reverse the movement and the rotation of inlet relative to exhaust would be the other way.

Movement of the tensioner body was by hydraulic pressure, controlled electro-mechanically, so that the change in timing could be mastered electronically. The system was capable of varying cam phase over a crankshaft angle range of 25°. It was exploited to improve exhaust emissions control at mid range and part throttle by providing some internal exhaust gas recirculation to lower combustion temperature and thereby reduce

The 1998 Carrera 3.4 had a completely new shape with distinctive headlamps.

The 1998 model Carrera 3.4 in Cabriolet and hard-top versions.

Above: Double wishbone rear suspension and subframe of 1998 model Carrera 3.4.

Right: Front suspension and subframe of 1998 Carrera 3.4 with steering rack and drilled ventilated brake discs.

generation of oxides of nitrogen (NOx) and, at higher speeds and load, to harness ram inlet effects for greater power.

A variable volume, therefore variable resonance, intake manifold to feed air to the engine used a new version of Porsche's variable resonance system first seen in the 1996 model year 911 Carreras, in this case providing two modes of operation. Fuel injection was sequential Bosch Motronic, relying on air-mass measurement and linked to drive-by-wire throttle control. For the first time ignition was solid state, using digital switching and individual coils on each plug (as pioneered originally by Saab). This confined spark (very high) voltages to the plug area only, ensuring far less vulnerability to short circuits due to any reason, including very damp under-engine-cover conditions. The lubrication system was an ingenious version of dry-sump, avoiding the necessity for a scavenge pump by putting the oil tank under the crankcase and using inclined slats from the crankcase to return oil.

The fruits of all this were a high specific power of 88.5PS/litre, which corresponds to 300PS at 6,800rpm and 350Nm of torque at 4,600rpm, good enough for *Autocar*'s 1 October 1997 road test of the 911 Carrera to comment: 'To 30mph it is untouchable by any two-wheel-drive car in our experience, recording a kidney-squeezing 1.8sec. But it's the way the 911 continues to pile on the giant-felling acceleration beyond three figures which is truly astonishing.' On handling, the magazine test team wrote: 'The extra stability and body control of the new ... chassis is not to be underestimated when it comes to dispensing with difficult obstacles tackled at speed, and is way above anything the old car had to offer.' The testers were not so happy about steering feel and behaviour: '... rather too much of the character that has distinguished the 911 as such a sharp driver's car over the years has been diluted.... The steering is the most obvious culprit. Although still extremely precise and accurate on lock, it is not as richly communicative as before, offering no more than satisfactory information about the road below.'

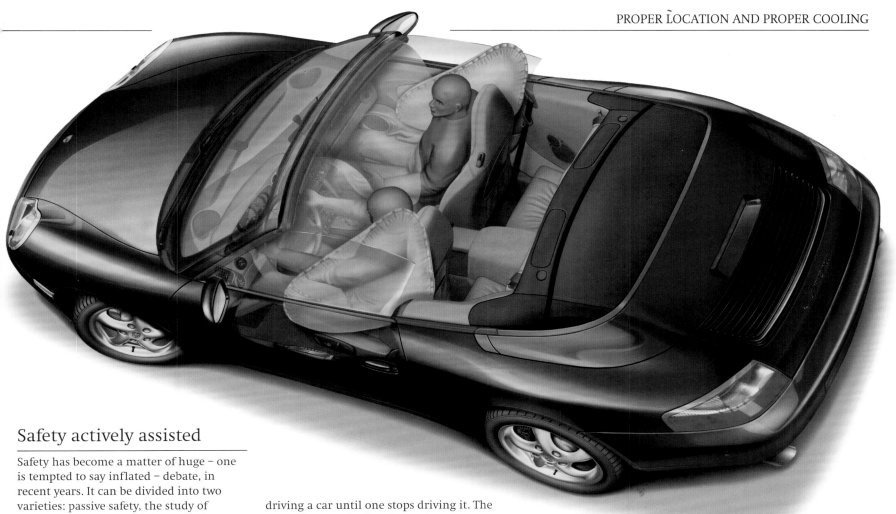

Safety actively assisted

Safety has become a matter of huge – one is tempted to say inflated – debate, in recent years. It can be divided into two varieties: passive safety, the study of providing the best possible protection of the occupants of a car should it be involved in an accident, and active safety, the science of making cars which steer, handle, and stop, again as effectively as possible, so that the driver can avoid an accident. There is an important difference between the two.

Passive safety – the impact-absorption properties of how the front collapses in a head-on collision, the effectiveness of seat belts and air bags and so – is only brought into play in an accident. Going by the unbalanced fuss made by government, some pressure groups, and even to their shame some car manufacturers, one would think that passive safety measures are the most important of the two. Yet obviously, active safety – best possible braking, roadholding, steering, and handling – is much the most valuable, simply because it is in action from the moment one starts

driving a car until one stops driving it. The 996 series was the first 911 to incorporate an electronically controlled aid to active safety, which goes by a variety of acronyms, most often ESP, standing for electronic stability program. Porsche's name for it was Porsche Stability Management (PSM) introduced on the Type 996 range in 1998 for the 1999 model year.

PSM, still fitted on current 911s at the time of writing, embraces traction control (TC in 911 speak) and automatic brake differential (ABD) in the customary way. It is fed by signals from anti-lock braking wheel-speed sensors and sensors of yaw deflection (movement of the car's direction), plus steering wheel angle and movement to provide an indication of what the electronic brain of the system sees as the start of any loss of control in terms of wheel-spin, brake locking, or the more challenging phenomena of understeer or oversteer. It then applies a single wheel

Above: POSIP (Porsche side protection system using side airbags) showing dummies with ghosted air bags inflated on a 2001 model Carrera 3.4 Cabriolet.

Left: Horst Marchart, pictured in 2000. He was the board member for research and development in 1991 and head of Porsche car development from 1992 to 2001.

brake whose eccentric effect on the car in turn applies an automatic correcting yaw effect – on the inside rear wheel brake in the understeer case and outside front in the oversteer case.

Porsche claims to have set PSM so that it only intervenes to control oversteer or understeer at a higher level than on less sporting cars. Since some drivers reckon they can control the car as well as any electronic system, or because, hopefully in appropriate circumstances, they enjoy provoking oversteer, Porsche provides a switch to disable PSM. However, it cannot be disabled totally, the system switching on again as soon as the brake pedal is touched, so left foot braking as part of one's cornering technique is not on. As on other cars so equipped, there is the usual provision of a warning lamp to remind the driver that it is off and it is automatically switched on again during re-starting.

Roll-over protection hoops erection mechanism on a 2001 Carrera 3.4 Cabriolet.

Super 911: the GT3

The third of the 911 top GT performance variations with deliberately introduced development for racing appeared first at the Geneva Show in 1999. Unlike the GT2 and particularly the GT1 that were overtly racing-biased from the start, the 911 GT3 began life as a production car, of which nearly 2,000 were built between the autumn of 1999 and the end of 2000. It was evolved from the first 911 Carrera Cup model, providing a basis for the racing 911 GT3 R and 911 GT3 RS variants.

It was not greatly stripped inside, as a number of the well-heeled people who wanted an extra high performance 911 had made it plain that they did not totally enjoy the bare essentials of Carrera RS ownership that went with such machinery. The soon-to-arrive R and RS GT3s would look after those who wanted the pure

sports-racing experience, unadulterated by sound deadening and upholstery. However, the plain GT3 did lose the somewhat useless rear seats and the needless luxury of power adjustment for the front seats, replaced with much lighter race-suitable Recaros.

Power for the GT3 came from the M96/76 normally aspirated 3.6-litre four-valve engine closely based on the twin-turbo 3.2-litre of the 1998 Le Mans winning mid-engined 911 GT1. A 100mm bore and 76.4mm stroke gave the required extra swept volume of exactly 3,600cc, using a crankshaft plasma-nitrided to ensure a more extensive carbon-enriched harder layer than conventional nitro-carbide nitriding. Here was another Porsche flat six whose Nikasil wet-lined cylinders, cylinder head on each side, and valve chest were spigotted and tied together by long through-bolts.

The same shot-peened titanium connecting rods as on the GT1 engine were fitted, each weighing 74 per cent of an equivalent forged steel rod. Forged pistons were cooled by oil spray from underneath. A torsional vibration damper was mounted at the back end of the crankshaft, backed up by a twin-mass flywheel at the other. The timing drive to the double overhead camshafts was a two-stage affair, with a gear-driven intermediate shaft from which duplex roller chains at the back of the motor took the drive to the camshafts. These were hollow, actuating the four valves per cylinder (set at a 27.4° included angle) on their double return springs via bucket hydraulic tappets.

The inlet camshaft was variably timed using a conventional oil-pressure-powered helical ramp, capable of altering the cam position through 12.5° advance or retard. Bosch Motronic ME 5.2.2 sequential fuel injection was combined with

the breakerless direct ignition system whose spark voltages were generated by individual coils on each plug. A third radiator mounted in the middle of the front of the car was added to ensure the required extra engine cooling. Transmission of the power available – 360PS at 7,200rpm and 370Nm at 5,000rpm – was through a higher torque capacity G96/90 gearbox. Also provided was a bigger 90-litre fuel tank and a weight-saving puncture repair bottle in place of a spare wheel.

Third generation 911 Turbo

Frankfurt Show 1999 was the setting for the re-introduction, four years after the launch of the previous Type 993 version, of the 911 Turbo in Type 996 form. Its 420PS from 3.6 litres – and, more relevantly, its 253PS/tonne laden one-up power to weight ratio – very sensibly persuading its makers once again that the four-wheel-drive system of the 911 Carrera 4 should be fitted as standard. The engine (as on the previous Turbo) used two turbochargers, each with its own intercooler, blowing at a maximum of 0.85bar into 9.4:1 (instead of the previous Turbo's 8.0:1) compression ratio combustion chambers, a high ratio for such a supercharging pressure. This was made possible by a combination of helpful factors: the more effective cooling using liquid as opposed to air, the greater turbulence and therefore better combustion of four valves per cylinder, comparatively small valve head diameters of 37mm and 32mm inlet/exhaust, and the then latest version of Porsche's variable lift and timing valve control system, Variocam Plus.

This system abandoned the curious and ingenious chain-tensioner-controlled valve timing system of the original Variocam of 1998 for a conventional helical spline arrangement, driven as before by engine-oil hydraulic pressure, acting on the inlet camshafts. This was capable of varying inlet cam angle relative to the exhaust cam by 15° either way, a total of 5° more than the previous system. The 'Plus' in the name referred to the extra facility of a two-stage variable inlet valve lift. Two amounts of valve lift – 10mm and 3mm – were provided.

Above: The GT3 was a production car with a 3,600cc engine developing 360PS.

Left: Exhibition cutaway version of the 1999 Turbo showing the 3.6 litre twin turbo engine, which delivered 420PS through four-wheel drive.

Triple cam-per-valve variable lift

Instead of the usual single cam per valve, the inlet camshaft was machined with three cams to each valve; the centre one provided the low (3mm) lift, the other two, either side of the middle one, provided the high (10mm) lift. Each inlet valve had two concentric tappets – the inner one working directly on the valve via its normal hydraulic zero-clearance device and operated by the centre cam, the outer cylindrical sleeve tappet kept in contact with the outer two cams, which operated it by its own separate return spring abutting on the main valve spring cap. In low-lift running, the outer sleeve tappet was moved up and down freely while the centre cam opened and shut the valve. To start high-lift running, the Bosch ME Motronic 7.8 DME electronic control system brought into play hydraulically operated pins that were pushed across into the sleeve tappet to lock it to the inner tappet and through that, to the valve, which then moved through a 10mm stroke.

The combination of the two features was used both to increase power at high load and speed and, as with the original Variocam system, to assist in exhaust emissions control by using valve overlap to generate some internally provided exhaust gas recirculation (EGR). EGR was as usual employed to lower combustion temperatures at small to medium load in order to reduce the generation of oxides of nitrogen (NOx).

As was becoming usual in many European engines at this time, as well as the main three-way catalytic converter, the engine was fitted with small primary catalytic converters. These were placed immediately outside the turbine exhaust, each one's low mass and position ensuring very early light-off to deal that much sooner with cold-start emissions. Beside the 420PS peak power figure at 6,000rpm, Variocam Plus helped the engine generate its maximum torque of 560Nm continuously between 2,700 and 4,600rpm – a huge aid to drivability and overall performance. All this was done

while meeting all three of the main current exhaust emissions standards: EU3, American LEV, and the more strict German D4 regulations.

The 996-series Porsche 911 Turbo was the first Turbo to be offered with the automatic Tiptronic transmission option. No ZF box existed to take the engine's power and torque, so a DaimlerChrysler epicyclic five-speed gearbox and lock-up torque converter was used, with a 580Nm torque capacity, allied to the now usual 4x4 transmission. The manual gearbox version of the Turbo shared its four-wheel-drive system with the contemporary Carrera 4. This included some minor changes, most obviously the deletion of the torque tube enclosing the propeller shaft and linking the gearbox at the back with the front differential. Besides saving some weight, this also made room for the radiator pipes. In front, the viscous coupling was moved to the back end of the front diff, slightly improving weight distribution.

Racing 911 miscellany

Porsche appreciated that designing, making and supplying fast road cars and competition cars to private customers and racing teams was vital for the firm's standing and reputation. The next fruit of this effort was the 911 GT3 of 1999, a production model developed as a homologated car capable of development as a rival to other cars in the GT3 class and already described earlier in this chapter.

What had by then become a minor Porsche racing tradition was revived again in the Cup model of the new Type 996 series 911. Production bodyshells were diverted to the racing department and fitted with a roll-over protection cage. The engine, however, was not that of the standard 996-series Carrera but a different version of the 3.2-litre GT1 engine. The two biggest differences were the capacity, increased to 3.6 litres, and

the removal of the turbocharging and Variocam systems, taking it close to the GT3's power unit.

Similarly, the GT2 993-series G50 transmission with its oil cooling system deleted was provided, mainly because it offered easily changeable gear ratios and had a higher torque capacity than the Type 996 G96/00 box. Valve gear was simplified as usual for racing by swapping the hydraulic tappets for a bucket tappet set-up. Deleting the air filter and the use of a less restrictive catalytic converter exhaust system helped both power and torque to increase by 10 metric units beyond the standard – 370PS at 7,000rpm and 370Nm at 6,250rpm. The 2002 season brought another dual 10 metric unit increase to 380PS and 380Nm, credited to a new stainless steel exhaust with two catalytic converters plus Bosch Motronic 3.1 engine management.

The GT3 R and RS

In 1999 Porsche also introduced R and RS versions of the GT3 production road car, which is what it was designed to spawn, for competition in the Le Mans LM-GT near-standard class and the FIA N-GT rules. Inlet restrictors were involved but nevertheless seemingly regardless of these, Porsche succeeded in extracting 420PS at 7,200rpm and 390Nm at 7,000rpm. The slightly later arrival of the GT3 RS, whose engine had larger titanium valves, more obviously racing valve timing, and an exhaust free of any catalyst, brought an extra 40PS.

A third racing variant of the GT3 came in 2002 in the Cup version. This had various aerodynamic improvements – a large rear aerofoil, sill skirt-like extensions, and a deeper front – as well as some lightening measures such as plastic materials used for the rear window, engine cover and door panels, only one

Recaro racing seat, and no interior trim. Later that year there was further lightening of the doors, a less heavy exhaust system, smaller rear-view mirrors, a small alternator, and thinner glass in the front windows. Springs and the usual Bilstein dampers were stiffer than in the standard GT3, anti-roll bar adjustment was provided, and the rear subframe's elastomeric mounts were swapped for plain bolting. Also the braking system was uprated with six-piston calipers, 350mm front and 330mm rear discs. By 2002 the centre-lock 18in wheels were 9J-rimmed in front and 10.5J rear.

Being the more extreme of the three variants, modifications to the GT3 RS were deeper. All suspension pivots changed to ball joints and dampers were Sachs-supplied. To adjust ride height as allowed by the various formulae, Porsche went to the unusual length of providing two different sets of suspension uprights,

with the same suspension link and in front, steering pick-up points to preserve geometry, but the front and rear hub bearings higher on the upright. The servo-assisted brakes relied on 380mm front and 355mm rear discs, again restrained by six-piston calipers. The brakes lived inside 18in wheels with 10J and 11J rims front and rear. Steering was power-assisted in both the R and RS, with the RS using electrical power for its hydraulic assistance pump, which was not absorbing power in straight-line running, of course.

Composites were used for front and back of the car, while aerodynamic measures included a more pronounced air dam in front and an incidence-angle-adjustable aerofoil behind. Within the body, inclining the radiator forward improved airflow through the matrix, after which it was led to exit from a slot just in front of the screen, encouraged by the low pressure area at that point. In the

cockpit, dial instruments gave way to a racing-style digital display. Weight reductions added up to 70kg, or six per cent less than the Cup model.

For the first time in the story of 911-derived racers, there was some variety introduced into the clutch fitted. The GT3 Cup model used the usual racing version of a single-plate clutch with sintered metal linings. However, for 2002 the GT3 R and RS models depended on a three-plate device whose tripling of the friction surfaces meant that its diameter and therefore rotary inertia could be reduced, benefiting gear-change speed. In the transmission itself, the pump and oil cooling system were retained for the Cup version, for owners interested in long-distance events.

Both the GT3 R and GT3 RS were successful in racing, particularly the RS, which in the 2001 Le Mans won the GT class, finishing sixth overall. In the previous Le Mans, nine RS and a lone R

A GT3 RS ready for the track with roll cage, 18in wheels, and adjustable rear aerofoil.

Above: A 1999 Carrera 4 3.4 coupé fitted with a Tiptronic gearbox and satellite navigation equipment.

Opposite: Cockpit of 2001 Carrera 3.4 Cabriolet from passenger side. There are driver and passenger airbags and also side airbags in the doors.

model were privately entered; a multiple crash eliminated one and the other nine finished in classified positions. The Le Mans début for the GT3 R was in 1999, when the very first example of this car was entered privately (if works-backed), won the LM-GT class race, and finished 15th overall. All of which was the best possible advertisement for how the Porsche 911 reputation for true reliability allied to always competitive performance is sustained to this day.

Changes in 2000

The year 2000 looked comparatively modest by Porsche 911 standards with the replacement of the traditional cable-connected throttle of the 911 Carrera 4 with an electric drive-by-wire set-up, principally to suit the recently introduced Porsche Stability Management (PSM) system described earlier, subsequently incorporated in the 911 Carrera and Turbo in the same year.

Second-generation GT2

In 2001 the second generation of 911 GT2 was introduced with more modest ambitions than the 1994 original. Instead it was aimed squarely at the GT2 less-modified production car racing class at Le Mans. It was based closely on the 996-series 911 Turbo, as part of the standard 911 line-up. Its M96/70S engine only differed from the Turbo in having larger blowers working at 1bar (0.15bar more than the Turbo). These demanded more effective intercooling, duly provided. Here was the first example of an idea used two years later on the 911 GT3, where the engine cooling radiator was inclined to ease the flow of high speed air through it. This air exited the front part of the car through a vent in the low pressure area in the nose, in the process eliminating a small loss of downforce. This may not have been a pure sports-racing 911 but it had near racing performance, with a close to 200mph top

speed. This was thanks to its 462PS at 5,700rpm and 620Nm maintained constantly between 3,500 and 4,500rpm.

While it could be modified readily for use in the original class, its makers did not encourage such action, not offering any RS variant, simply because by this time, competition in the class was using and dependant on ground-effect-generating underbodies, which the layout of the 911 clearly did not permit, since the engine in the tail got in the way of a half-venturi profile to the underside. There was however a Club Sport version equipped to FIA racing standards that could be bought.

Left: The second-generation 2002 model GT2 with 462PS offered near-racing performance.

Ceramic brake discs arrive

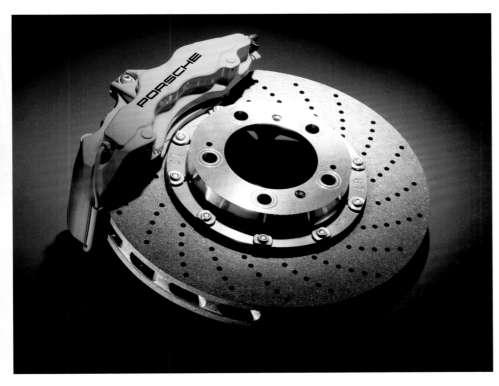

The GT3 was probably the first 911 to be offered as standard with Porsche's now famous composite ceramic brake discs, supplied by SGL Brakes GmbH of Meitingen in Germany. Besides its claimed resistance to fade and distortion and, of course, corrosion, ceramic composite discs are roughly half as heavy as a steel or cast iron disc, saving both overall weight and, important from the suspension's point of view, unsprung mass. Other weight savings were gained from deleting the front half of the Turbo's four-wheel-drive system, using lightweight racing seats instead of power-assisted ones, eliminating the occasional back seats and the spare wheel. Racing did not require the Porsche Stability Management system either. Externally, the car was identified by its front air intakes, the bigger rear aerofoil, and a black bottom edge to the front air dam.

Far left: Porsche first used ceramic brake discs on the GT3.

More powerful engine

The first power increase for the standard M96 water-cooled engine occurred in 2002. It was achieved first of all by increasing the stroke from 78mm to 82.8mm (the bore stayed at its original 96mm), giving a capacity of 3,596cc, and installing the Variocam Plus inlet valve and lift system first seen in the 911 Turbo and GT2 engines. What was known internally as the M96/03 accommodated the extra stroke by

shortening the between-centres dimension of the connecting rods (by 3mm to 142mm) and fitting new pistons in which the gudgeon pin axis was raised slightly. A similar increase in crankshaft main bearing diameter preserved crank strength in view of the higher output, and the crankcase was enlarged to keep windage losses due to the bigger crank throw under control.

In the original M96 engine the two camshafts in each cylinder head were linked by their own short chain drive, the drive from the two-thirds speed reduction intermediate shaft running to the exhaust camshaft. This was altered in the 2002 engine, where the addition of the Variocam Plus system was accompanied by driving both shafts with the same chain. The control program for Variocam Plus

Opposite: Racing-style shell seat, but with normal three-point colour co-ordinated seat belts, of a 2001 model Carrera 3.4 coupé.

arranged its timing and lift not only to boost mid range and maximum power, but also to generate some internal exhaust gas recirculation (EGR) as part of this engine's compliance with Euro 4 exhaust emissions. It also contributed usefully to the M96/03's healthy 300PS at 6,800rpm, a 20PS gain on the original, and 370Nm at 4,250rpm.

In this same year, some small modifications were made to the six-speed gearbox with a higher-strength steel for the gears and a four-planet gear in the differential instead of two, both improving torque capacity. An extra bearing for the input shaft just behind the clutch was interposed to eliminate a source of vibration in the shaft. On the Tiptronic front, the higher torque of the current engine encouraged Porsche to standardise on the DaimlerChrysler automatic first used in the latest Turbo, but with lower final drive gearing to suit the less powerful engine.

Seven 911 models

For the 2005 model year, Porsche offered a seven-model range – four were variously new or modified in the 996-series and two were the new 997-series models. The Type 997 version of 911 came in 3.6 Carrera and 3.8 Carrera S versions and was distinguished from the Type 996 by a wider track (21mm more in front and 34mm at the rear), and some minor body changes.

The 3,596cc engine was mildly improved with power raised by 4PS to 325PS at 6,800rpm and 370Nm at 4,250rpm on 98RM fuel. It drove through a new six-speed manual gearbox, a development of the previous transmission, uprated in torque capacity with wider gear pairs running on larger shafts. The synchromesh followed long-established Porsche practice formerly only seen in competition 911s, in changing from phosphor bronze synchro rings to steel ones; the lower three gears, the most heavily loaded by virtue of their ratios, were all

The more powerful M96/03 engine introduced in 2002 had a longer stroke, giving 3,596cc, and Variocam Plus valve timing.

carbon-coated to provide further improved wear resistance. The gear change was claimed to have been improved in quality and reduced effort needed, and also had less lever movement thanks to a combination of lower friction cables from gearshift to selectors and a higher-geared lever, by moving the position of the gear-lever pivot.

For the first time on a 911, variable ratio rack and pinion steering was fitted. ZR-rated tyres, on 18in wheels, were 235/40 front and 265/40 rear. Brakes were more powerful, with a higher servo boost (increased by 17 per cent for less pedal effort), 318mm diameter front discs and 299mm rear discs, both cross-drilled and ventilated, braked by four-piston calipers. One could specify – at a price – the option of ceramic composite brakes (PCCB). The largest change was an

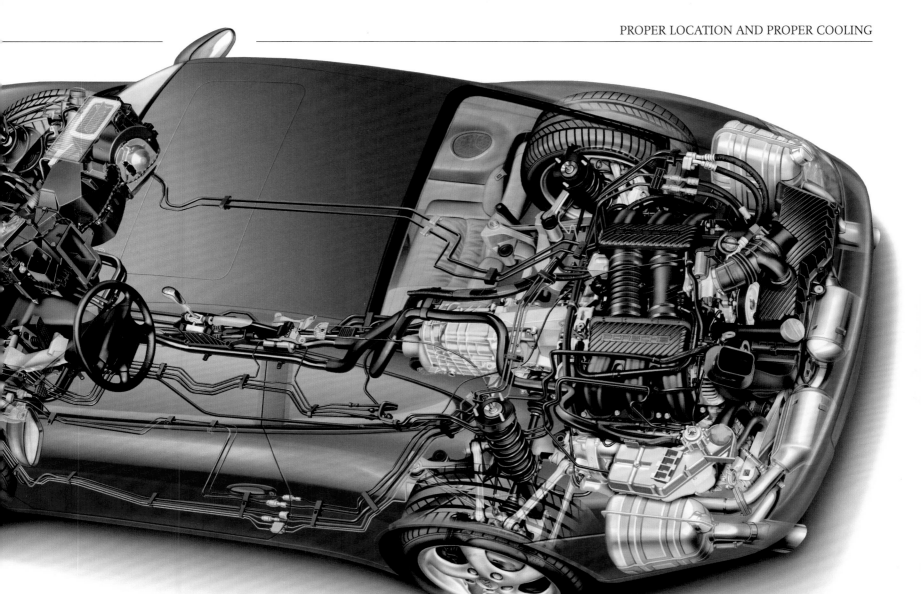

Mechanicals of a 2001 Carrera 3.4.

option, Porsche Active Suspension Management, a fancy name for electronically controlled driver-selectable variable damping, combined with sports suspension lowering the car by 20mm, and a differential locking facility.

Porsche's stability management system (PSM) was now standard from the base 911 upwards. An adjustment to this which would please the really enthusiastic driver was that if one switched off PSM, its re-engagement on using the brakes was now not made until one was braking hard

enough to initiate anti-lock action. What at first looked like something of a sports-car gimmick was the analogue-digital stopwatch, which featured prominently on top of the dashboard. In fact, pressing the control button brought in various enthusiast-driving bonuses: engine behaviour under load change was altered, PSM intervention points were set higher, control maps of the damper variation and Tiptronic S transmission options altered. You could also time journeys or laps according to whim.

Safety and more aerodynamic styling

Structurally, passive safety was improved with further reinforcements of the body, in particular with an eye to offset collision. Seat belt restraint was backed up by no less than six airbags, two two-stage main bags, a thorax bag on each side housed in the seat squabs, and, most unusual, an 8cu dm head-protection bag in each door. On inflation in a side impact this formed a flat cushion

Above: The new 997 series models came in 3.6 Carrera (left) and 3.8 Carrera S versions and had wider front and rear tracks.

Right: Instrument layout of the 997 Carrera with new three-spoke steering wheel and stopwatch mounted above the centre console. Digital clock and air temperature readouts are in the bottom sector of the combined water temperature and fuel gauge.

providing both impact protection and a shield from flying glass.

Inside, there was the long overdue introduction of height, as well as reach, adjustment for the steering wheel. Pedals were moved forward to improve legroom for taller drivers and seats had more side support, the sports option seating even more so, with a claimed 50 per cent added. Instrument layout was made clearer with wider spacing between the five dials. A display monitor was part of the Porsche Communication Management system, basically a trip computer idea in principle.

Body styling was different, with separated headlamps in front, more accentuated wheel-arches, door mirrors on elaborate double arms, a new rear aerofoil, and detail changes to the shape. That not all of this was just styling is proved by the reduction in drag coefficient, for the first time on a road-going 911 brought below 0.30, to 0.28. Combined with the 2.00sq m projected frontal area, the effective frontal area (CdA) was 0.56sq m. Finally, from the viewpoint of the more frugal owner, service intervals were increased by 50 per cent, from 20,000km to 30,000km.

The 3.8-litre Carrera S

The other 997 series 911 was the Carrera S. Its engine had a larger bore (99mm instead of 96mm) for the same 82.8mm stroke giving a swept volume of 3,824cc, uprating the output figures by 9.2 and 8.1 per cent respectively to 355PS at 6,600rpm and 400Nm at 4,600rpm. The higher compression ratio of the larger engine, 11.8 instead of 11.3:1, was a further contributor. Gearbox and final drive ratios and clutch size were the same, the only difference in overall gearing being due to the ZR-rated rear tyres, larger in diameter (19in instead of 18in) and section (295/30 instead of 265/40). Brakes were bigger too, at 330mm diameter both front and rear, and 34mm thick in front and 28mm rear. At 1,420kg, the 911 Carrera S was 1.8 per cent heavier than its 3.6-litre brother.

Claimed performance figures showed commensurate differences – the 3.6 managed 0–100kph in 5.0sec, 0–160kph in 11.0sec, and a 177mph maximum speed. Corresponding figures for the 3.8 model were 0–100kph in 4.8sec, 0–160kph in 10.7sec, and a 182mph maximum speed. *Autocar* tested the 3.6 Carrera S in its 5 October 2004 issue, returning 0–60mph in 4.6sec and 0–100mph in 10.8sec. Weather conditions prevented verification of Porsche's claimed 182mph maximum. The testers' views on the car's handling were basically highly complimentary – '... even better than the excellent 996's and ride quality and refinement have been transformed...' – but alloyed with a few reservations about steering character – '... the 911's is still a great helm: beautifully weighted, crisp on turn-in and fearsomely accurate. But subjectively some of the life seems to have been squeezed out of the system. No longer does it writhe gently in your hands at even modest speeds, and only when traversing more challenging roads does the wheel come alive, gently tugging at your wrists and streaming details back through your fingertips.'

Above: There were detailed changes to the shape of the 997 Carrera with more accentuated wheel arches.

Left: The 997's new body was more aerodynamic with a drag coefficient of 0.28 and now had separate headlamps.

157

The new Type 996 Targa had an electrically operated sliding glass roof panel. A lift-up rear window gave access to the rear load space.

Specifications: 2005 Carrera S (Type 997)

ENGINE

Capacity
3,824cc

Bore and stroke
96.0mm x 82.8mm

Compression ratio
11.8:1

Maximum power
355PS @ 6,600rpm

Maximum torque
400Nm @ 4,600rpm

Fuel system
Bosch DME sequential injection

TRANSMISSION

Gearbox
Six-speed manual

BRAKES

Front
Ventilated disc, 304mm

Rear
Ventilated disc, 330mm

PERFORMANCE

Top speed
182mph*

Acceleration
0–60mph	4.6sec
0–100mph	10.8sec

KERB WEIGHT
1,420kg

*Manufacturer's claimed figure.

The 996 series changes

Changes in the 996-series (first launched in 1997), in ascending order of power, started with the introduction of a re-created Targa on the basis of the 911 Carrera coupé 996. The rear window could be opened for access to the 230cu dm load space, lit automatically upon opening at night. The roof now contained an extensive laminated glass panel, which could be moved back by up to 0.5m. The engine was the 3.6-litre giving 320PS at 6,800rpm and 370Nm at 4,250rpm.

Next, very much further up the power scale, came the Turbo S in coupé and Cabriolet versions. The 'S' denoted 450PS at 5,700rpm and 620Nm constantly between 3,500 and 4,500rpm, improvements respectively on the standard 911 Turbo of 7.1 and 10.7 per cent. The gains were due to larger turbos and more effective intercooling, plus revised engine management. To match the

increased go, standard brakes were Porsche Ceramic Composite discs, providing a reduction in unsprung weight, better fade resistance, and freedom from wear and corrosion. The discs were 350mm diameter front and rear (330mm on the plain Turbo) and were braked by six-piston calipers. Comparing 0–200kph standing start times, the 'S' arrives in 13.6sec, 0.8sec faster than the standard Turbo, while maximum speed was the same at 190mph.

Improvements to the 996-base 911 GT3 were similar to those making up the 911 Turbo S, with power from the earlier 100mm by 76.4mm 3,600cc engine boosted from 360PS at 7,200rpm to 381PS at 7,400rpm, and torque from 370Nm to 385Nm at the same 5,000rpm. This was enough to provide a 0–200kph time of 14.3sec and again a 190mph maximum. Brake disc size in front was increased by 20mm to 350mm, with six-piston calipers instead of four; PCCB discs were an option.

Changes to the body – a redesigned front, new sill extensions, and a different aerofoil – brought the drag coefficient down to 0.30.

Finally, the 996-series GT2 had 5.2 per cent more power, at 483PS at 6,800rpm, if slightly reduced torque, a steady 640Nm (instead of 670Nm) between the now usual 3,500 and 4,500rpm – good enough to give this king of 911s a 0–200kph time of 12.5sec and a top speed just 2mph short of 200mph.

The Type 996 Turbo S Cabriolet with the coupé in the background. The Cabriolet's bodyshell was reinforced with high-strength steel (used for the first time on a Porsche sports car), resulting in the stiffest and strongest of all 911s.

The 911 Carrera S (Type 997) and its rivals

Make and model	Top speed	0–60mph	0–100mph	Standing ¼ mile	Fuel consumption
Aston Martin Vanquish	*196mph	4.4sec	10.5sec	13.3sec	12.6mpg
Audi TT 3.2-litre V6	147mph	6.8sec	17.2sec	15.2sec	16.0mpg
Bentley Continental GT	*196mph	4.9sec	11.8sec	13.5sec	13.9mpg
Ferrari 550 Maranello	*199mph	4.6sec	10.1sec	12.9sec	12.3mpg
Porsche 911 Carrera S	*182mph	4.6sec	10.8sec	13.0sec	20.9mpg

*Manufacturer's claimed figure. Other performance figures from *Autocar*

Index

Aherns, Kurt 43
Alfa Romeo 64
Aston Martin
   Vanquish 159
   V8 51
Audi 68, 81
   Quattro 99
   TT 3.2-litre V6 159
Austin-Rover K-series
   engine 19
Auto Union 10-11, 16
Autocar road tests 6-7, 28, 30,
   32, 34, 44, 47, 51, 54, 63,
   73, 77, 80, 86, 103, 136,
   138, 144

Barth, Jürgen 45, 49
Bentley Continental GT 159
Bien, M. 45
BMC Mini 12, 26
BMW 71, 117
   M3 123
   2002tii 58
Böhringer, Eugen 28
Bott, Helmuth 79, 97
BPR series races 138
Braseur, 92
Bridgestone tyres 96

Caterpillar 79
Chevrolet 117
Cisitalia 12
Citroën 41
Cooper-Climax 11
CSI 64

Daimler-Benz 10
DaimlerChrysler 154
Daytona 24-hour race 55
De Tomaso Pantera 51
Detroit Show 141
Dr. Ing. h.c. F. Porsche
   GmbH 11
Dunlop tyres 96

East African Safari Rally 34,
   44-45, 58, 61
Elford, Vic 33, 35, 40, 43
European GT Championship
   59, 70
European Rally
   Championship 45
Eyb, Wolfgang 16

Falk, Peter 28
Ferrari
   348 104
   348tb 123
   365 GTB/4 Daytona 51
   550 Maranello 159
FIA 137, 148, 153
FISA 83
Ford 71, 142
Frankel, Andrew 136
Frankfurt Show 14, 31, 79,
   92, 106, 136, 140, 147
Fuhrmann, Prof Ernst 45, 71,
   73, 75-76, 79

Gall, 41
Geneva Motor Show 53, 79,
   130, 146
German National Championship
   2-litre class 71

Gregg, P. 55
Group A racing (production
   touring cars) 83
Group B (small-production
   GT cars) 83
Group C ('free' prototypes)
   83, 92, 96
Group 3 racing (Production
   GT cars) 49, 58
Group 4 racing (Special Gran
   Turismo) 49, 69
Group 5 racing (modified
   production cars) 69-70, 78
GT racing 64, 113, 137, 149
   Group N 112
GT3 racing 136
Gulf-Ford V8 64

Haywood, Hurley 55, 117
Heisser Schnee Rally 59
Helmer, Lars 40, 54
Hettman, Richard 61
Heyer, Hans 77
Hezemans, Toine 77
Hillman Imp 26
Hockenheim 33, 36, 71
Honda NSX 123
Hooke joint 21

Ickx, Jacky 71, 92
IMSA Championship 59, 117
Issigonis, Alec 99

Jaguar
   D-type 14
   E-type 47, 54
JaguarSport XJR-S 104
Jensen FF 99

Kassmaul, 92
Kauhsen, W. 43
Kern, Hans 61
Kirn, Karl 61
Komenda, Erwin 14
Kremer, Erwin 41

Lamborghini Miura 47, 51
Lamoyne, Dominique 92
Larrousse, Gérard 40, 44, 55
Le Mans 24-hour race 43, 59,
   78, 83, 113, 117, 133,
   135-138, 146, 149
Lehto, K. 40
Lerner, 92
Linge, Herbert 28, 61
Lohner-Porsche 10
Loos, Georg 49
Lotus 117
   Esprit S4 123
   Esprit Turbo SE 104
Ludwig, Klaus 77-78
Lyall, J. 61

Marathon de la Route 55
Marchart, Horst 145
Martini Racing 55, 70, 78
McLaren F1 GTR 136
Mercedes 11
Metge, René 92
Miles, John 77
MIRA test track 6, 47, 80
Monte Carlo Rally 28, 33, 35,
   40, 54-55, 77
Monza 54

Morgan 13
Morris Minor 99
Müller, Herbert 59

Nadella 21
New York Show 43
Nicholas, Jean-Pierre 77
Nissan 117
Norisring 71
Nürburgring 1,000km race
   49, 59, 69, 77

Opel/Vauxhall Corsa 136
Oulton Park 6

Paris-Dakar Rally 92, 96
Paris Salon 48, 62
Perramond, J. C. 40
Peugeot 14, 26
Piëch, Anton 10, 75
Piëch, Ferdinand 19, 39, 75,
   79, 99
Piëch, Louise (née Porsche)
   10, 61, 73
Pirelli tyres 52, 117
Pontiac 117
Porsche 10, 12, 61
Porsche Design GmbH 117
Porsche GmbH 73, 75
Porsche heating 22
Porsche KG 39, 75, 117
Porsche synchromesh 21,22
Porsche 356 12, 14-15, 18, 27,
   35, 61
Porsche 365 16, 28, 31, 41
   Super 90 29
   365C coupé 15, 27
Porsche 901 11, 13-16, 19-20,
   26, 39, 48
Porsche 904 28, 39, 54
Porsche 911
   2.0 coupé 15, 18, 26-28, 30,
      34, 36
   2.4 45
   2.7 53, 75
   2.7 coupé 65, 67-69
   3.2 58
   A-series 22, 42
   B-series 26, 39
   G-series 20, 53-54, 87
      2.7 coupé 60
   H-series 58`
      Carrera 54
   L-series 75
   O-series 42
   Cabriolet 58
Carrera 86, 107, 133, 144, 150
Carrera 2.7 Targa 65
Carrera 3.0 67, 75
Carrera 3.0 coupé 71
Carrera 3.2 (Type 953) 80,
   87-89, 92
Carrera 3.2 Cabriolet 89,
   93
Carrera 3.2 coupé 88
Carrera 3.2 Speedster
   106-107
Carrera 3.2 Targa 87
Carrera 3.4 141, 143-144,
   155
Carrera 3.4 Cabriolet 140,
   143, 145-146, 150
Carrera 3.4 coupé 140, 150,
   153

Carrera 3.6 122, 156
Carrera 3.6 Cabriolet 123,
   127-128, 130, 135
Carrera 3.6 coupé 127-128,
   135
Carrera 3.6 Tiptronic S 128
Carrera coupé 60
Carrera Cup 146
Carrera RS 49, 50-52,
   54-55, 59, 61-62, 112,
   142, 146
Carrera RS (Type 964)
   116-117
Carrera RS Touring 51
Carrera RS 2.7 55, 61, 103
Carrera RS 2.7 coupé 49-52
Carrera RS 3.0 49, 58-59,
   62
Carrera RS 3.6 86, 112-113
Carrera RS 3.8 112, 114,
   128-129
Carrera RS 3.8 Clubsport
   129-130
Carrera RS 3.8 coupé 129
Carrera RSR 55
Carrera RSR 2.8 49
Carrera RSR 3.0 59
Carrera RSR 3.8 113, 116
Carrera RSR Turbo 2.2 59
Carrera S 3.6 135
Carrera S 3.8 156-157
Carrera 2 (Type 964) 58,
   101, 104, 109-111, 115
Carrera 2 Cabriolet 111
Carrera 2 coupé 82,
   111-112
Carrera 2 Cup 116
Carrera 2 Targa 111
Carrera 2 3.6 110
Carrera 2 3.6 Cabriolet 111,
   121
Carrera 2 3.6 coupé 112,
   121
Carrera 2 3.6 Targa 111
Carrera 4 (Type 964) 86,
   99, 101-105, 110-111, 115,
   127, 133, 147, 150
Carrera 4 Cabriolet 101,
   111
Carrera 4 coupé 111
Carrera 4 Targa 111
Carrera 4 3.6 102-103, 105,
   110, 130
Carrera 4 3.6 coupé 99,
   104, 121, 124-126
Carrera 4 3.6 Targa 100
Carrera 4S 3.6 128, 133
Speedster 86, 106, 121
Targa 31, 33, 34, 60
Targa 3.6 128, 135-137
Targa 3.6 coupé 130
Turbo (Type 930) 58, 62-64,
   67, 69-70, 72, 75, 80,
   82-83, 103, 107, 110-111,
   115, 147, 150
Turbo 3.0 coupé 62-64, 68,
   71
Turbo 3.2 81
Turbo 3.3 71, 73, 75, 79,
   86, 91, 108, 111, 114
Turbo 3.3 Cabriolet 86, 90
Turbo 3.3 coupé 72-73, 80-
   83, 88, 90, 93, 97, 108
Turbo 3.3 Targa 90

Turbo 3.6 114, 117, 121,
   128, 131-133, 135
Turbo 3.6 coupé 114-115, 131
Turbo 3.6 IMSA Super Car
   116, 123
Turbo S 113, 116-117
Turbo S Le Mans GT 116
911 Cup 86, 115, 148-149
911 Cup 3.8 135-136
911E 37, 39-41, 43
911E 2.0 coupé 41
911E 2.0 Targa 40
911E 2.2 coupé 42
911E 2.4 45, 47
911E 2.4 coupé 46
911E 2.4 Targa 47-48
911 GT1 133, 135-136, 138,
   146, 148
911 GT2 133, 135-136, 146,
   150, 153, 159
911 GT2 Club Sport 153
911 GT3 133, 135, 146-149,
   153, 159
911 GT3 Cup 149
911 GT3 R 146, 148
911 GT3 RS 146, 148-149
911L 37
911L 2.0 coupé 37
911L 2.0 Targa 37
911 LM Turbo 117
911S 29-30, 32, 39-41, 43,
   50, 142
911S coupé 44-45, 60
911S Targa 37
911S 2.0 36, 45
911S 2.0 coupé 29, 40
911S 2.0 Targa 34, 39
911S 2.2 44
911S 2.2 Targa 43
911S 2.3 coupé 54
911S 2.4 44-45
911S 2.4 coupé 46, 48
911S 2.7 53
911S 2.7 coupé 65
911S B-series 35
911SC coupé 75, 79
911SC 3.0 61, 75, 79-81
911SC 3.0 Cabriolet 79
911SC 3.0 Sport 77
911SC 3.0 Targa 75-76,
   82-83
911SC 3.0 Turbo coupé 75
911T 32-33, 35, 43, 46
911T 2.0 coupé 32
911T 2.0 Targa 36, 41
911T 2.2 44
911T 2.2 coupé 42
911T 2.2 Targa 43
911T 2.4 45, 52-53
993 series 6, 99, 109, 117,
   120-123, 130, 132, 147
Carrera 3.6 121
Carrera 4 123-124
Turbo 135
996 series 136, 140-141,
   145, 148, 153-154, 158
Cabriolet 138
Carrera 148
Carrera coupé 158
Targa 158
Turbo 138, 147-148, 150
Turbo S 158-159
Turbo S Cabriolet
   158-159

Turbo S coupé 158-159
997 series 153
Carrera 6, 156-157
Carrera 3.6 154
Carrera S 6, 159
Carrera S 3.6 157
Carrera S 3.8 154, 157
Porsche 912 27-29, 32, 65
   912E 65, 75
Porsche 914 11, 65, 141
Porsche 917 43, 49, 58-59
Porsche-VW 924 67, 73, 75, 81
Porsche 928 58, 73, 75, 141
Porsche 934 69-70
Porsche 935 69-70, 83
   935/2 'Baby' 71
   935/76 70
   935/77 70
   935/78 'Moby Dick' 78
Porsche 944 81, 141
Porsche 956 92
Porsche 959 86, 92-96, 99,
   102, 120, 131
Porsche 961 93
Porsche 962 117, 137
Porsche 968 141
   Turbo RS 116
   Turbo S 114
Porsche 995 135
Porsche Boxster (Type 986)
   11, 135, 141
   2.5 roadster 135, 140
Porsche Carrera GT 138
Porsche Cayenne 141
Porsche F-type (Type 114) 12
Porsche engines
   Type M64 3.6 100-101, 109,
      111, 114, 125-126;
   M64/05 125;
   M64/06 125;
   M64/21 133;
   M64/22 133;
   M64/81 135;
   M96/01 141-142;
   M96/03 153-154;
   M96/76 146
   V10 1.5-litre 12; 5.5-litre
      138
   2-litre flat-six 35
   2-litre fuel-injected 911S
      39-40
   2.7-litre 67, 142; 3-litre 58;
   3.2-litre 79, 89, 101
   3.3 Turbo 72, 76, 80, 90;
   3.6 Turbo 147
   3,386cc flat-six (Carrera
      3.4) 141-142
   3,596cc 154
   356 Carrera 73
   901/02 29; 901/20 29, 54
   910/01 54
   911 92;
   911E 46-47;
   911S 47;
   911SC 76;
   911T 46-47
   930 92
   935/76 92
Porsche, Brigitte 61
Porsche, Dorothea 61, 82
Porsche, Dr Ferdinand 10-13
Porsche, Ferdinand
   Alexander 'Butzi' 13, 37,
   39, 43, 61, 82, 117

Porsche, Ferdinand Anton
   Ernst 'Ferry' 10-13, 15, 39,
   61, 73, 79, 82, 99, 107, 117
Porsche, Gerhard 82
Porsche, Hans-Peter 39, 82
Porsche, Wolfgang 82
Preston, Vic 61

Reimspiess, Franz Xaver 61
Renault GTA Turbo 104
Rohrl, Walter 117
Rolls-Royce Merlin aero
   engine 19
Rothmans 92
Rzeppa CV joints 22

Sarthe 24-hours race 138
Schurt, Wagen 11
Schutz, Peter W. 79
Sears Roebuck 44
Sebring 12-hour race 55, 117,
   123
Spa Francorchamps 24-hour
   race 41, 113
Specifications
   1966 911S 30
   1973 Carrera RS Touring
      52
   1975 Turbo 63
   1983 Carrera 83
   1989 Carrera 2 105
   1993 Carrera (Type 993)
      121
   2005 Carrera S (Type 997)
      158
Stenzel, R. 59
Steyr 10
Stommelen, Rolf 43, 78
Stone, David 33, 35, 40
Stuck, Hans 117

Targa Florio 31, 54-55
Thorszelius, N. 61
Toivonen, Pauli 28, 40
Tour de France Automobile
   44
Trans-Am Championship 70
'Turbo Look' bodywork 82,
   89, 106-107, 111

Volkswagen (VW) 10, 15, 21,
   27, 68
   Beetle 12
   KdF-Wagen 11
VW-Porsche 914 65

Waldegaard, Björn 40, 44,
   54-55, 61
Watkins Glen 70
Weissach establishment 103,
   115, 136, 141
Whittington brothers 78
Wiedeking,
   Dr Wendelin 121
Wölfle, Gustav 61
World Championship of
   Makes 71
World Rally Championship
   77
Wütherich, Rolf 28

Zasada, Sobieslav 44-45, 61

911 Cup races 117